CONCRETE: A SEVEN-THOUSAND-YEAR HISTORY

CONCRETE

A SEVEN-THOUSAND-YEAR HISTORY

REESE PALLEY

THE QUANTUCK LANE PRESS NEW YORK

BEYOND DEDICATION

It is not sufficient to say that this book is dedicated to Marilyn Arnold Palley. While she was central to the eventuality of this book, acting as critic, stylist, mirror, and cheering section, she has much more deeply touched, nay extended, my life in as many dimensions as one can imagine.

The years beyond those normally granted that were necessary to construct this history were a physical and emotional gift from Marilyn. Without her I would not have lived so long or, if I had, I would not have found the strength to carry this project to completion.

Thank you seems insufficient but will have to do.

Copyright © 2010 by Reese Palley

Layout and Composition:
    John Bernstein Design, Inc.
Manufacturing by
    South China Printing Co., Ltd.
All rights reserved
Printed in China
First Edition

Library of Congress
    Cataloging-in-Publication Data

Palley, Reese.
    Concrete : a seven-thousand-year history / Reese Palley. — 1st ed.

    p.   cm.
    ISBN 978-1-59372-039-1
1. Concrete—History.   I. Title.
    TA439.P245 2010
    620.1'3609—dc22

                    2009037430

The Quantuck Lane Press, New York
www.quantucklanepress.com

Distributed by:
W.W. Norton & Company
500 Fifth Avenue, New York, NY 10110
www.wwnorton.com

W.W. Norton & Company Ltd.
Castle House, 75/76 Wells Street
London, W1T 3QT

1 2 3 4 5 6 7 8 9 0

Cover photo:
Aerial view of the Millau Viaduct over the River Tarn, France.
Courtesy of photographer, Cyrille Lips.

OTHER BOOKS BY REESE PALLEY

Wooden Ships and Iron Men: The Maritime Art of Thomas Hoyne by Reese Palley and Marilyn Arnold Palley, The Quantuck Lane Press, 2005

The Best of Nautical Quarterly, Vol. I: The Lure of Sail by Reese Palley and Anthony Dalton, MBI International, 2004

Call of The Ancient Mariner, McGraw Hill / International Marine, 2004

Unlikely People, Sheridan Press, 1998

There Be No Dragons, Sheridan Press, 1996

Unlikely Passages, Simon & Shuster/Seven Seas Press, 1984

The Porcelain Art of Edward Marshall Boehm, Harry N. Abrams, 1976

Concrete *ab ovo*

Shallow seas fill with minerals and shells.
Aeons pass.
More sediment, huge pressures, endless time.
Changing of sea to land, shell to rock.

Thrusting upward of the crust.
Exposure
Once again to air and organic life.
In the blink of an eye men find and extract
the vast layers of hydraulic lime,

Crush it, fire it in kilns,
Grind it to a fine powder.
Five hundred pounds of rock
Morphed into a fifty-pound bag.

A fifty-pound bag
Transforms the world.

CONTENTS

Preface

8

The Great Agglomeration

10

CHAPTER 1

Pyramidiots

The Pyramid Wars · Decline and Fall

12

CHAPTER 2

Between Egypt and Rome

The Nabateans

24

CHAPTER 3

Roman Concrete and
Its Impact on World History

Pouring the Coffers · Herod's Dream

30

CHAPTER 4

Vitruvius and Giocondo,
1445–1525

38

CHAPTER 5

Joseph Moxon, 1627–1691

42

CHAPTER 6

Concrete in the
Eighteenth Century

The New Stone Age · The Eddystone Lights ·
The Nineteenth Century

45

CHAPTER 7

The Twentieth Century

Control and Communications Bunkers ·
The Maginot Line, The Siegfried Line, and
The Mannheim Line · An Exercise in Futility ·
An Exercise in Deceit · Subterranean England ·
Kelvedon Hatch · The Greenbrier Spa ·
"A Hard Lesson to Learn" (A Short Story by
Betty Overocker) · The Sicilian Vespers

58

CHAPTER 8

The Wizard of Menlo Park

Edison's Concrete Modular Houses

90

CHAPTER 9

What Is Art?

Flights of Concrete Fancy · Roots of Grass ·
Rachel Whiteread · Picasso · Architecture · San
Simeon · Shelters · Idiosynchronicity · Liturgy
in Stone · Le Corbusier · The Church of the Poet

98

CHAPTER 10

Flagler's Folly

Ships · Method of Construction ·
Powell River Breakwater

140

CHAPTER 11

A Woeful Century

The End of the Era of Profligacy · All About
Sustainability · CRC and Other New Concretes ·
Our Senile Infrastructure · Cost of Profligacy

161

CHAPTER 12

The Industry

Hopeful Developments

192

CHAPTER 13

Lunar Transit

Engineers, the Invisible Men

203

Epilogue

212

APPENDIX I

Mercer

214

APPENDIX II

Roman Underwater

216

APPENDIX III

David Moore

217

APPENDIX IV

The Builders of Eddystone

218

APPENDIX V

Timeline

A Chronological Sequence of the History
of Cement and Concrete

224

Chapter Notes

226

Bibliography

228

Index

229

PREFACE

oncrete runs through all the histories of human affairs. It links our most distant past to our looming future in space. Emerging in the empty reaches of ancient primitive desert cultures, the use of concrete swells and ebbs in impact and in importance. Now and then, for arcane and unknowable reasons, its use mysteriously disappears.

The conceit that stone could be made by man and turned to the uses of man was a concept that powered volcanic religious and cultural and economic movements. In its early uses it was the private and powerful domain of Egyptian priests and the equally secret and closed fraternity of the engineers of Rome. Concrete was, from the start, more alchemy than science.

The use of concrete disappeared from Egypt as the power of the later kingdoms waned and the knowledge of the priestly secrets that built the great Giza pyramids were lost.

There is a curious historical symbiosis between concrete and wood. When wood was plentiful as a quintessential building material the uses of concrete disappeared, as in the dark and middle ages. As wood became scarce and expensive, its use shifted from building with wood to burning the wood that fires limekilns, the precondition to artificial stone. Should the source of wood fail entirely, concrete will again go underground and entire cultures and dynasties may dwindle and die.

It was not until the middle of the nineteenth century that concrete began to reappear in the industrial soup of England.

It took the explosive growth of industry, construction, and population in the twentieth century to reawaken the ancient art of stone making. Today, the use of concrete has swelled into a torrent, which is sweeping away all before it. The world is being paved over.

Now, in the twenty-first century, we are overcome by an avalanche of artificial stone. In the industrialized world the demand for dams, roads, bridges, and skyscrapers, essentially slab upon slab of precast artificial stone, grows from year to year as more uses of concrete are developed and as engineering skills unravel the endless potential of concrete. Modern uses of concrete stretch from the mundane to the unthinkable, from ordinary sidewalk slabs to the walls of buildings that translucently replace windows for lighting and concrete that sucks the pollutants out of the air we breathe.

The developing world has long since outstripped the developed in adopting concrete to the housing of its people. As unlovely as Stalin's housing for the proletariat may have been it was the true progenitor of the mushrooming condos that are crowding out skies around the world.

When a prescient Thomas Edison in 1926 built a concrete Victrola he opened the gateway to recondite uses for concrete that are daily changing our world. Concrete that light passes through and concrete that absorbs sound and concrete that is soft and concrete that is a palate for artists are the legacy of Edison's Victrola.

From the floor of a millennia-old peasant hut to the achievement of landing on Mars is but a blink in the eye of history, but it is in this span that we see the old beginnings and the new beginnings of concrete. The peasant who accidentally tamped his mud floor into a primitive form of concrete was the ancestor of the astronaut who will step out onto the indigenous concrete of Mars.

Space is the future of concrete. Spaceships today can barely transport the life systems of its occupants let alone the materials that will be needed to sustain humans in a Martian environment. But the makings of concrete will be under the very feet of Martian explorers. Rock and sand, trace chemicals and limestone are the stuff of Mars as they are of earth. Most important, the recent discovery of polar ice on Mars rounds out most all that will be needed to commence the colonization of the solar system.

Concrete will be with us wherever we journey because there is no place we may go where the makings of stone are not already there.

THE GREAT AGGLOMERATION

A few billion years ago the earth, for our purposes, can be viewed best as a monster Ready Mix concrete truck. Having been filled by someone, somewhere, with all of the ingredients that make up our planet, earth rumbled about the universe mixing, homogenizing, and differentiating the stuff that, in the fullness of time, became the planet's core, mantle, and crust. Earth was agglomerating into mostly solids. In other words...rocks.

Ultimately the agglomeration settled into the familiar geological structures that make up our planet home. The way the eternal concrete maker made the earth is essentially the same way that we concrete makers function today. We take various-sized pieces of rocks of various chemical properties, add some liquid, and reagglomerate them into concrete—artificial stone.

This reagglomeration is made much simpler for us because of natural, billions-year cycles that have existed since the earth first began its hardening process, a process that is still going on. The process is called the rock cycle. The cycle makes it unnecessary for us to chop up and pulverize the oldest and the hardest rocks, the igneous, in order to make them into what they were initially.

The rock cycle works like this. Igneous rock lies closest to the core of the earth and, at places and at times, it partially melts and is uplifted to form a softer rock, the plutonic. These rocks weather and are reduced to sediment, which, through compacting over long periods of time, become sedimentary rock. To complete the cycle both sedimentary rock and igneous rock, when pressed down toward higher temperatures in the depths of the earth, become again what they started out as—igneous rock.

Thus we are presented with rocks of varying chemistry and content, and it is from these rocks that we reassemble bits and pieces into the convenient slabs and shapes of man-made concrete. Rather it is man reagglomerated into what we call artificial stone, which, however, is not artificial at all, as it cannot be geologically or chemically differentiated from natural rock except by its lack of stratification and by the possible inclusion of materials not seen in the natural processes.

The very first evidence of man-made stone discovered so far is the floor of a primitive shelter that has been dated to around 5,600 BCE, found in present-day Yugoslavia.

It may be too much of a stretch to assume that the creation of this strangely isolated slab was the product of the intent of its builder. It is more likely that it came into being when there was a generalized movement of population westward and one of the refugees from the East brought with him or found, by accident or for a different use, some of the natron salts that were available in the lakes of Europe.

The common flooring of the time was pounded earth. It is interesting to conjecture that this particular builder, in order to lay the dust during pounding, wet down the surface, which, by the process of hydration, became a time-resistant concrete. This fortuitous concatenation of events resulting in a concrete floor seems to stand alone in an era when construction was the piling of one natural stone atop another. It was not until two or three thousand years later that concrete, essentially artificial stone, appeared as a reproducible industrial technique.

It is also possible that over the years there existed a faint cultural memory of how to make soft sand hard. Little specific evidence of man-made stone during these empty years has appeared but that may be due to the difficulty of defining what is man-made and what is not. There are occasional archaeological hints, dotted about between this early floor and the time of the pyramids of Giza, that individual builders knew what they were doing when they occasionally laid down concrete slabs.

CHAPTER 1

PYRAMIDIOTS

We now know that the use of concrete rose in the upper reaches of the Nile River thousands of years before the Christian era. It will be argued that the secrets of the making of the concrete stone blocks that were incorporated into the pyramids were held by the highly organized and highly secretive priesthood of the pharaohs.

Until an obscure French chemist placed scientific research against historical mythology the theories of how and why the pyramids were built ran from the fantastical to the theological.

Egyptologist Zahi Hawass, in exasperated response to the soaring flights of fancy concerning the construction and the uses of the Great Pyramids, reportedly coined the term "pyramidiots." In the absence of any acceptable explanations that could bring some sense to the many mysteries of the construction and uses of the pyramids, an entire mythology, part fatuous, part ludicrous, attracted surprising communities of believers around the world. There is, at least in America, a hunger for complete and easy answers to vexing problems.

Egyptology burst on the world's academic horizons when Napoleon exhaustively recorded what was discovered during his campaigns in Egypt. Unlike most conquerors, intent on destruction, Napoleon arrived in Egypt with a retinue of artists, historians, geologists, theologists, and other scientists and philosophers intent on recording what remained of four thousand years of Egyptian history. The record of these remarkable studies, which defined early questions about the ancient cultures of that remarkable country, are gathered together in Napoleon's official report.[1]

On November 25, 1922, a rich amateur archaeologist named Lord Carnavon, accompanied by an already famous Egyptologist, Howard Carter, broke into the underground tomb of a relatively unimportant pharaoh in the Valley of the Kings. When the two men opened the final seal there lay before them the unimaginable riches that even a minor Egyptian royal could command on his death.

The pharaoh was King Tutankhamen, who, at about age seventeen, had had his skull crushed either by accident or by design. He was mummified and laid to rest amid treasures and more archaeologically valuable goods, which Tut was to take with him into the his immortal life in the underworld.

The tomb was the most complete burial to have been found. Save for two minor incursions into the tomb² shortly after the young king's death a pristine royal tomb was, in terms of pharaonic history, a monumental discovery.

The mysteries that were inherent in the discoveries and the more delicious mysteries that were thereafter concocted led to an explosion of interest in all things Egyptian, which has continued down to our own time.

As if Carnavon had opened the Cave of the Winds rather than a mere royal burial, the outrush of commercial and intellectual creations submerged both good taste and, more important, good sense.

The spate of paperweights and wallpaper, lamps and furniture and other gewgaws led the Bauhaus artists into a holography of derived images that not even an Egyptian high priest would recognize. Fortunately the madness lasted only until the Great Depression put an end to such waste of resources, but the intellectual damage was done.

Although Tut's tomb was unrelated to any pyramidical structure, the discovered mysteries of Tut were quickly overshadowed by the still buried mysteries of how and why and by whom were the pyramids built.

The discovery of this tomb led, illogically, to a hard-edged almost indestructible belief, by the public and Egyptologists alike, that the pyramids were built as tombs for the royals. That no burials were ever found in any pyramid did not deter the development of an enormous literature to support this thesis. Entire professional careers and reputations were underpinned by the "evident logicality" of the concept of pyramids as tombs. No one could come up with any other reasonable answer to the question of why they were built so the most obvious—the burial thesis—took firm root.

Even now, when the lack of evidence of burials in the pyramids is beginning to seep into our understanding of the archaeology of Egypt, there has yet to be any theory that adequately argues a supportable motive for their construction. This mystery of exactly why the pyramids were built remains effectively unsolved.

There have been some interesting concepts concerning their function and there have been some that are interesting only in their unlikelihood. The most intriguing suggests a link between the stars and religious belief. All of the pyramids are situated precisely north and south and in Cheops pyramid "shafts" (a misnomer) were discovered that precisely link the North Star to both the "king's chamber" and the "queen's chamber." Two similar shafts pointing due south link both chambers to Orion, which, in the Egyptian pantheon, is related to Osiris. That they were not sighting shafts is evident from the fact that the northern shafts in both chambers arch around the main gallery of the pyramid. The precision and planning for these "useless shafts" equals the best we can do today with all of our sophisticated engineering machinery. These shafts, more than anything else, deepen the mystery of why the pyramids were built. A further puzzlement is that no similar shafts were ever discovered in any of the other pyramids.

Another curiosity, another mystery, is that there is little evidence in the pyramids of a solar orientation. The pharaoh Ahkenaten, the first monotheist, believed that there was only one god and that was the sun. Ahkenaten ruled during pyramid-building years but seemed to have little impact on the theism of the Egyptians or on their reasons for and methods of pyramid construction.

On the wilder shores of Egyptology, imaginations have run rampant. Our racial memories are replete with magic makers, witches, wizards, Titans, aliens, and other godlike creatures who could do things we can no longer do.

Erich von Däniken, a leading pyramidiot, published a book in 1968 entitled *Chariots of the Gods?*,[3] which dispensed with every known mystery of prehistory by posing the curious question "Was God an astronaut?" His solution to every curiosity, every contradiction, and every unfinished investigation into man's past was that "the spacemen did it." We were, according to von Däniken, visited by superior beings in "chariots of fire" between ten thousand and forty thousand years ago who provided the technology to build the pyramids.

As imaginative and unprovable as all this sounds, it twanged a chord among readers the world over. By 1970 four million copies of the book were sold, a serialization in a national yellow journal was published, and even Hollywood jumped on the bandwagon. This is a testament to the very human need to find our proper place in the dark vastness of the eternities of time and space. None of us wants to be alone.

Von Däniken's enormous effort to codify all the occultations of our history, however, remains little more than the substitution of the constructs of an invented, anthropomorphic race of beings not unlike the more recently developed teleologies of the Christian/Judaic worldview. When a mystery confounds history we tend to invent a God.

Another most arcane flight of fancy was offered as late as 1998 in a book entitled *The Giza Power Plant* by Christopher Dunn, whose arguments have pleased many pyramidiots. It is interesting to note the back cover blurb by Jeffery D. Kooistra of *Analog Science Fiction and Fact* magazine.

Dunn, like many others, was stymied by the question of how the pyramids were built with only human labor, inadequate materials, and primitive technologies.

As with other attempts to explain the unexplainable, Dunn invented a mysterious, sophisticated, highly technological civilization, which, he alleges, was destroyed in prehistory by an unnamed cataclysmic event.

Dunn argued that the Giza Pyramid was an enormous machine that was attuned to the thermal, magnetic, and gravitational energies of the earth. As these forces ebbed and flowed, Dunn argued, the Giza Pyramid resonated to these planetary forces and, somehow, through hydrolysis created hydrogen, the source of the extra-human energy that Dunn argues was required to accomplish the enormous tasks of pyramid building.

Hydrolysis, of course, requires all sorts of materials and constructions, none of which were found in the pyramid or anywhere else in Egypt. This absence of the mechanical structures required to create the chemical release of hydrogen from water is explained by Dunn in a manner that is both unarguable and unprovable. Dunn claims that all evidence of this technological marvel inside the Giza Pyramid was totally, and conveniently, destroyed by an enormous explosion when the machinery producing hydrogen got out of control. Sort of a serendipitous meltdown.

The energy created by the "Giza power plant" was the power source Dunn needed to explain the mystery of how the pyramids were built.

It is insightful that most, if not all, of the attempts to explain the why of the pyramids originated with the inability of Egyptologists to explain how they were built. The popularly accepted thesis that hundreds of thousands of men toiled for twenty years to quarry millions of blocks of hard stone using only copper tools was based on a report on the pyramids by Herodotus. He visited Egypt around the beginning of the Christian era and spoke with the local priests whose stories, now three thousand years old, were the basis for the carved stone theory.

Herodotus reported:

> The work went on in three-month shifts, a hundred thousand men to a shift. It took ten years of this oppressive labor to build the track along which the stone was hauled, a work in my opinion of hardly less magnitude than the pyramid itself. For it is five furlongs [660 feet] in length, sixty feet wide, forty-eight feet high at its highest point, and constructed of polished stone decorated with carvings of animals.

> To build the pyramid itself took twenty years.

There was no other evidence of the hewn-stone theory than this oral recounting of events passed along by sixty generations of priests. The image of whipped slaves hauling impossibly heavy stones caught the historical imagination of the public and has proven almost ineradicable.

As it became clear that the hewn-stone theory could be adequately explained only by the magical intervention of super-beings, a lonesome few inquiring scientific minds began to think of the only possible alternative, that the pyramids were poured concrete. This was initially greeted with some derision but, because of a careful second reading of Herodotus, a glimmer of historical evidence began.

Moustafa Gadalla, an independent Egyptologist, in his book[4] has marshaled all of the arguments that opt against hewn stone and for a pouring process. He states that the initial error occurred in a mistranslation of Herodotus, when the Greek historian reported on the method by which the pyramids were built.

"The pyramid was built thus, in the form of steps. After preparing the foundation they raised stones by using machines made of short planks of wood, which raised the stones from the ground to the first range of steps. On this range there was another machine which received the stone on arrival. Another machine advanced the stone on the second step." And so on upward.

Gadalla argues that the confusion lies in the Greek word *mechane*, which is a "non-specific term indicating a type of device." Herodotus's translators recognized the word as *machine* rather than the more general term *device*.

Herodotus's statement that the stones were raised by a machine using "short planks of wood" makes no sense at all unless *machine* is translated as *mold*. Then the report by the Greek historian becomes clear that the Egyptian priests were speaking of a wood mold made of short planks into which stones, in the form of a liquid, were poured.

Joseph Davidovits, the originator of the theory of poured stone, presents a series of arguments that leads to the new theory that the stones were *poured in place*! These arguments can be summarized as follows.

The Great Pyramid of Khufu contains approximately 2.6 million blocks. These blocks weigh between two and seventy tons apiece. While it may be possible for a gang of men to lift two-ton blocks to the ever increasing height of the pyramid, the problem remains to explain the seventy-ton monsters that provide part of the roof of the king's chamber, how they were cut to such precision with only copper tools, and how they could be raised and put in place with the accuracy that the pyramid constructors required.

THE PYRAMID WARS

In 1974 Joseph Davidovits, an amateur in the eyes of established and respected Egyptologists, produced a material in his laboratory in Saint-Quentin that seemed to approximate natural stone. Dr. Davidovits unwittingly redefined his entire future when he sought the opinions of geologists concerning the "reclaimerate" sample he had produced.

"In June, 1974, I realized that what we were producing were materials that were very close to natural cements, such as rocks based on feldspars, the feld spathoids. One day, as a joke, I asked my scientific partners at the Musée d'Histoire Naturelle de Paris what would happen if we buried in the ground a piece of the product that we were synthesizing in the laboratory at the time, and an archeologist were to discover it in 3,000 years time."

Without yet relating his discovery to Egyptian history, Davidovits, by his choice of a time period of three millennia, was already linking reagglomeration to prehistory construction techniques.

The reply of the geologists was startling and precise: "Their answer was surprising: the archeologist would analyze this object disinterred from the garden of a ruin in Saint-Quentin, and the analysis would reveal that the nearest natural outcrop of the stone was in Egypt in the Aswan region!"

At this point Davidovits took an enormous, instinctive leap forward. He had, in his own words, "built up a whole scenario:

blocks of soft limestone extracted from quarries, when broken up with water, could give a limestone mortar easily transportable in baskets. The mortar, mixed with ingredients including kaolin, natron salt and chalk, could be poured out and compacted into moulds just as concrete is, directly on the site of the pyramids."

Concrete! The pyramids, he reasoned, were poured concrete. This was a frontal attack on the professional reputations and long-held beliefs of eminent Egyptologists. If proven, entire careers could be destroyed.

The initial battle took place in 1982 in Toronto at the Third International Congress of Egyptologists. Lined up on one side were approximately three hundred recognized Egyptologists of substantial professional reputations and, on the other, stood Dr. Joseph Davidovits, chemist, amateur Egyptologist, and a self-described enfant terrible in the field.

The opposition was led by the doyen of all Egyptologists, Jean-Phillipe Lauer, an eighty-year-old scholar long recognized as the ultimate authority on all millennia-old matters Egyptian. Lauer proclaimed the Davidovits theory "ridiculous" and announced that "there are many ridiculous surveys, not stupid but impossible." And reflecting the opprobrium laid on Davidovits as being and amateur he added, "Not many are serious."

The most serious charges that can be mounted in academia are the lack of seriousness and the lack of academic standing. Toronto was a rout for Dr. Davidovits but he had managed to put his foot in the door. He realized that in order to gain a serious hearing from the Egyptologists it would be necessary to meet them on their own ground.

The comforting concept that all the stones of history, Greek and Roman and Renaissance, had been carved out of natural material allowed the established Egyptologists to slide over and dismiss some subtle considerations. Davidovits, a careful scientific researcher and observer, looked beyond the easily accepted view of pyramid building. He invented a word, "geopolymer," and set up a research organization, the Geopolymer Institute of Saint-Quentin. In order to answer his detractors, of which there were many and of which there are still not many fewer, Davidovits then posed eight unanswered observations. Each of his observations tends to weaken the carved-stone argument and each tends to strengthen the suggestion that the stones of the later New Kingdom pyramids were cast.

Davidovits argued as follows.

1. Almost none of the pyramid blocks match the Giza bedrock chemically or mineralogically. Until Davidovits raised this most obvious point the chemistry of the stones of Giza had been largely ignored.

2. Limestone, like all natural rock, is stratified. The limestone that was used in pyramid building was deposited, in millennia past, from the waters that covered the Giza plain. This process, over millions of years, creates the familiar stratification that is found in all stone throughout the world. That the pyramid blocks contain no strata is a powerful indication that these stones were altered from their natural state.

3. Geochemical analyses have shown that the properties of the pyramid blocks match those of at least twenty different Egyptian quarries. If this is true then the suggestion that the "core masonry of the pyramid was quarried from local bedrock" can no longer be supported.

4. There are about ten standard block lengths among the stones of the pyramids. Carving by hand with copper tools, such uniform dimensions strain credulity. If the stones were cut, there would be no reason why the masons would have gone to the agonizingly time-consuming process of cutting standard lengths. Standardization by molds are the logical answer to this precision.

5. The longest blocks in the pyramids *always have the same length*. This could hardly have been accomplished by carving since strata and defects would make uniform dimensions impossible.

6. A central objection long overlooked by early Egyptologists is that copper tools cut limestone, if at all, inefficiently and slowly. New Kingdom masons had only copper available to them as cutting tools. It was not until a millennium later that bronze appeared in Egypt, much too late for the Aswan pyramids. Using copper tools the builders would have been unable to produce the millions of limestone blocks within the historically established span of the twenty years that the Great Pyramid was abuilding.

7. Even using modern tools, carving of limestone blocks to a rigid standard results in at least one failure for every block cut. There should be, therefore, evidence of millions of cracked blocks lying about. Observers in antiquity as well as modern archaeologists have made no such discovery.

8. Finally, Davidovits observed that the pyramid blocks are 20 percent lighter than the local bedrock limestone. Cast blocks are always lighter than natural stone due to the presence of trapped air bubbles.

It is only recently that professional Egyptologists, faced with the logical, have begun to accept the poured concrete concept. The general public, however, still clings to the romantic image of carving and hauling and lifting impossibly gigantic stones and laying them down with impossible precision. The common wisdom is that the pyramids were simply the application of enormous amounts of treasure and human energy to build burial monuments for pharaohs. That no burials were ever found and that the impossibility of masons cutting and lifting and placing two and a half million stones in twenty years do not seem to touch accepted beliefs. Indeed, when crypto-Egyptologists accept the impossibility of carving and setting they go off on tangents involving aliens from space and highly technological prehistory cultures that were wiped out by an enormous explosion of one of the imagined energy machines, which, conveniently, destroyed all evidence of the advanced technology. A sort of Atlantis in the desert scenario.

The story of stone-built structures starts with Imhotep, the great scribe and architect of the Zoser pyramid. Imhotep was a wellborn, highly educated engineer who became high priest to pharaohs. He has been credited with the first advance from sundried, frangible bricks to the hard stone bricks that make up most of the building blocks of Zoser's step pyramid. In his book[5] Dr. Davidovits identifies and locates all of the materials for stone making that would have been available to Imhotep in the third millennium before Christ and he describes the process by which these materials, all at hand, could have resulted in the production of the small hard stone bricks of Zoser's pyramid.

In the ancient mythic pantheon of Egyptian gods one stands preeminent. The ram-headed god Khnum is the deity called the Divine Potter, who formed humanity out of the earth. Khnum is depicted at a potter's wheel forming ordinary mortals out of the common silt of the Nile and creating more exalted nobility out of harder materials. Later in Egyptian history Khnum, the potter, lost position to the god Amun who is depicted as creating man by carving him out of stone. The change in emphasis between these two gods paralleled the progress from soft copper tools to harder bronze.

The discovery in the inner chambers of the step pyramid of thirty thousand stone vessels that were impossible to turn on a wheel was left unexplained by Egyptologists. These objects, perfectly smooth and formed in such a manner inside and out, seemingly defied explanation. Eventually the thought began to permeate the literature that these were not turned objects but

were, indeed, molded. Davidovits describes these vessels thus. There are unique and enigmatic hard stone vessels, made of slate, diorite, and basalt. Some of these materials are harder than iron. No sculptor today would attempt to work with these materials. "Their design is extremely beautiful and impossible to carve. No tool marks are found on their surfaces. They must have been cast in molds."

Another startling find was a wafer-thin cup made of anorthositic gneiss, a very hard stone. It is only one of tens of thousands of hard stone vessels found in the Aswan plain but, while the method of construction of many other Egyptian vessels can be argued, there is no possible explanation for this cup other than that it was cast and formed in a soft state that then set into one of the hardest of geological materials.

Great overarching theories such as the Davidovits theory and, indeed, the Einsteinian general theory of relativity are ultimately proven or disproven by the smallest of pieces of evidence. Einstein's work gained strength and support when, as predicted, the light passing across Venus in an eclipse was observed to have been bent by the gravity of Venus. Likewise the geopolymer theory finds justification in this simple cup, idly fashioned by one of the masons of a great pharaoh.

And yet in spite of mounting evidence of the cast stone premise there still remain sincere people prepared to go to extreme lengths to prove that the stones of the pyramids are natural.

One of these is Dr. Menno Blaauw, a researcher at the Delft Interfaculty Reactor Institute. Blaauw applied the very latest nuclear technology to investigate a piece of stone from the Khufu pyramid. According to Dr. Blaauw the stone was stolen from the pyramid and smuggled out of Egypt by his father, an Egyptologist himself. The small stone lay about for years until the younger Blaauw, intrigued by the theories of Dr. Davidovits, brought all of the sophisticated technology of his institute to bear on the stone. Was it natural or was it man-made? As a result of a battery of carefully constructed scientific tests Dr. Blaauw declared the sample to be natural stone.

When queried on this pronouncement Dr. Davidovits pointed out, "Of course, the studies revealed that the stone was natural, since all of the material that went in to casting the sample in antiquity were natural to begin with." All of the scientific effort Blaauw brought to bear to disprove the casting theory merely ended up proving that a stone, cast or cut, that is made up of natural materials will, quite obviously, test as natural.

DECLINE AND FALL

The Giza pyramids represented the high-water mark of the use of cast stone in construction in Egypt. For the next three millennia, construction of tombs and monuments generally involved the use of common brick. There is considerable mystery surrounding the absence of evidence of cast stones throughout Egypt during these long years. The art was lost or forgotten or suppressed as the pharaonic empires lost their strength and ability to organize life along the Nile.

There are few supportable suggestions concerning this loss but at least two of them have the charm of relating to changes in the ecology and the geology of the area. One additional theory is based on the suggestion that, when the Egyptian high priests lost their ability to discipline the priesthood, secrecy could no longer be maintained and there was no other body to whom the art could be safely passed.

The manufacture of artificial stone requires the calcining of limestone. This is a simple process of burning limestone over fires stoked by wood and then grinding the product into a powder. Shortly after the last of the great pyramids were built the limited supply of wood began to decline as its use for construction and heating and calcining of lime overtook the ability of the limited forests of Egypt to replenish themselves. By Roman times whatever extensive forests that had flourished in the third millennium BCE had all but disappeared. Furthermore as the power and the reach of lesser pharaohs declined the import of wood from abroad became more expensive and less dependable. Thus, one logical explanation of why the art of casting stones fell out of favor could have been due simply to the declining availability and the increasing cost of fuel for the kilns.

The casting of stone like mummification and other Egyptian arts shrouded in mystery, was a closely held secret guarded by an all powerful priesthood. As the carefully tiered structure of the priesthood unraveled, much of the cultural and technological record of Egypt was lost. It is reasonable to assume that, rather than let priestly secrets melt out into the general population, the chain of knowledge was at some point broken and the art was lost.

A third explanation has both romance and reality. For thousands of years, Egypt and other cultures worked the fabled mines of the Sinai. The output of these mines, which have come to be known as King Solomon's Mines, would diminish just about the time the great pyramids were being built. The casting of large stones such as those used in the Aswan pyramids required the arsenic minerals contained in the varied output of the Sinai mines. These minerals were the medium that allowed the rapid hydraulic setting of Egyptian concrete. When the essential chemicals were no longer available the manufacture of large artificial stones ceased.

It would take almost three thousand years before the widespread use of reagglomerated material—concrete—was rediscovered and then, astoundingly, it would be lost for another two thousand years.

BETWEEN EGYPT AND ROME

A fter the decline of the great pharaonic empires in the third millennium BCE, construction in Egypt reverted to the use of the sun-dried bricks that had preceded the limestone-based, poured concrete of some of the pyramids.

However, some of the closely held techniques of the Egyptian priesthood leaked to Asia Minor and parts of Europe where mosaics, which required the use of cementitious materials, evolved into high art in the first millennium BCE. There is sporadic archaeological evidence, especially in Syria and Greece, of the use of these agglomerated materials during this pre-Roman period.

Mosaic construction, a process by which hard, decorative elements are embedded into a cementitious base, was already in evidence in the second millennium BCE in Chaldean architecture. Since mosaics deal only with the surfaces of structures they had little impact on architecture other than as adornment. The process of making the mortar that held the baked clay mosaics in place is essentially the same mixing of materials that produces concrete.

In the Chaldea, columns were covered first with a mortar material into which were impressed small cones of fired clay. In the beginning these cones were set in repetitive patterns and in some cases painted. Later in Chaldean history the use of mosaics evolved into what were to become perseverative themes, those of war and victory.

Ultimately the best-known and best-preserved mosaics came from the buried city of Pompeii where the newly rediscovered lime mortar concrete was in evident use in building construction as well as surface decoration. The Pompeian mosaics matched the luxury and the opulence of the city itself. The most noted of all is the depiction of the defeat of Darius by Alexander the Great. This mosaic involved the setting of over one million pieces of tile into a lime mortar base.

The close connection between lime mortar concrete and mosaics is demonstrated in the diagram of mosaic stratigraphy.

It is clear from this diagram that the second layer, rudus, and the third layer, nucleus, which underlie the actual image of the mosaic, are, simply, concrete. The first layer, statumen, is a form of plaster not dissimilar to plasters used today.

It can be argued that this use of cementitious material during the thousands of years before the rise of the Roman empire had kept some of the techniques of agglomeration barely alive. Why knowledge of the making of concrete keeps disappearing and reappearing throughout recorded history is a mystery. But its appearance and disappearance significantly altered cultures and civilizations. Had Egyptian concrete making survived, the post-pharaonic period would likely have given rise to more settled and less vagabond cultures. It is fascinating to contemplate how effective concrete might have been to defend against the attacks of the Visigoths and other invaders from the north. Indigenous tribes all across Europe would have had concrete structures and concrete defenses that may have allowed them to survive, grow in power, and extend their territories. It is likely new and powerful cultures would have arisen to challenge the rise of Greece and Rome and, indeed, might have interdicted the gestation and growth of both of these cultures so seminal to our own time. Without Greek philosophy, polity, and literature and without Roman governance, militarism, and engineering we would be hard pressed to define the sources for the democracies of later centuries, or whether, in the end, the democratic ethos would have risen at all.

MOSAIC STRATIGRAPHY

The following stratigraphy is adapted from ancient literary sources. It is to be used only as a general reference in this document. In practice, all mosaics do not necessarily display this stratigraphy.

A mosaic can be built on natural ground made of soil or rock, or on top of a previous pavement. The mosaic itself is composed of a variety of foundation or preparatory layers and a layer of tesserae.

1 • **Statumen** · First preparatory layer, which is made of large stones laid on the ground, previously leveled and rammed. This layer only exists if the mosaic has been constructed on a natural soil.

2 • **Rudus** · Second preparatory layer, which is spread over the statumen. This layer is made of a lime mortar with large aggregates.

3 • **Nucleus** · Third preparatory layer, which is spread over the rudus in a thinner layer. The nucleus is made of a mortar with fine aggregates.

4 • **Bedding layer** · Fourth preparatory layer of mortar, which is very rich in lime, and thinly applied in small sections over the nucleus. Tesserae are inserted in this layer before the mortar sets.

5 • **Tessellatum** · Layer that constitutes the mosaic surface and is composed of tesserae and mortar filling the interstices between them.

SOURCE: WWW.GETTY.EDU/CONSERVATION

THE NABATEANS

The Nabateans were a desert tribe of traders who flourished in the arid regions between Palestine and present-day Jordan. They numbered about ten thousand, a very large population for the first millennium BCE, an impressive number to have been supported by their barren desert homeland.

They seem to have emerged in about 800 BCE after having been driven from the more lush regions of coastal Palestine. Faced with untillable desert land and very little water in their new home, and hemmed in from the east and the west by larger, more powerful tribes, it is a wonder that they managed to survive as an independent empire for a thousand years.

An important element of their survival was that their neighbors had no design on their barren land. Had it been rich and yielding of crops we might never have heard of the Nabateans as they would have soon been conquered and absorbed into the tribal roils of the time.

Survive they did and the lovely places they left to us supports the argument that technology leads culture. In the case of the Nabateans their survival was guaranteed by another inexplicable rise in the use of concrete. The rediscovery of the technology of a concrete that holds water was related to the fact that the Nabateans were desert traders whose function was to link the spices of the Far East to the coast of the Mediterranean via the ancient spice route and thus on to Europe.

One route would certainly have been across the Sinai and on into the fertile Nile Valley where the use of concrete must have survived. Somehow, this desert people, driven by their desperate need for retaining water, were able to draw from dim tribal memories of ancient Egypt and duplicate and even improve on the achievements of the great pharaohs of Giza.

But Egyptian concrete was made of porous limestone, which was not designed for nor capable of retaining water. The Egyptian agglomerations required the addition of the minerals that would create such a cement.

It is not unlikely that the Nabateans, as desert travelers familiar with the barrens to the south of them, were able to locate and extract the small quantity of required raw materials that rendered concrete impervious to water from the mostly exhausted mines of King Solomon in the Sinai desert. Also, in the Hisma desert near Wadi Rum, there are deposits of silica that served as a substitute for the volcanic ash from the area of Pozzuoli in the vicinity of Vesuvius, later discovered by the

Romans. They had limestone aplenty and there is archaeological evidence in Nabatea of limekiln pits used for burning limestone, the essential process in the making of concrete.

This isolated tribe developed or acquired the knowledge for making waterproof pozzolan concrete hundreds of years before the process was rediscovered by the Roman engineers, and, as we shall see, it was this discovery that allowed the Nabateans to thrive in the desert without water.

Around 850 BC, King Mesha of Moab conquered a considerable territory east of the Jordan. In the famous Moabite Stone the king proudly declared, "I made two reservoirs in the midst of [Qerkhah]. Now there was no cistern in the city, so I said to all the people, Make you every man a cistern in his house."

These household cisterns located within the Nabatean cities were supplied by open catchments and by pipes running down from rooftops. This may be the first time that water cisterns are mentioned in a text, but the device itself must have been invented considerably earlier.

These individual cisterns were the forerunners of the great Nabatean secret cisterns that extended out beyond the cities into the desert and, brilliantly hidden from their enemies, were designed to supply their camel caravans across the spice routes in the deserts.

Recently, archaeologists made a remarkable discovery in the Nabatean desert. They unearthed a stone mill designed for the making of olive oil. This suggested that the area at one time supported olive groves, which would have required much more water than existed in the desert at that time. The puzzle was from whence the needed water came.

The Greek historian Diodorus Siculus wrote about the Nabateans around 50 BCE, "They are conspicuous lovers of freedom and flee into the desert using this as a stronghold. They fill cisterns and caves with rainwater, making them flush with the rest of the land. They leave signals there which are known to themselves and not understood by anyone else…so that they do not constantly need water in waterless regions."

These cisterns, like the vast cisterns of Rome that came later, would leak like a sieve without a coating of waterproof cement. Such cisterns allowed the Nabatean culture to grow and blossom and bequeath to us the marvel that is Petra.

"If ever a dead city held romance it is Petra….Hewn out of solid rock in the midst of a mountain wilderness like a great carved opal glowing in a desert, this lost caravan city staggers the most experienced travelers."[1]

"The four Nabatean towns of Haluza, Mamshit, Avdat and Shivta are spread along routes linking them to the Mediterranean end of the Incense and Spice route. Together they reflect the hugely profitable trade in frankincense and myrrh from south Arabia to the Mediterranean, which flourished from the 3rd century B.C. to 2nd century A.D. With the vestiges of their sophisticated irrigation systems, urban constructions, forts, and caravanserai they bear witness to the way in which the harsh desert was settled for trade and agriculture."[2]

Assyrian records imply that the Nabateans were moving regular camel caravans through the waterless deserts as early as 700 BCE. Absolutely essential to this kind of trade would have been water sources along the caravan routes hidden from other traders.

The cisterns had to be fed, however, and the only source of water was the light and intermittent rains that sprinkled the area. The water from these rains is immediately absorbed into the dry ground. Rainwater caught on the surface would, in moments, be evaporated back into the atmosphere. The Nabateans needed to somehow funnel what little water there was into their cisterns. Their solution was ingenious and effective, rendered the cisterns essentially invisible, required no human activity, and was made possible only by waterproof cement.

Large areas surrounding the cisterns were dug out of the desert and then covered with a thin layer of concrete. This waterproof layer was sloped down into a cistern. The entire catchment was then covered with the desert sand, which left no mark aboveground yet provided a slow but continual replenishment of the water levels in the cisterns. The light rains and dews that gathered onto the sand above the catchment would seep down to the waterproof layer and be guided by the slope of the concrete into the cistern. By keeping the water underground and interdicting it from disappearing in the depths of the desert sands, the Nabateans were able to water their camels on the long trek from Jordan to the Mediterranean carrying the spices of Arabia to Europe.

In Egypt the invention of lime-based concrete had created great monuments. Later in Rome the extension of empire was made possible by volcanic ash from Vesuvius. But only in the Nabatean desert was the very existence of a thousand-year-old empire entirely dependent on a thin skin of cementitious material.

The Nabateans are a curious link between the Egyptians and Romans. They straddle the two major cultures in both geography and time. From a thousand years after Giza to a thousand years before the Roman empire, this desert people and their caravans of plodding camels were the chiefest link between the two regions. As the Egyptians lost the skill to make artificial stone, their neighbor and trade partner the Nabateans converted the porous concrete of the pyramids to a material that would hold water.

If the Nabateans had not made this portentous discovery and become perhaps the agency from which the Romans picked up the hint, consider how history might have been different. Without Roman empire building with waterproof concrete, Greek culture rather than Roman might have intersected with the Judeo-Christian tribalisms of the first century. What could have emerged from that marriage might have been more Greek, or more Jewish, or more Christian than the Roman profile we now know.

ROMAN CONCRETE AND ITS IMPACT ON WORLD HISTORY

Place a perfectly round hoop upright on a surface. Rotate it around its vertical axis. The result is a sphere. Dispose of the bottom half of the sphere. The result is a dome. Build a wall around the bottom rim of the dome of the same height as the dome. The result is the pantheon, the most perfect geometric, hollow structure ever devised by man.

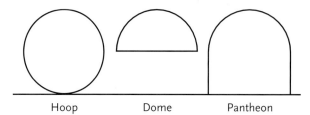

Hoop   Dome   Pantheon

PANTHEON MODEL

COURTESY CITY OF ROME

The two-thousand-year-old Pantheon was first conceived of and constructed in 27 BC by the consul Marcus Vipsanius Agrippa. It was destroyed by fire in AD 80 and was reconstructed in its present state by the emperor Hadrian about 124 AD.[1] It is the only building in the entire classical world that survived intact from the Greco-Roman period. It is the largest dome built in antiquity and it was not surpassed for a millennium and a half until Brunelleschi constructed the dome of the Cathedral of Florence, completed in 1436.

The dome is a coffered, unreinforced concrete structure, 43.3 meters in diameter.

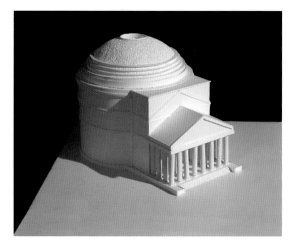

At its peak is an opening (*oculus*) that allows light in and smoke to get out. The height from the oculus to the floor is the same as the diameter of the dome. The floor of the Pantheon is a circle also exactly 43.3 meters. It is as if the Roman engineers set this task for themselves, to "create a structure entirely defined by a perfect circle and confined within a 43.3 meter cube."

The circular aesthetic is equaled by its execution. The unreinforced, unsupported concrete dome was constructed of Roman concrete that exceeds in tensile strength that of most modern concretes. The deep coffering serves to eliminate excess weight of material while retaining the strength supplied by the walls of the coffers. The high tensile strength of Roman concrete appears to come from the way the concrete was applied as well as the inclusion of volcanic ash. It was laid in very small amounts and tamped down to remove excess water. This prevents the debilitating voids that normally form in concrete as the material dries, thus enormously increasing its strength.[2]

In a construction so committed to geometry, the overall size of the original circle might be expected to conform to a whole number that is readily convertible to circular measurement by degrees. In the Pantheon, however, the circle is 135.5177 *pedae* (Roman feet) in diameter, which relates to nothing circular. In addition, there is a "legal" ped that puts the diameter at 162.6596, which also relates to nothing. This is odd since the probability that the Roman engineers would lay out a purely arbitrary size for so rigidly conceived a building is practically nil. In addition, engineers of the Pantheon would have had to deal with dividing the circular dome for the placement of the coffers, which are not only exquisitely arranged but diminish in size as they approach the apex of the dome. This problem is reminiscent of the latitude lines of the earth, which diminish to a point (zero) in circumference as they approach the geographic poles. The dome of the Pantheon is a cameo re-creation of the lines of latitude and longitude, which would be dealt with in succeeding millennia.

PANTHEON INTERIOR

UNKNOWN ARTIST

POURING THE COFFERS

The siting of these layers of concrete a hundred feet in the air required brave and sophisticated masons. An astounding fact is that the Pantheon was completed in only six years. (Other undocumented sources give construction time as seven years.) Compare this to St. Peter's in Rome, which took fifty years, and St. Paul's in London, which took thirty-five years, both of which were built of cut stone. In contrast St. Sophia in Istanbul, a smaller concrete dome of 32 meters constructed centuries later, took only five years to complete. The use of concrete proved many times more efficient than cut stone, but the secrets of the material and the technology of unreinforced concrete, which had been lost for millennia, were to be rediscovered anew, improved, and refined by the engineers of Rome.

Consider the problems of pouring a concrete structure that is both very large and curved. There was no possibility of pouring it in place as one piece, not only because of its span but also because concrete is a liquid that requires time to set and, as a liquid, it requires at least one level surface; it cannot gel as a curve. Furthermore one of the strengths of Roman concrete is that the air bubbles, formed during pouring and mixing, were removed by tamping and tamping could also be accomplished only if the setting concrete had at least one level surface. Thus the roof was poured in individual molds known as corbels, either on the ground or aloft, supported by a timber network.

The Pantheon roof, resulting from the clever shape of the corbels, was both enormously strong and light in weight. In

PANTHEON ROOF/OUTER DOME
PHOTOGRAPHS REESE PALLEY

order to pour and tamp, the molds were poured upside down. The indented area at the top dramatically cut the weight and the thickened edges dramatically increased the strength. The corbels were poured in decreasing size and thickness and, when dried, were turned over and became the smooth shape of the top surface of the dome. The individual corbels had to be exact in both the vertical and the horizontal and the curvatures of each had to mesh precisely with its neighbor to create the overall curvature of the dome.

The hollowed-out corbels, seen from below, when set in place give the unique and pleasing characteristic pattern to the ceiling of the Pantheon. What are now the curved tops, carefully dimensioned so as to fit one to the other, create the domed outer surface.

HEROD'S DREAM

Outside of Egypt, and except for the bookishness of the Jews, much of the recorded history of the world between 3000 BCE and 500 BCE is a tabula rasa. Starting in the fifth century BCE, religious cultures, led by Judaism, emerge from the confusions of polytheism. A social upheaval of religious thought began that was to form our sense of ourselves for two and a half millennia. During this roiling period Rome developed from republic to empire, Greek literature and philosophy began the search for reason, Jews were kings, and Christianity eventually conquered all.

For the purpose of this book, however, the trace of concrete from Egypt to Rome is far from clear. We do know some things. The Egyptians lost the art and until the eighth century BCE almost all construction was rubble and sun-dried brick. Around 800 BCE, as noted earlier, the Nabateans emerge from the mists of the Judaea desert with a sophisticated knowledge of waterproof cement.

Rome, sometime later, discovered the magical qualities of volcanic ash from Vesuvius. With this discovery and its use in aqueducts and cisterns came the rise of the Roman empire. Unless one subscribes to the theory of simultaneous discovery, of which there is ample evidence in history, there might well have been a link between Rome and the Nabatean desert tribe. Trade and transport between Palestine and Italy was active and, in the case of King Herod's family, as we shall see later, intermarriage was common. All of the conditions for the sharing of the secrets of making concrete between Rome and Palestine were in place.

That the transfer took place in Palestine is amply supported by the construction of a wondrous city and port in the first century BCE. Herod, king of the Jews and loyal liege of the Romans, had his engineers design and construct Caesarea, a city that could not have been built better nor more logically even in our own time.

It is likely that the actual construction was designed and supervised by Roman engineers abetted by the knowledge of waterproof cement handed down to Herod by way of his Nabatean mother.

The difficulty in writing of a commodity such as concrete with its long and rich past is that there is a constant temptation to wander down the side roads of subjects that may be important and fascinating but marginal in the perspective of concrete's millennia-long record.

The city of Caesarea, and its port Sebastos, was a marvel not only in its construction but also in the logicality of its design. Caesarea, contrary to almost all of the accidental growth of cities

PORT OF SEBASTOS TERINGO
COURTESY NATIONAL GEOGRAPHIC

in the known world, was laid out in regular geometric "islands" with straight and parallel streets connecting the city and its scores of storage vaults to the harbor. The storage vaults, which lined the harbor and extended even under the Temple of Augustus, were warehouses for the grain, the wine, and the construction materials that flowed back and forth between Europe and Palestine and beyond into the Arabian and Mesopotamian regions far to the east. There were at least fifty of these structures, designed by King Herod and his architects in his Herod's dream of an essential port city.

Sebastos was the central justification for the city itself. Herod chose to combine the port with a major city for its protection thus securing a safe and defensible outlet on the Mediterranean coast.

The port activities as well as the population of the city required a regular and plentiful supply of water. In his planning for the Caesarea, Herod included an aqueduct, which arose in the faraway slopes of Mount Carmel. This aqueduct was made feasible by the use of water-proof cement, which lined the canals of the structure. As the city grew and prospered, more water was required so the engineers, most probably Roman, simply duplicated exactly the original structure, a solution seen in so many modern "mirrored" constructions such as the former World Trade Center Towers. The line joining the two aqueducts can be clearly seen under each of the vaults.

Harbors on the Palestinian coast were then, as now, rare. The region's Mediterranean coast is straight, low, and sandy for

CAESAREA PLAN

Two quays surround a well-protected harbor with a narrow entrance designed to keep the worst of stormy seas out. The lighthouse on the end of the southern quay beckons the seaman as does the enormous temple, extreme left, which Herod built to glorify his lord and master, the caesar Augustus.

CAPTION C. BRANDON

most of its length, so a protected harbor had
to be built from scratch. Choosing an
ancient landing area known from antiquity as Strato's Tower, the city of
Caesarea was created to glorify Herod
and to further his commercial
exploitation of the spice route from
Arabia to Europe, of which Herod's
kingdom was the transfer point.

   Both the quays and the harbor are
of enormous importance to this historical
record as they were both constructed upon
foundations of poured concrete.

   "Josephus's 'massively built tower' and 'blocks of
stone' that supported the colossal statues flanking the harbor
entrance turned out, on investigation, to be made of concrete.
The best example, however, is the giant concrete block that
forms the western end...of the northern breakwater....The block
is 11.5 by 15 meters long and wide, and 2.4 meters high. When
the team exposed the vertical faces of this block, they also discovered parts of the wooden forms into which the builders had
poured the concrete. The formwork had been constructed from
large wooden base beams with uprights and horizontal planking
inside and out. The elaborate carpentry includes lap joints and
mortising. To prevent collapse during pouring, the builders had
passed tie beams through the volume to be filled with concrete"[3]

   The concrete foundation of the quays were *poured underwater.* This was likely accomplished in two ways. The first, for
small installations, required divers, free diving without oxygen,
to construct the wooden forms under the unprotected sea.

   Long wooden planks were driven through the loose sea
bottom silt down to bedrock. These had to be reinforced under
water with the horizontal members. The spaces between the
planks required caulking to prevent the escape of the liquid
concrete. All of this hard work had to be accomplished by men
holding their breath.

   The second method was designed for the very large blocks
that were found underwater in the harbor.

> Thousands of workmen, both slaves and conscripts, would have
> labored at a furious pace to bring the project to completion in twelve
> years or less. In places they used stone blocks quarried in the vicin-
> ity in sizes they could easily manage from boats. For the larger
> works workmen put together the forms for the concrete on or near
> shore and then sledged and towed them into position. Professional

FILLING UNDERWATER CAISSONS

In this illustration the wooden
caissons were sited by the use of
eight oared galleys. They were then
filled with concrete, in sections, from
huge barges.

ILLUSTRATION C. BRANDON

divers (called urinatores by the Romans because of their predictable physiological response to spending long periods under water) had already prepared the sea floor to receive the framework. Workers inserted mortar into the cavity between the inner and outer planking of the forms, causing the forms to sink into place. Others lowered the stone aggregate (caementa) and mortar, probably in leather buckets, into place beneath the sea's surface. As each huge concrete block was completed, stonemasons laid down a pavement of limestone blocks above it, fragments of which…were found. Still other laborers dropped stones along the block's outer edge to create a sloping barrier, or berm, to protect the base of each block from undercutting by the sea. The berm protected the wooden formwork as well. Fragments of it have enabled modern archeologists to reconstruct the ancient engineering.[4]

The strength of Roman concrete depended as much on the technique of the pouring as it did on the material itself. In the case of Caesarea the layering and especially the tamping had to be done underwater. On land the tamping process was made possible by the gravity-induced weight of the tamping equipment. Underwater buoyancy canceled out much of the useful weight. As a result the tamping process became a major complication to underwater pouring.

The concrete used in Caesarea was of the pozzolan type used in Rome. There is a suggestion, not unlikely considering the amount of sea trade activity in the eastern Mediterranean, that material from the foothills of Vesuvius in the region of Pozzuoli was actually imported by Herod. It is also just as likely that similar arsenic salts to the pozzolan material were still available from the fabled mines of the Sinai. In any event Herod built his great city and port of solid concrete, which, modern underwater archaeologists tell us, is still lying on the bottom of the sea and, after two thousand years, still affords some protection to the coast.

Herod was a Roman zealot. He admired all things Roman and in his new city were included the architecture, the entertainment, and the commercial zeal that characterized Roman culture. The temple he built was Greco Roman and the concrete itself was either Roman in origin or imitation.

Herod was a bold builder. In addition to Caesarea he built Masada, Herodian, the Holy Temple in Jerusalem, and the huge Temple Mount upon which the temple was constructed.

The jewel of all of his Herculean efforts was the great city of Caesarea. Conceived in toto as an artist would conceive a sculpture, Herod cast his city in timeless Roman concrete. His vision lives on today as archaeologists rediscover, stone by stone, the dream city on the shore of Palestine.

CHAPTER 4

VITRUVIUS AND GIOCONDO, 1445–1525

World-altering changes most often occur as the result of very large events. Wars, geography, invasions, disease, and weather profoundly alter the way the world works. Once in a while, however, the course of history is determined by the unlikely confluence of talents that emerge in one person who, at the same time, has the public power and influence to apply those talents.

In the history of concrete this fortuitous, isolated, and rare coexistence of talent and power had been present in the Egyptian high priest Imhotep. Architect, engineer, and theologian, he was privy to all of the secrets of empire, one of which was how to mix sand and lime with the waters of the Nile to create some of the man-made stones that have been identified in the pyramids. And he had the ear of the pharaoh.

Later, another historical singularity, the Roman architect Vitruvius, combined literary skill and the knowledge of architecture in his book *De architectura* in which the secret of waterproof cement was preserved, hidden and safe, for a thousand years. Finally, it was Fra Giovanni Giocondo, a thousand years after the Roman empire had declined, who translated and edited Vitruvius's newly found manuscript. Giocondo, an extremely skilled Renaissance man, had the wit and knowledge to realize the value of this text. This many-faceted and subtle man was among the very first of the Europeans to use waterproof cement in bridge construction. And he had the ear of Frances's Louis XII.

Giocondo was a Franciscan monk born in Verona who came of age during the seminal years of the fifteenth century. He was, among other pursuits, a fellow of the order of the Frères du Pont, a group of engineer friars who had come together under the aegis of the papal authority in the twelfth century to preserve and advance the art of bridge building.

The group was formed as the popes came to understand the importance to the papacy of easing the difficulties of travel within the developing empire. Few persons of that dark century ever ventured much past their immediate village. Travel, such as it was, was the luxury, if such hardship can be so described, of royalty and the Church. Except for a few Roman roads, not lost to disuse, roadways at that time were not much more than tracks in the forest. Indeed, no more was needed for the then primitive modes of transportation required of mostly self-contained communities. While bad roads were an acceptable nuisance, unfordable rivers could not be tolerated. Out of this developing need for better communications the order was born.

Giocondo, besides being a monk, engineer, and member of Frères du Pont, was an architect, antiquary, and archaeologist long before such a science even existed. He was a classical scholar adept in Latin at the moment in the history of the West when the gifts of Rome were being rediscovered. Above all, Giocondo was fascinated by her faded glories the bare-bones remnants of which were scattered across the face of Europe.

He was a man of prodigious energy whose role in the history of concrete was ensured when he came face to face, across half a millennium, with another remarkable figure, the Roman Vitruvius, whose notes on how to make Roman concrete emerged as the only surviving written record.

Architect Marcus Vitruvius Pollio lived in the first century BCE. He is a shadowy figure of whom nothing has survived, not even a portrait, except for a single copy of *De architectura*, the portentous ten-volume document that allowed the use of concrete to come forth from the mists of the dark ages. That manuscript, lost for so many centuries, was rediscovered in a remote monastery in Switzerland in 1411. It was the fragile thread that brought the history of architecture forward from Rome to pre-Renaissance Europe and helped to define much of the relationship between the classical world and our own.

Vitruvius recorded everything known about architecture by the Roman engineers: construction techniques, skills, and the materials that were used. Among all of this wealth of information and detail, one short paragraph set down the actual formula for the making of the single most important architectural discovery of the Roman empire, waterproof concrete.

Other translators of Vitruvius, insensitive to the import of the formula and unfamiliar with the names of the materials, ignored this simple passage in favor of the more dramatic descriptions of the ancient buildings of Rome. Those who dipped into the manuscript in the fifteenth and sixteenth centuries, including Leonardo da Vinci, were taken with the arguments of Vitruvius concerning the relationship between the human form and the dimensions of buildings. One of the most famous images that comes down to us from this era, one that was derived from the notes of Vitruvius and published by Leonardo da Vinci, is that of the so-called Vitruvian man.

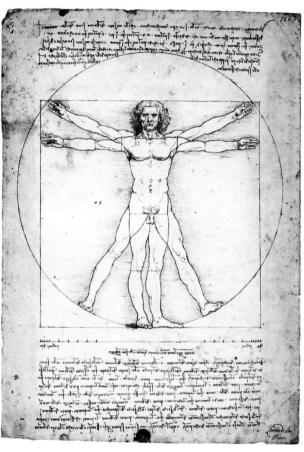

DA VINCI'S VITRUVIAN MAN

The original drawings of Vitruvius of Roman antiquity, the Roman Forum, temples, theaters, triumphal arches, and their reliefs, did not survive the centuries in the Swiss monastery. Giocondo, being an architect and a draftsman, was well equipped to reconstruct the originals from the text. The reimagined images were then converted by Giocondo's publisher into woodcuts. The book and its reimagined illustrations quickly became a major inspiration for Renaissance, Baroque, and neoclassical architecture.

All the translators of the time missed the esemplastic power of Vitruvius's explicit instructions describing how to make artificial stone. But Giovanni Giocondo, already a famous architect trained in humanist philology who had been called to lead the construction of St. Peter's in Rome, had that rare combination of talents that enabled him to recognize the consequence of the formula. His translation of Vitruvius, in 1511, was the first attempt to establish a critical text of this treatise of classical architecture. It was as a result of this translation, in which he was praised by critics as more of an editor than a mere translator, that the classical world was opened to all. There was no longer any reason why the use of concrete, a cheap and available material so much more strong than anything in use at that time, should not have come into general use.

As we have seen, however, the curious and often interrupted history of concrete required another century or two to pierce the veil of traditional and deeply embedded masonic skills. So slow was the community of constructors and so resistant to change that, remarkably, no seismic changes would occur in the use of concrete until the nineteenth century.

Giocondo himself obviously knew of the technique prior to the publication of his edition of Vitruvius and actually used water-proof concrete in a bridge in Paris. Why he waited to dabble in concrete until he was summoned to Paris by Louis XII is a matter for conjecture. It can be argued that Giocondo, wiley and political, preferred to experiment with this newly found and little known material in a far off land rather than risk his reputation in Rome.

In any event, the piers that supported the Pont Notre-Dame that connects the Ile-de-France to the right bank were poured concrete. The bridge was rebuilt several times in exactly the same location and the rebuilders found that they would not need to hew out Giocondo's concrete. They found Giocondo's concrete foundations essentially intact. As with the foundations of Sebastos, the first-century harbor of Caesarea built by King Herod, Roman concrete, poured under water, tended to stay around for a very long time.

Giocondo returned to Italy around the turn of the sixteenth century and was involved in many structures in Rome, Venice, and Verona but, again curiously, there is no evidence or indication that he ever used concrete again.

This pattern of discovery, use, and disuse of so elegant a material is repeated through history. No other important technological discovery has had so many seemingly accidental starts and just as many unexplained disappearances. Similar technologies such as brick making, pottery making, and metal refining lasted and evolved over continuous and contiguous centuries. Not so for concrete.

JOSEPH MOXON, 1627–1691

A special pleasure of attempting a disciplined but limited survey of a historical process is that the writer is often seduced by personalities, perhaps tangential to the study but, by their exceptionality, impossible to ignore.

In scanning the years between the fifth and the eighteenth centuries, there are few references to cementitious materials. There is, however, one curious clue, repeated in skeletonized time lines and dated 1678, concerning the inquiries of one Joseph Moxon. The note refers briefly to "the hidden fire in heated lime that appears upon the addition of water." Since the burning of limestone has been for millennia the core method of creating cementitious materials, this lone clue demanded investigation. Little information was learned until a true copy of Moxon's eighteenth-century treatise *Handy-Works* drifted in off the Internet.

In this work, Moxon emerges from the bipolar seventeenth century as a precursor of the Renaissance man. The seventeenth was a century drawn hindward by blind religiosity and pushed forward by tentative essays into the emerging scientific method. In this flux Moxon, like Benjamin Franklin a hundred years later, made seminal efforts to answer very real workaday concerns as well as investigate more rarefied, more academic topics.

Moxon essentially repeated the work of Fra Giovanni Giocondo, in which the secret of Roman concrete was revealed. Giocondo used the formula in the late fifteenth century and then, inexplicably, never used it again. Nor did anyone else. A fair explanation is that Giocondo's translation was in Latin and unavailable to mechanics and masons of the time.

Moxon was born at Wakefield, Yorkshire, in 1627 and died as the century came to a close in 1691. His father, James, was an impassioned Puritan and was caught up in the royalist difficulties of the time. The family moved to Holland in 1638 in order to print English bibles without interference from the Crown.

In 1646, at the age of nineteen, Joseph and his brother John set up a print shop in London. With one exception, all of their publications were Puritan works. The one exception, which appeared in the year after the print shop opened, was a treatise on the printing and coloring of maps and prints. This was the work of Joseph Moxon, rather than of the Moxon print shop, and it presaged the direction of the rest of his life.

Following his separation from publishing Puritan theological tomes around 1654, he became known in literary and mathematical circles for his excellent maps, charts, and globes and for republishing popular scientific books. In that year, and until 1686 when he moved out of London, he wrote and published a shelf of books on subjects of great sophistication that dealt with the subtleties of the emerging sciences of astronomy, mathematics, and navigation. He was among the first to attempt to regularize the formation of letters of the alphabet "Shewing how they are compounded of geometrick figures…by rule and compass." At the other end of the literary scale he produced a deck of playing cards, published in 1676, that "instructed ladies and gentlemen in the delicate and complicated art of correctly carving at table."

In the midst of all of this activity Moxon wrote and published six volumes of the book for which he is best known. This book, which dealt in detailed terms and explanatory drawings with the practical problems of most of the current crafts, was entitled *Mechanick Exercises*, or the *Doctrine of Handy Works*.

In one volume, on brick making, he nonchalantly unraveled a process in plain English that had been lost for a thousand years. Vitruvius's writing in Rome in the time of the empire carefully recorded the formula by which resilient and waterproof Roman concrete was made. With the decline of Rome Vitruvius's document, along with libraries filled with other manuscripts of classical times, was lost, as we have seen. This document, written in Latin, was first translated into modern Latin and then later into most European languages by academics and classical scholars. Except for a brief moment, the import of the concrete method so clearly described was completely overlooked for another two hundred years, not until Moxon, in 1685, included the Vitruvius writings on concrete in his *Handy Works*. Written in readable English nothing could have been more clear than this route map for the making of mortar leading to the making of concrete.

"*Lime* mixt with sand is much used in buildings," and *Vitruvius* says, "That you may put three parts of Sand that is digged and one part of *Lime* to make Mortar." But *Vitruvius* his Proportion of Sand seems too much, altho' he should mean the *Lime* before it is slacked; for one bushel of *Lime* before it is slacked *will be five Pecks after 'tis slacked.*

Here at *London*, where for the most part our *Lime* is made of *Chalk*, we put about thirty six Bushels of Pit-Sand, to twenty five Bushels of Quick-Lime, that is about one Bushel and half of Sand, to one Bushel of *Lime*.

And *Lime* mixt with *Sand*, and made into *Mortar*, and if it lye in a heap two or three years before 'tis used, it will be stronger and better, and the reason of so many insufficient buildings, is the using of the *Mortar*, as soon as tis made, as *Agricola* saith.

Moreover there is other Mortar used in making of Water-courses, Cisterns, fish-ponds, etc. which is very hard and durable, as may be seen ot Rome, at this day, which is called Maltha, from a kind of Bitumin Dug there; for as they build most firm walls thereof naturally, so they use it in making of Cisterns to hold Water, and all manner of Water-works."

While it is obvious from Moxon that a form of mortar or plasters was in wide use in England at the time, the short step from mortar to concrete hadn't been taken since classical times. All this in spite of the paragraph that precisely describes Roman pozzolan concrete.

What is astounding is that the secret of concrete, with the brief exception of the suggested use of a material similar to the Roman pozzolana by Venetian constructors in the fourteenth century and in a single instance by Giocondo in Paris in the sixteenth, concrete lay undescribed and essentially unused from 1411 to 1685. What is more astounding is that the secret, having been revealed in plain English by Moxon, was thereafter again forgotten for another hundred years, until the industrial revolution stirred the curiosities of Englishmen such as John Aspdin and Joseph Smeaton.

While other crafts such as glassmaking, bricklaying, carpentry, metal working, and the use and cutting of hewn stone have had an unbroken history throughout the world since Egyptian times, not so concrete, employed only during discrete eras and in disconnected places.

Industrial secrets and closely held craft techniques have consistently failed to be kept secret. In the case of concrete the secrets were kept, the secret holders died out, and what were simple and easily repeatable formulations of the uses of concrete had to be endlessly and laboriously rediscovered.

CHAPTER 6

CONCRETE IN THE EIGHTEENTH CENTURY

F or some seventeen hundred years, cultures, upstart empires, and regional potentates failed to appreciate the gift of concrete. During these years, at least once a century, odd but prescient folk did grasp the import of man-made stone and wrote and spoke loudly about how to make concrete, how to use it, and how important it might become. In spite of these occasional insights and exhortations, nobody in power listened and concrete, available for the taking, remained sans takers.

At the opening of the eighteenth century the groundwork of the industrial revolution was being laid, communications had vastly improved, and the interests of the state and the interests of individuals began to converge. "Everyone," to paraphrase Adam Smith, "will act in his own self interest and the self interest of each will become the self interest of all."

The blessed eighteenth century, thrust up by the Enlightenment, rationalist philosophers, and the industrial revolution, was lubricated by blossoming scientific curiosity. The common man was changing from servant, subject to random ills, to master of his fate in the intellectual turmoil of Europe at the time. A flood of investigations ensued and among them was a rebirth, this time sustained, of interest in the manufacture of artificial stone. But before concrete could become the dominant "medium of everything" another two hundred years were needed to complete the process by which concrete would become the most ubiquitous building material.

There is an aggravating question in this iterating need for rebirth before concrete could finally enter the mainstream of construction. Brick and wood and iron had leaped fully blown like Venus from the seas of discovery and their uses flowed without suspension from century to century. It is almost as if there existed a spiritual reluctance to take on the power of making rock, which had heretofore been a central act of creation by the many gods of man. It was as if this alchemic imitation of Genesis was too hubristic for mere mortals.

As the Middle Ages waned and the scientific method, defined by research and observation of nature, spread throughout Europe, the sporadic invention and reinvention of concrete became less capricious. Good minds turned to proofs and formulas and the history of the development of concrete became more chemic than alchemic. The work of earlier experimenters was observed, recorded, and passed down so that history need not be monotonously relived.

Real change came as the laws of patent rights developed. With patents a man's work could be protected and income from his experiments could be stretched into the future. Suddenly the "kitchen dabblers" became respected inventors with legal protection for their inventions. This was a seismic alteration in how the fruits of investigations were dispersed. Along with this boon came the observation to be precise in descriptions and to be able to offer repeatable proofs. At the same time that ideas were being made more public, the creators of the ideas were being covered with a mantle of protection.

Ideas entered irrevocably into the financial mainstream of the emerging capitalist economies. Ideas became, for the first time, pieces of assessable equity. The deus ex machina of this upheaval was the invention of the patent office, which sought to guarantee that inventors would benefit, over a long period, from their inventions.

Until this concept became established, inventions were protected by guilds that were committed to secrecy. Techniques and processes were the guarded private secrets of groups of craftsmen. By its nature this close guarding of industrial technologies served best to limit the uses of creativity. And besides, in the long term, secrets could not be kept.

The earliest known grant of a patent was in 1449 when Henry VI put his great seal on a twenty-year "monopoly" for a Flemish glassmaker's process for making stained glass. It is interesting to note that the grant was considered not a protection but the recognition of a monopoly, with all that implies. Even in this, its earliest beginnings, the patent concept set the rights of the public in the use of inventions against the rights of inventors to enjoy the fruits of their labors.

This mutually exclusive conflict, in which the public interest became progressively more subservient to industry, dragged on for a century and a half until, in 1610, James I was forced by the obvious abuses of the system to revoke all previous patents. Declaring that "monopolies are things contrary to our laws" he nevertheless allowed a major exception for "projects of new invention," which are not "mischievous to the State by raising prices." His good intentions were feckless as all patents and all restraints on the free dissemination of ideas are, essentially, "mischievous" to one party or the other in an economy.

This royal assertion, however vague, of the concept of the public good was inserted into the Statute of Monopolies in 1624 to help balance the egregious impact of monopolies on the emerging capitalist system. But by the mid-nineteenth century, the statutory process needed to obtain a patent had become so arcane and expensive that only the very rich or the politically powerful had access to patent protection.

In essence patents again became "mischievous to the State." Charles Dickens, in the English journal *Household Words*, wrote a scathing spoof of the tortured journey of a patent applicant. Entitled "A Poor Man's Tale of a Patent" he described visits to thirty-four offices (including some abolished years before) and the repeated returns to these offices, two separate occasions when the actual signature of the queen was required, and the six months it took and the then enormous sum of 100 pounds it cost in fees, all of which were far beyond the resources of any but the very rich.

Shortly after Dickens's spoof was published the Patent Act of 1852 completely overhauled the system. Legal fees were reduced, procedures were simplified, and patents were extended to all of the United Kingdom. With this act both the public and the patentee were protected from abuse by bureaucrats and the need for privileged connections.

Obtaining a patent no longer depended on the goodwill of the ruler. Kings and emperors and presidents no longer had the power to grant monopolies. Instead of privilege flowing down from the centers of power, the advantages flowed up from the creative minds busily propelling the industrial revolution. In limiting the power of sitting kings, the Patent Act of 1852 narrowly mimicked the great thrust forward of the Magna Carta. In a real but more limited sense power was reverting to the people.

It was in this context that the early patents for the making of cementitious materials were being sought. In the late eighteenth and early nineteenth centuries dozens of dabblers in both England and France appeared with formulae for cement of varying qualities.

American interest developed later as there was wood for construction and for kiln fuel to be had for the asking anywhere on the North American continent.

This blooming interest was built on the suggestions of Joseph Moxon a hundred years earlier. But while Moxon was an observer, this new breed were skilled in their trades and eager to capture markets for their inventions.

A subtle but seismic change was altering the political landscape of the eighteenth century. Power and wealth were moving away from the traditional structures of inherited influence. The use of concrete, always sensitive to the course of history, was about to surface once more, never again to fade from the works of man.

A new stone age was on the horizon.

THE NEW STONE AGE

After the turn of the nineteenth century there appeared, as if by agreement, hundreds of half scientists, half alchemists busily messing up their wives' kitchens. Quite ordinary citizenry, autodidacts all, in England and France became enchanted with the conceit of turning free water and free limestone into usable, valuable rock.

For the first time in the history of cementitious materials, the secrets of rock making were no longer in the hands of closed cliques, cults, guilds, priests, and potentates. The secrets were being unraveled by disorderly and dedicated searchers intent on hauling themselves over the social and financial barriers that, until almost their yesterdays, had been considered the inviolable manner in which society had forever been organized.

In the field of concrete, as in a hundred other fields in which wealth flowed from the application of intelligence rather than from inheritance, a profound topsy-turvydom was in the making. Suddenly, the freemen of England and France, no longer serfs or peasants but not yet their own masters, were finding that their own independent, self-interest-driven efforts were capable of building fortunes and elevating them into positions of power and influence. A new middle class was aborning and inventors within that class were becoming the "unacknowledged legislators of the future."

History does not neatly conform to man's description of it. The eighteenth-century experience with concrete commenced in 1779 when one Bry Higgins was issued a patent for a hydraulic cement used to waterproof walls. This material, stucco, still in use in essentially the same formulation, kept water from entering porous wood and brick. The exclusion of water from the abodes of mankind has been the goal of all housing, but until stucco came into common use houses remained wet, moldy, uncomfortable, and unhealthy. In the American Southwest the local building material, adobe, was dried mud, which worked just fine in the aridity of the semi-desert areas. But in the mists and dank of Europe stucco made a prodigious and salubrious contribution to the comfort and well-being of the emerging middle classes. Since stucco was both cheap and widely available it acted as a leavening agent between rich and poor, the powerful and the powerless. While a measure of dryness had been achieved at great expense in the homes of the mighty, it would become, after millennia of mold and moisture, easily available to all.

Bry Higgins's patent was granted to him in 1779 under arcane conditions, which required dozens of functionary signatures and royal seals. Bry, a man of means, paid out of pocket the 100 pounds sterling fee that was required. Subsequently, in the next year he published a how-to book based on his patent grant. The treatise was entitled, "Experiments and Observations Made with the View of Improving the Art of Composing and Applying Calcereous Cements and Preparing Quicklime."

Bry—probably short for Bryan—Higgins was a physician and chemist who reported in his book that he "was motivated…to recover or to excel the Roman cement, which, in aqueducts has withstood every trial of fifteen hundred or two thousand years." Higgins started from the Roman experience, which was demonstrably far superior to the cementitious materials hitherto used in traditional building practices in England. After much research and experimentation he settled on a formula of "well slaked lime, sparingly used, combined with fine and coarse sand, bone ash and water."[1]

The publication must have had a wide distribution because in the notes of George Washington dated 1784 was found a "very complete and careful summary of Bry Higgins on calcerous concrete."[2] It is interesting to note that although the process of making cementitious materials was known to our first president, a respected engineer in his own right, the conditions that would lead to its widespread use would not develop for another hundred years in the United States.

There was something of a footrace going on among the new alchemic entrepreneurs. Higgins seems to have won in the short run as his published patent dated from 1779 while John Smeaton did not enter the fray publicly until 1793. In the long run, however, Higgins's haste produced a cement that proved much inferior to that of Smeaton who, in the early days of experimentation, came closest to aping a Roman pozzolan cement. Hard on Smeaton's heels was James Parker, who patented a natural, Roman hydraulic cement in 1794, just a year following Smeaton's announcement. Parker's cement was superior to Smeaton's but, as we shall see, both Joseph Aspdin, another entrepreneur who arrived in 1824, and Smeaton were more savvy about market acceptance.

There were numerous formulaic variations of cements brought to market between 1779 and 1824. Two experimenters outside of England made interesting contributions. Antoine-Joseph Loriot published an essay on "a cement and artificial stone justly supposed to be that of the Greeks and Romans, lately re-discovered by Monsieur Loriot."[3] Loriot was "Master of mechanics to his most Christian Majesty" and with the king's backing should have had a great success with a material that was, in his words, "cheap, easy, expeditious and durable construction of all manner of buildings, and formation of all kinds of ornaments of architecture, even with the commonest and coarsest of materials."

In retrospect, considering our present vast array of the uses of concrete, this was a curiously prescient statement of its benefits. However, even with the active support of his monarch and a full understanding of the potential of his new material, Loriot seems to have missed the historical boat. He may well have been an accomplished chemist but he was vague on the history of concrete as the Greeks made almost no contribution to Roman cement.

While Loriot was generally ignored by the marketplace, a French compatriot named Louis Vicat had a better sense of the dramatic. In 1817 he announced the invention of a new artificial cement to which he fortuitously attached the name "white gold." White gold, perhaps by virtue of its name, enjoyed a brief popularity but was superseded by the Portland Cements of England. However, as history sometimes perversely turns, Vicat is known to this day as the inventor of a simple and direct method to test concrete and cement for hardness. The device, the Vicat needle, consists merely of a frame and a movable rod weighing 300 grams with a 10 mm plunger on one end and a 1 mm needle at the other.

Drop the needle into setting concrete and the distance it penetrates is an exact measure of the temper and solidity of the mixture at progressing moments of the solidification process. This primitive apparatus, devised by Vicat merely to further his experimentation, would become his pertinacious claim to a place in history. Vicat's needle remains, in a form not distant from the vision of its inventor, in common use today.

VICAT NEEDLE

THE EDDYSTONE LIGHTS

Nothing is more telling of the importance of waterproof cement than the long tale of the attempts to mount a light on the Eddystone Rocks. From almost the beginning of the eighteenth century until near the close of the nineteenth, repeated attempts were made to place a lasting structure on the rocks that lay astride shipping lanes barely fourteen miles from England. The rocks, almost invisible to approaching ships, rise only a few feet above the waters of the channel. Hundreds of ships have foundered and thousands of sailors drowned almost within sight of their island home. "Eddystone," Adam Hart Davis said, "was a perfectly

EDDYSTONE STUMP

COURTESY P. STEVE

EDDYSTONE LIGHTS

COURTESY ANDRAS KALDOR,
DARTMOUTH, ENGLAND

| Winstanley | Second Winstanley | Rudyard Light | Smeaton Light | Modern Light with Smeaton Stump |

placed peril." Sailors paid for the peril with their lives. It became clear that a light must be placed on the "wicked reef of twenty three rust red rocks…around which the sea constantly eddies."[4]

Many attempts were made but all except one were constructed of inadequately cemented stone, rusting iron, or the hard woods of Britain's forests. Iron and stone, the material of the Winstanley Light, were swept away, along with its builder, in a channel storm. Rudyard's Light, built of wood waterproofed with pitch, burned from the top so fiercely that the lead used in construction melted and rained down on the lighthouse keepers.

The full and fascinating stories of the colorful men who were so typical of that period in the development of the industrial revolution in England are told in an appendix to this book. Winstanley, Rudyard, and Smeaton deserve full treatment and their lives, in their own way, define the development of English waterproof cement.

It was not until John Smeaton proposed a stone tower cemented with "hydraulic lime" that the problem was solved. Smeaton's Tower was to be attached to the rocks "as stone is to stone." At that level the rocks and the base of the tower would be almost constantly wet by driven seawater so it was only by the use of a pozzolan material, which he imported from Italy, that the tower was able to survive.

Indeed, it survived so well for 121 years that, in 1877, it had to be rebuilt because the very rock on which it was situated had been worn down by the tougher tower to which the rock was attached. Smeaton went on to great engineering achievements, including the invention of the science of civil engineering, but it was Smeaton's Tower that has caught the historical imagination. The tower survives to this day on the Devon coast, carefully taken down, stone by stone, and rebuilt on land as a memorial to the final conquest of the Eddystone Rocks.

So important was Smeaton's Tower to the sense of Victorian self-image that, on the gold medal struck on the occasion of Queen Victoria's diamond jubilee, an illustration of Smeaton's tower is included among the images of empire.

The Keeper of the Eddystone Light

Me father was the keeper of the Eddystone Light,
And he slept with a mermaid one fine night
Out of this union there came three,
A porpoise and a porgy, and the other was me!
CHORUS:
With a yo-ho-ho, let the wind blow free,
It's all for the life on the rolling sea!

One night, as I was a-trimmin' the glim
And singing a verse from the evening hymn
I see by the light of me binnacle lamp,
Me kind old father lookin' jolly and damp.
CHORUS:
With a yo-ho-ho, let the wind blow free,
It's all for the life on the rolling sea!

A voice from starboard shouted, "Ahoy!"
And there was me mother sittin' on a buoy
Meanin' a buoy for ships what sail,
And not a boy what's a juvenile male.
CHORUS:
With a yo-ho-ho, let the wind blow free,
It's all for the life on the rolling sea!

"Well, what became of me children three?"
Me mother then she asked of me.
Well, one was exhibited as a talking fish,
The other was served as a savory dish.
CHORUS:
With a yo-ho-ho, let the wind blow free,
It's all for the life on the rolling sea!

The phosphorous flashed in her seaweed hair
I looked again and me mother wasn't there,
But her voice came echoing out of the night,
"To hell with the keeper of the Eddystone Light!"
CHORUS:
With a yo-ho-ho, let the wind blow free,
It's all for the life on the rolling sea!

SMEATON LIGHTHOUSE ON VICTORIAN PENNY

1863 English penny showing Smeaton tower to the left of the shield.

COURTESY BRITISH MUSEUM

THE NINETEENTH CENTURY

There are good centuries and there are bad. There are centuries of light and centuries of darkness. There are centuries when mankind aspires to the stars and others when the high hopes of good men are drowned in the base turmoil that engulfs them.

The nineteenth century neither rose to moral heights nor fell below the radar of decency. It was a century during which mankind was involved with the fascinating toys of the industrial revolution. It was a century when these toys wrought unassailable fortunes and lent immortality to the names of quite common men.

Chief among the toys with which men conjured in this pedestrian century was concrete. In this period of explosive growth concrete moved from alchemy to chemistry and from the kitchen stoves of patient wives to the enormous rotary kilns of Thomas Edison.

It was also the century when the tools of modern capitalism were being honed. Twenty-five years before the century turned,

Adam Smith defined, for all time, the way in which the capitalist world works when not constrained by governments, monopolies, or cartels.

> It is not from the benevolence of the butcher, the brewer, or the baker that we expect our dinner, but from their regard to their own interest. We address ourselves, not to their humanity but to their self-love, and [they are], in this, as in many other cases, led by an invisible hand to promote an end which was no part of his intention. Nor is it always the worse for the society that it was no part of it.

All over Europe and America the entrepreneurial spirit was moving ordinary men to get involved in powerful economic movements that were just beginning to mature. One such man among the burgeoning dabblers in concrete was Joseph Aspdin.

Aspdin was an ordinary mason and bricklayer whose contribution was central to the production of a useful waterproof "natural" cement. In 1824 he burned, at a high temperature, finely ground chalk in his kitchen oven along with clay and lime. The heat removed the carbon dioxide, a weakening agent, from the mixture and produced a superior hydraulic cement.

Aspdin was preceded by others of his century, including Edgar Dobbs (1810) and James Frost (1822) who developed "natural" cements in England. In France Louis Vicat (1817) developed an "artificial" cement. However, all of these men lacked the understanding of the market displayed by Joseph Aspdin.

With a stroke of marketing genius, Aspdin patented his new concoction as "Portland Cement" and with this seemingly incidental gesture his contribution dominated the entire universe of cement production for the next hundred years down even to our own century, in which the name "Portland Cement" retains an indestructible marketing power.

Not fully trusting the protection of his patent, Aspdin pursued a secretive, almost paranoid, manufacturing process. He likely did not understand the chemistry as he was a "kitchen" experimenter arriving at his successful formulation mostly by trial and error. Although hazy concerning the science, he very well understood the developing competitive market. To discourage and confuse his competitors, he spread the disinformation that, in addition to the well-known content of his Portland Cement, he sprinkled "secret salts" into the slurry.

To further throw off the competition he would not allow visitors to his mill and quite alone, without even his workmen, he would make the final mixture. This is much like the current company-inspired myth that there is a secret formula for Coca-Cola.

Portland, in the county of Dorset in southern England, had long been known for the high-quality building stone that was quarried in the area. The insinuation that Aspdin's cement quality was somehow related to the naturally occurring granite of Portland, and the incidental similarity in color to that stone, was worthy of Madison Avenue. The name Portland Cement instantly gained acceptance in England and later, when concrete came to America, the name stuck and for all time it defined English cement as superior to all others.

For decades thereafter Portland cements continued to be imported at great expense from England although the process was well known in America and waterproof cements were being locally produced. However, even at a cheaper price, these local products could not overcome the powerful branding of the word *Portland*.

The natural cements that preceded Portland Cement are products to which no compounds or minerals have been added. Essentially they are derived from burning limestone at moderately low temperatures and reducing the resultant product into a fine powder. Because limestone deposits are widespread and natural cement requires much less fuel, this cement was fast to make, cheap to sell, and easy, with great care, to pour.

Furthermore natural cement has a unique advantage/disadvantage, depending on the method of its delivery and the needs of the user. Early natural cements set in minutes and therefore had to be mixed and watered on site, which not only involved very careful timing but required an on-site production facility. On one hand the instantaneity of the material was a potential threat and on the other it tended to reduce construction time and costs.

Natural cement was widely used in the United States prior to the impact on the market of Portland Cement. It played an important part in the great canal-building fever that commenced in the earliest days of the eighteenth century. The Erie Canal system and eventually much of the Panama Canal was poured with natural cement produced in the eastern part of the United States. The industry was well established by the mid-1800s with hundreds of production facilities, characterized by vertical "bottle" kilns located at limestone quarries.

Fayetteville, in Onondaga County in New York, was the site of the first natural cement manufactured in the United States. A man curiously named Canvas White discovered a limestone deposit that could be heated easily and ground into a powder that, when mixed with almost anything, made a respectable concrete. The price was 20 cents a bushel, which White considered fair. For some reason New York State purchased his patent for $20,000 although it would have been possible for the state to produce its own version of a natural cement as many other natural cement makers were doing. At the time $20,000 was a very large sum and the deal suggests that Canvas White, in order to effect the sale to the state, had considerable influence.

Actually it was the fever to build inland waterways that popularized local American natural cement. In response to this demand, and as a result of the simplicity of the manufacturing process along with the ubiquity of limestone deposits, dozens of cement producers appeared across the nation. In addition to its use in canal construction a symbiotic relationship arose: "While this new article of commerce was gaining a foothold through canal construction it was being brought to the market by the same medium. There was at the time no cheaper or faster mode of transportation than the new popular waterways."[5]

Between 1818 and 1829 there were only 300,000 barrels of natural cement produced in all of the United States, but by the end of the century cement plants from across the country were spewing out almost 9 million barrels. Considering the slow, inefficient, and unreliable method of production, it is surprising that the constantly increasing demand for natural cement could be met. Vertical kilns were used and a week's production of each kiln rarely produced more than 150 barrels. Taking into account cooling times, weather, holidays, and other interferences, it is estimated that three thousand vertical kilns would be necessary to maintain the close delivery schedules that quick-setting natural cement required.

As individual entrepreneurs discovered that banks would make loans in response to a rapidly expanding economy, small-time industrialists with little more than a fistful of orders suddenly could access easy capital. In the cement business, responding to seemingly unlimited demand, almost anyone could get signed orders to take to the bank. The gap between order and delivery was quickly shortened by the rapid construction of these brick bottle kilns of which thousands sprang up designed to produce both natural and Portland types of cement. In just a couple of decades along the east coast of the United States wherever limestone could be mined the landscape was dotted with, and besmirched by, these smoke-belching monsters. The ease of erection of the kilns and the availability of both orders and capital led to the enormous increase in cement output during the first two decades of the nineteenth century.

However, problems such as rapidly depleting sources for cheap fuel and the high labor intensity required to load, tend, and empty the vertical kilns quickly brought the first age of American cement to a close. The entire industry in the United States appeared and essentially disappeared in the relatively short space of only seventy-five years. New processes, such as the rotating kilns developed by Thomas Edison and a rising clamor for standardization of formulations and setting times, ended vertical cement production in less than a lifetime of a man. Such was the pace of industrialization in America.

As a sidelight it is interesting to note that during the century when cement was transported on canal boats, the containers had to be waterproof lest the cement arrive solid and set. Canal boats, operating in a marine climate, were sometimes uncovered and oftentimes leaked, hence expensive packaging in barrels was required. It was not until the covered cars of the nation's new railroad system came into play and the delivery of cement was no longer carried by wet barges that the cheaper cloth and paper containers appeared.

Similar revolutions in packaging appear regularly in the history of commerce in response to new technologies of transport. As long as carriers were water based, weight and to a lesser extent volume had little influence in effecting end user costs. With the shift to delivery by rail in which volume and weight were limiting factors compared to the canal barges, these considerations became paramount. Cement delivery toward the end of the nineteenth century was almost exclusively by rail as more and more kiln clusters began to be serviced by railroad spurs directly to the cement factories. Cement delivery remains today one of the mainstays of the faltering American rail system and, with the recent enormous increase in the uses of cement and concrete, it may well help to save and extend profitability of rail.

During the early part of the century Portland and natural cements were being produced and sold in the burgeoning market. That came to an end as the power of the Portland brand caused the natural product to decline in spite of the fact that Portland Cement was sometimes offered at a higher price than the natural product, demonstrating that marketplaces and consumer habits change very slowly. Natural cement all but disappeared in the twentieth century. Very recently, when scientific regimens of chemical retardants and accelerants were developed to control its speed of setting, natural cement use has staged a small comeback, which further proves the reticence of craftsmen to abandon known technologies and to resist unfamiliar new stuff.

CHAPTER 7

THE TWENTIETH CENTURY

For the purpose of this book the man who turned the page on the twentieth century in America was a reclusive bachelor who forswore marriage after contracting a sexual disease in his youth and which deviled him for his entire life. Excluded from connubial involvements, he turned his vast energies and analytical talents first to the study of classical archaeology and then, almost single-handedly, he invented a new archaeological discipline, the study of the recent rather than the distant past.

Around the turn of the century, Henry Chapman Mercer became disturbed that the ingenious hand tools and techniques, spewed out in all their artless simplicity during the industrial revolution, were being rapidly replaced by machinery more conducive to mass production methods.

The homely wood and iron tools that facilitated Western man's hobble into our own time were being shelved for new and more cunning inventions based on technologies rather than techniques.

Fearing that all of the intense effort and ingenuity that carried man through history into Mercer's time might be lost, he poured a seven-story concrete progenitor of the Guggenheim Museum, spiral ramp and all, and proceeded to fill it with what was fast becoming the detritus of the industrial revolution.

The Mercer Museum in Doylestown, Pennsylvania, was among the first poured concrete structures in America. It is a building that looks forward to the hegemony of concrete while

FONTHILL, DOYLESTOWN, PENNSYLVANIA

PHOTOGRAPH REESE PALLEY

the collection that it houses casts a longing glance backward to a time when a mechanic in need of a tool was more likely to fashion it than to buy it.

The twentieth was the miracle century. What was unthought in 1900 became commonplace in 1999. Before the twentieth century all the world was gently lit by fire. By its end many of the fires that lit the world were the terrifying fires of the atom. From his desk in a Swiss patent office, Albert Einstein struggled, as the century rolled over, toward a "unified theory" of the physical world. By the end of this century "theories about everything," string theories, and other pansophies abounded. Even the concept of a solid, tactile physical world was under attack.

Buildings leaped from under ten stories to over a hundred in only the first three decades of this improbable time. The paired steel rails that had reduced weeks to days were suddenly replaced with propellor-less aircraft that reduced days to hours. The great liners, built with such pride, fell into desuetude as the sweeping lines of the great ship *United States*, the most graceful ocean liner ever built, idled away at a dock in Philadelphia.

Bridges were thrown across vast chasms and wove the ubiquitous American system of roads into every cranny of every country. "From sea to shining sea" was no longer a mere song lyric; it had become a short and metaled reality.

The handful of horseless carriages that lurched about on roads worse than Roman had become a lemming spate of sweetly engineered runabouts for all, which, in their uncounted millions, were eating up the atmosphere. By the end of the mirabile dictu century the seven league boots of legend were worn by all, rich and poor alike.

One of the breathtaking mechanical marvels of the nineteenth century was the Linotype machine, which replicated the robotic gyrations of a man picking and setting type. This delicious compendium of cogs and wheels and levers and arms, dancing to a satisfying clanky music, was replaced not by mechanics in imitation of man but by the quiet, unhuman pixels of everyman's computers.

When this author was in school in England in mid-twentieth century, a young Australian had spent years of his postgraduate life to build a room-sized hydraulic construction of glass and liquids and valves designed to predict the macroeconomic flow of capital and interest. It worked fairly well but, with the passing of a handful of years, computers of credit card size could predict a thousand times faster and a hundred times better. During only the last quarter of the twentieth century, bottomless computers leaped full grown from the nubile minds of youth and changed a century that itself was changing the world.

Diseases were wiped out at such an astounding rate that new diseases had to be invented by the bacteria that had invented us, reinforcing a dismal Malthusian doctrine. In apposition, agrarian science so exploded the food supply that Malthus was vindicated in reverse.

Most of the diseases of childhood faded with the memories of our mothers. A century that opened with medicine men shaking the rattles of primitive cures came to a close with the unraveling of DNA, the ultimate biological mystery. Today we hold the beating hearts of patients in our surgical hands and fix them or replace them or insert devices to steady their rhythm.

The century opened with wheeled juggernauts striving to reach the goal of a mile a minute and ended with NASA's "Chariots of Fire" aspiring to the stars and tinkering with the conceit of the speed of light. The moon and Mars became familiar landscapes to the earthbound and the space station evolved into a true home for earthmen in space. In the twentieth century the gravitational shackles that have held us tight to the surface of our globe were broken. The results of this break portends as unimaginable a twenty-first century as the twentieth was from the nineteenth.

The flow of knowledge not only raged forward but spread wide filling the incidental gaps between sciences and changing forever the topology of ideas. The compendia of events and records and documents stored on our computers and available to all grew from billions to googols. This exponential growth will soon require us to restrain the flow of data lest the volume of pure information overwhelm our ability to access anything.

Today the imaginations of millions are on fire as one spectacular event succeeds another. Hot button discoveries and developments are the stuff of headlines. They come on us unexpectedly giving us frissons of pleasure. They are the loud and resurgent revolutions we have come to expect of our time. They are changes that take on the mantle of habit.

However, there is one quiet, very quiet, revolution that has crept up on us with none of the hullabaloo associated with the others. Concrete has more deeply and personally affected more daily lives in the twentieth century than almost any of the other more dramatic enchantments of our time. Metastasizing during the first five decades, concrete imperturbably spread over the surface of our planet, well hidden from us by its lack of drama. And yet almost no one has been untouched by the ubiquitous creep of concrete. Concrete was remaking the face of the world and we hardly noticed it.

When the expansion is as explosive and chaotic and world changing as is the story of concrete in the second half of the twentieth century, reportage is possible but a grand view of history is not. What will come of this burst of energy and invention will take shape and make sense only to some lucky historians of the next hundred years.

All a reporter can do, as he watches the shape and content of his world melt and reform about him, is to try desperately not to miss the central themes. But when all changes and discoveries are eye popping and unfamiliar, the only recourse of the observer is simply to report everything and hope that the seminal changes are not missed.

So here is a report of the untamable proliferation of concrete in the twentieth century. The pen can scarcely record, let alone analyze, the spate of discovery.

To observe that concrete has changed the world in our century is to understate the obvious. That conversion has happened is a true fact nailed down by some billions of objects that range in size from earrings to China's Three Gorges dam. The simple mass of 50 *billion* cubic feet of concrete that is the current annual rate of production is a dimension that, pari passu, must have a social impact. The changes that this volume of material and constructions have wrought are as immutable as the earth itself, having been made, essentially, of the earth itself.

The question remains as to why this rush of concrete commenced to cover the land only around 1900, some thousands of years after it was first used in an organized fashion. Profound historical changes are rarely self-generating; they are urged on, indeed, commanded by some force or a concatenation of forces.

With the emergence of the enormous and homogenous American marketplace, propelled by a universal language and unhampered by the restrictions of national borders, something had to change. A mass audience was beginning to demand uniform, interchangeable, and quickly produced, and as quickly reproduced, products. Craft unions, the heirs of the guilds, were giving way to industrial unions and, subsequently, as the century came to a close, to no unionism at all.

One social scientist[1] equates the beginnings of the demise of craft unions with the sudden growth of the use of concrete in industrial construction. Amy E. Slaton uses as a paradigm the thousands of standardized reinforced-concrete factory buildings that proliferated after 1900. These structures were intended to create settings for the various new technologies of mass production. They were meant to be minimally decorated, easily replicated, and simply converted internally to changing demands in the marketplace.

What was being sought by the burgeoning American economy was "a uniformity wrought by economy: to simplify and standardize to conserve effort or expense."[2] The need to standardize and the search for competitiveness, two sides of the same coin, both in the construction and in the uses of these poured concrete buildings, would be accomplished if the skill-based workers, creating one-at-a-time projects, could be replaced by less-trained workers operating in a technology in which hands-on knowledge and experience was less important.

Poured concrete fit exactly the new demands of the marketplace. Concrete construction required the least amount of technical expertise on the part of the actual constructors, which directly affected the cost of labor and construction in general.

This revolution of construction technology had enormous implications in terms of how the workforce is organized and how, and how much, labor is paid. Since pouring times and finishing times could be more easily estimated, the construction of factories (and other buildings) required new skills that had little to do with actual hands-on labor of construction.

Scientific methods of measuring strengths and durability of concrete that allowed standardization of formulations of concrete soon created a university-educated group of experts who controlled construction technologies by experimentation and the resulting publication of standard methods. Thus a class of higher-paid technicians arose. This new class was created to replace the master craftsmen of the building trades. From 1900 onward the spread between the well-being (read real income) of trade unionists and the new class of scientists and managers widened until, by the end of the century, the spread became a chasm and the opportunity to escape directly from labor to management declined. Trade unionism, unless supported by political protectionism as during the New Deal era, died a slow, century-long demise.

Starting as early as the first decade of the twentieth century concrete buildings sprang up using large numbers of untrained workmen, a new underclass, supervised by a scientifically trained and very highly paid upper class of technocrats and managers. Slaton describes the almost volcanic upheaval:

> To comprehend this alteration of modern work, we must first recognize that between 1890 and 1920 the idea of uniformity came to exert a remarkable hold on American industrialists. The era brought

an unprecedented level of regularity to the quality of raw materials used in the industry, the procedures of production, and the character of finished products. In manufacturing and food processing, in mining and construction, predictability—and not coincidently profits—reached heights not seen before. This transformation can be pictured in part as a physical one. Tidy assembly lines replaced cluttered workbenches; standardized screws and teakettles replaced idiosyncratic models. The steady flow of concrete replaced the piecemeal accumulation of bricks. But it was indisputably also a social transformation, in which the work experiences of many Americans changed dramatically. For the highly paid technical and managerial experts of the period, as well as the much lower-paid rank and file, the daily tasks of industrial employment called for new skills and workplace behaviors.[3]

The most far reaching social changes took place in the materials used in industrial production. Not only was science and technology transforming societal relationships throughout industry but, in the special case of construction, concrete burst onto the scene giving legs to the mounting social changes.

There was at least one other development that hastened the denigration of skilled labor in the construction industry. This was the standardization and materials control that replaced personal knowledge of methods and materials with simply printed instructions. Prior to the twentieth century materials were mixed, formed, or selected according to the experience and the skill of craftsmen. These skilled workers brought their own individual, unscientific methodology to their work. Repeatability was limited to the working life of an individual craftsman or, in some cases, how he happened to feel that day. Apprentices absorbed the skill of their masters but were rarely able to inherit the art. What was missing were the rigors of scientific method, which demanded publication, repeatability, and standard methods to reach the desired identical results.

This "murkiness" in production was supported by the medieval guilds, which used secretiveness as a form of protectionism. The growing influence of craft unionism in the first half of the century turned to the protection afforded not by secretiveness but by the strictures of local building codes. Very early techniques and methods, inherited from the craft unions, became embedded in local building codes from which, even today, they have not been extricated. To counter the industrial search for efficiency in construction, the trade unions turned, successfully, to protectionism from local governments.

By mid-century the craft unions were under severe attack, especially during economic downturns, by the increasingly efficient methods of precasting and casting on-site of concrete for large industrial projects. As a result of the Great Depression of the 1930s, federal regulation and protection of the trade union movement saved for the unions a less than significant place in large projects and a death grip on small-scale production such as private housing.

The surge in new technologies, however, especially in the timely delivery of dependable concrete, ate away at the effectiveness of federal controls. By the end of the century the trade unions retained only marginal involvement in large-scale construction.

In the construction industry politics is intensely local and the grip that the trade unions have by way of local building codes is the last, but seemingly indestructible, bulwark against the scientific rationalization of home building. But even this institutionalized monopoly is beginning to crumble in the face of factory-built housing.

Nevertheless, the class-based social revolution instituted in large part by the coming of concrete has widened the chasm between the rich and the non-rich in America. Low-skilled, low-paid labor predominates. The big bucks are reserved for the managers and the entrepreneurs and the new technicians who reign over vast means of production, both in labor and in capital, and who earn salary windfalls that are often in the order of a thousand times the income of the employee who tamps concrete for his living.

The creative, idiosyncratic skills in the making of objects that was the signature of the nineteenth century survive mostly in the handwork of craftsmen/artists who have little or no impact on industrial processes.

By the end of the twentieth century a million fecund minds, reacting perhaps unconsciously to economic, population, and scarcity issues, were spewing out ways that the old earth rocks of creation could be reaggregated to serve, in a thousand new forms, the requirements of the dawning twenty-first century. From the turn of the century until just after World War II, the applications of concrete in the industrialized West were intermittent and, to a certain extent, experimental. Wonderfully conceived buildings appeared, concrete bridges were thrown across large spaces, and great dams (such as the Hoover) began to appear.

Steel, stone, and brick were still the preferred materials of construction in industry and, in spite of Edison's foray into home building, wood and brick remained the way homes continued to be built in the industrialized world. Changes were coming but it took a number of parallel events and movements to break old dependencies on iron and steel.

Probably the single most important developments were the huge road building programs of Europe and America. The autobahns of Germany led the way. Built by Hitler, they were a farsighted preparation for the mobility that the Wehrmacht would require to fight a two-front war. Built mainly of concrete, they seamlessly connected the many frontiers of Germany. The efficiency of the autobahns added to the horrendous death and destruction of the war by enabling the Wehrmacht to fight on even beyond any hope of final victory. Without this network of concrete Germany, dependent solely on the German rail network, might not have been able to attack Russia to the east while threatening the Allies to the west, thus shortening the war by half and more than likely saving millions of lives.

Between 1939 and 1963 no autobahns were built and it can be convincingly argued that, absent a war, when costs and capital expenditures are not the operative considerations, there would have been little motivation to undertake a public building program of such magnitude. Intriguingly, concrete built the roads that contributed to the destruction of Europe and then concrete, carried on these same postwar roads, was the primary material that rebuilt Europe after World War II.

The total amount of concrete sucked up by the autobahns was vast but did not begin to compare to the flood of concrete that was incorporated into the American Interstate Highway System.

The interstate discussions go back to the mid-1920s when the American car builders began to lobby for better roads. But it took a serious war to get Washington to move. In 1940, with war looming, President Roosevelt appointed a group to study the project but no funds were provided until 1944. As in Germany, all road building halted during the profligate war years. Even after the war, nothing much happened until Eisenhower, who had had an intimate relationship and an enormous respect for Hitler's autobahns, lent his popularity to a program that jump-started the interstate system. It might well have taken another decade to come to fruition if the U.S. Defense Department had not pushed for a national defense program called STRAHNET, the Strategic Highway Network. "Strategic" is a motivating word for the U.S. Congress and when it is combined with the concept of national defense there are few legislators who were able to find the will to say no. All of this was leavened by the fat contracts to be had in their home constituencies.

The Interstate Highway System alone spread out over 45,000 miles and the STRAHNET added another 15,000. These projects, commenced in 1956 and declared complete in 1991, cost the taxpayers, in dollars of the years they were spent, almost $130 billion. When it is considered what that sum would represent the highway system was a great bargain. Of the total spent, $100 billion was for construction, a significant portion of which was accounted for by the purchase, the delivery, and the installation of concrete.

From this one aspect of concrete consumption, and this only in the United States, the dimension of the use of concrete in the twentieth century becomes clear.

PILLBOX, DOVER COAST, ENGLAND

COPYRIGHT © BIGSTOCKPHOTO

The twentieth century opened with the sprouting of concrete silos for the storage of American grain that could feed the world and passed its midpoint with concrete silos for nuclear-tipped missiles that could end the world.

The uses of concrete in the service of war, throughout the twentieth century, were wildly prodigal. The autobahns did their bit to lay waste to most of Europe and the potency of the atom bomb promised to complete the job worldwide. As we shall see this threat of annihilation caused uncounted tons of concrete to be fecklessly poured into holes in the ground.

To guarantee the continuity of the holders of political power, no matter what the devastation of war or the threat of a nuclear holocaust, millions of tons of concrete were poured for this precise purpose. Defense was the name of the war game and concrete was the obvious and effective means to protect a political elite.

The building of defenses against attack up to 1900 was accomplished primarily by wooden stockades and stones piled up upon one another. Inaccessible placements such as the Masada and the hilltop castles that dot most of Europe were the best past defenses against intrusion.

In preparation for the wars of our busy century the war planners abandoned wood and substituted concrete in the development of the essentially defensive program of hundred-mile-long walls and hardened gun emplacements. The face of Europe became ineradicably scarred by the ubiquitous concrete defensive positions of the pre–World War II period, all made of poured concrete and all as indestructible—this was their intent—as the rocks on which they were sited. In the end those pillboxes proved as ineffectual as they were indestructible.

Hoxha, the Albanian dictator, alone, is said to have built a hundred thousand of these concrete caves. Even neutral Switzerland, not wanting to depend solely on the more effective defenses of cash and credit, sought to ward off invasion with concrete pillboxes set along the slopes of the Alps.

Pillboxes were little more than the extension of the trench warfare of World War I. The slaughter of the men in the trenches gave rise to the concept of a more protected defensive position. Pillboxes were simply a trench firing step hardened (with concrete) to protect against small arms fire and grenades and raised a little to improve the field of fire. Their huge numbers reflect the fact that they were envisioned as an impenetrable line of riflemen stretching across the great distances and depths to be defended.

Fixed defensive positions, as those throughout the history of warfare attest, are the usual mode of the losing side in war. Examples such as Troy and Thermopylae come down to us from classical times to which war planners paid little attention. The pillboxes of World War II did little more than momentarily delay the German blitzkrieg. Hardened positions that could not easily be overrun from the front could, as demonstrated in the 1940s, be flanked by the highly mobile forces of the Reich. The pillboxes, sown like concrete dragon's teeth across all of Europe, proved to have little bite. In the end they have found usefulness as occasional storage for farming equipment or, more widely, as homes for bats.

Spectacular remnants of a quickly outdated technology were the three "listening ears" at Denge near Dungeness in Kent, the best known of the various acoustic mirrors built along Britain's coast. A forerunner of radar, the sound mirrors were intended to provide early warning of enemy airplanes (or airships) approaching Britain. The smallest and earliest were about twenty feet

WORLD WAR II—ERA CONCRETE LISTENING POST, DOVER, ENGLAND

wide. Later examples ran up to an enormous two hundred feet of solid poured concrete. The mirrors worked, in a fashion, if listeners stood at a precise and invariable distance in front of the dish. Radar, developed by the British early in the war, quickly rendered them obsolete for military or almost any other application.

However, in 2001, the Manchester *Guardian* reported on an art project using concrete ears.

CONTROL AND COMMUNICATIONS BUNKERS

As the need to control ever swelling armies and to develop and protect the communications that keep the military from treading too badly on its own toes, untold millions of tons of concrete were poured throughout the world to protect the administration of war in these tactical nerve centers. As the ability to devastate grew and offensive weapons grew ever more offensively, control bunkers, designed to protect these folk well out of the killing fields, burrowed deeper and were covered with increasingly thicker feet of concrete.

In Germany the Führer's bunker, in the end, became more of a hidey-hole than a center from which a modern war could be waged. While the Allies were grinding Berlin to shards and cutting all communications, the Führer's bunker was reduced to sending out couriers to pass instructions to what was left of the Wehrmacht. In that instant, Hitler was waging a war in the twentieth century with communications that were available to Lee and Grant a hundred years earlier.

The bunker, buried in a mound of concrete that could have built a small town, protected Hitler to the last. Other than allowing him the time to accomplish the death of additional millions, his bunker, and thousands of others of the same ilk, had little effect on the wining or the losing of the war. The Allies had learned from Hitler, almost too late, that warfare was a matter of the rapid movement of masses of men and machines that required an offensive rather than a defensive mind-set. Since the bunker is the product of a defensive mind-set intent on defending unholdable ground, the Allies were, late in the war, still fighting the last war. The Russians never fell into this trap. They used their destroyed cities as positions from which to extract the highest cost of the Germans in men and material and their mobility in retreat finally ground the Wehrmacht to a halt. The Russians had learned well from Napoleon's disaster in his stretching of lines of supply to the breaking point and they also used the power of the same Russian winter that had helped to defeat Napoleon. The Germans missed both of these lessons and the endless land mass of Russia and the intolerable Russian winter crushed even their vaunted blitzkrieg.

Like the Russians, the English never did build a defensive wall. Churchill knew from the beginning, as did Rommel in his assessment of the German Westwall, that defense was futile once the enemy had taken the beaches. England's response was to oppose Germany where she was most strong, in the air, and sacrifice London, one of the great cities of the world, in the ultimately successful defense of one of the great democracies of the world.

THE MAGINOT LINE, THE SIEGFRIED LINE, AND THE MANNHEIM LINE

"Fixed fortifications are monuments to the stupidity of mankind," stated General George S. Patton.

In the annals of war, the theory of defense defines the nature of offensive strategy. For millennia the best defense was the concept of the keep, a place that could be easily defended for a very long time. When the chief defense strategy was a tower or a fort or a castle that involved great piles of stones sited atop inaccessible heights, the only way to get at them was the siege. Troy took ten years and Masada even longer but even they in the end both fell to a patient army, which could wait for starvation or thirst to do its fighting.

The ancient concept of the siege was patently useless in any war that extended across great areas for which encirclement was not possible. When old tactics became impractical, the generals planning the carnage that was to become World War I invented trench warfare in which waves of infantry were committed to the killing grounds where well-balanced forces decimated each other.

It had become clear, even to the generals at the end of that war, that trench warfare, using unprotected riflemen, was a mode of warfare that came and went in the few years between 1914 and 1918. Starting around the late 1920s the less aggressive, or perhaps the more exhausted, nations of Europe pondering the impenetrable power of concrete started to reinforce and define their borders with fixed fortifications designed to repel invaders and keep defenders from harm.

These concrete defenses were the Rubicons and the Alps of the twentieth century. They culminated in the great military structures that girdled the borders of Europe. The best known of these, the Maginot Line, the Siegfried Line, and the Mannheim Line, addressed the problem of invading infantry and were conceived to be secure against head-on assault.

These concrete constructions, which ran for hundreds of miles and were built in succeeding lines of defense, providing murderous enfilading fire, did indeed prove impervious to frontally advancing troops and their strength and the ease of shaping pourable concrete structures resulted in defenses that resisted even the largest of the big guns of the time.

Protecting the core of the nation and being sustained, fed, and munitioned by the heartland, these once built and never to be destroyed monuments to a reactive theory of warfare could have been conceived and developed only as a result of the endless supply of concrete that was available to the industrialized world. These great defensive military lines were the logical extension of the properties of poured concrete. Without concrete, Europe would have even more impoverished itself by building defensive lines of scarce and expensive steel.

In the event, this logical and ultimately inevitable use of concrete came within a cat's whisker of plunging human polity back a thousand years. The German generals, looking across the Rhine at the glowering outposts of the Maginot Line, recognized that they were beaten before the first shot was fired in an attrition war composed of static fronts.

AN EXERCISE IN FUTILITY

And so, once again and this time in direct response to the spread of cheap and durable concrete defenses, German military theory reinvented itself in the form of the blitzkrieg. The Maginot Line was named after its chief proponent, André Maginot, who was France's minister of war in the years 1928–31. Sensitive to the horrendous cost in lives that resulted from unprotected trench warfare, the thinking at the time was to build concrete "trenches" that were to become the Maginot Line. It is significant that Charles de Gaulle, considered a modernist by the French army, opposed the static concept and pushed for more investment in armor and aircraft. Hitler took de Gaulle's advice, to the ultimate distress of the French nation, and did just that—invested in airpower and fast and mobile tanks. The German approach harkened back to the fluidity of the Roman legions while the French risked the very existence of France on the reincarnation of crenellated forts and castles of the Middle Ages. It was a badly calculated risk that very nearly cost France its soul.

The construction of the Maginot Line was started in 1930 and largely completed by 1935 at a cost of 3 billion French francs. The fortifications stopped at the Ardennes forest, which the French believed was an impassable natural defense. It was exactly here on May 10, 1940, in the foggy woods of Ardennes, that the Wehrmacht mounted the blitzkrieg offense that reduced the Maginot Line to a monument to the military habit of preparing for the last war rather than the next one. Nor had the line been extended along the border with Belgium since a treaty signed in 1920 stipulated that Belgium would be an ally of France and the French army would defend that area against a German threat. With war looming between France and Germany, Belgium abrogated the treaty and declared itself neutral in 1936. This banned France from defending Belgium and left the northern end of the Maginot Line dangerously exposed.

During the "Phony War" the Germans placed a decoy force opposite the Maginot Line intended to signal that they were taking the line very seriously, especially since there had been German frontal forays against the line that the French easily repulsed. Thus comforted, the French settled down behind their concrete defenses intending to allow the Germans to exhaust themselves in attempting to breach them.

In the invasion of 1940 the Germans never planned on a frontal attack. While the decoy force held down the bulk of the French army the Germans, in lightning forays, simply rolled around the line at locations that had been considered unnecessary to defend strongly. They ripped through a futilely declared neutral Belgium and a defenseless Netherlands and quickly left the French army sealed in its concrete tomb. On June 22, with the Maginot Line still intact and with its guns pointed the wrong way, the French government sued for peace and Hitler danced a jig on the Champs-Élysées.

Even before the invasion the very reason for the existence of this very expensive wall of concrete had already been degraded by German foresight in rejecting static warfare. Blitzkrieg was born with its dependence on fast and mobile machines of war. The Germans refused to waste their legions by throwing them upon impervious walls of concrete. Warfare once again redefined itself after mid-century and, except for deep command and communications bunkers, concrete was abandoned as a serious means of deterrence in war.

AN EXERCISE IN DECEIT

After rejecting static warfare and concrete defenses in favor of a mobile force, the Wehrmacht, in spite of the success of the blitzkrieg theory of warfare, embarked on the huge fortifications known as the Westwall or the Siegfried Line. It remains a puzzle that the Germans failed to heed the lessons of their own success. Instead, they poured thousands of tons of concrete into a static defense system that ran for almost four hundred miles along the German borders with the Netherlands, Belgium, Luxembourg, and France.

This line of eighteen thousand bunkers, tunnels, and tank traps was constructed even though the Germans might already have been comfortable that no attack would come from the defensively oriented West. Netherlands was never in play, Belgium had declared itself neutral, and France had, with the Maginot Line, signaled its strategy of "defense only."

It can be argued that, in its construction, the Siegfried Line was built ultimately to be inadequate even to a frontal attack. The majority of the fortifications were outdated even before completion and could, at best, protect only against shrapnel. However, sprinkled among the thousands of structures were "Type 10" bunkers, which were more strongly constructed. These bunkers, started in 1938, had sufficient room for ten men and, contrary to the rest of the Siegfried Line, were sealable against poison gas. These Type 10s, although built with walls and ceilings feet thick, and consuming three thousand square yards of concrete each, were indefensibly scattered and dispersed among inadequate fortifications that would be easily overrun. They had no supporting protection on their flanks. It is a puzzlement why the Germans bothered.

If the Siegfried Line was indefensible and far from structurally able to withstand the armaments of the time, the only reasonable explanation was to convince the Western powers that the wall was unbreachable. This signaled a defensive posture with which the West was familiar and comfortable. It served to allay the fears of western Europe that the Germans sought expansion westward. The timorous Allies, ever eager to grasp at any straw suggesting that Hitler's intentions were nonaggressive, took the bait. The disastrous "peace in our time" mentality prevailed.

If deceit was the intention of the Westwall, this exercise in disinformation worked perfectly for the expansionist strategy of Germany. With the armed forces of the West bottled up behind their concrete comforters, the Germans were able to take their offensive to the East and start their long-planned expansion into the USSR.

The Siegfried Line, an utterly profligate military failure, was perhaps one of the most effective propaganda victories of Hitler's Reich.

After World War II the probability of a looming nuclear holocaust changed the game.

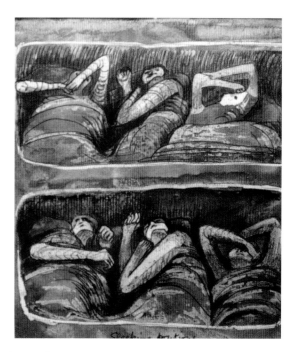

DETAIL OF *DEEP SHELTER* BY HENRY MOORE

PHOTOGRAPH MARILYN ARNOLD PALLEY

SUBTERRANEAN ENGLAND

There is hardly a square mile of the United Kingdom that is not caverned by either a bunker, a tunnel, or some other structure designed to hide people from the bombs of World War II and beyond. England, borrowing a term from fox hunters, went to ground. Looking both backward and forward they dug great holes in the ground and filled them with concrete.

Since there was little experience in the bombing of great cities prior to World War II, the air raid safe houses of the time were, for the most part, simply the identification of already constructed concrete buildings or, the great savior of much of London's population, the very deep London underground in which thousands of Londoners lived and slept.

There does not seem to have been much initial planning for the London underground to be used as a bomb shelter since, when the German raids commenced, the authorities actually tried to prevent people from sheltering in the "Tube." As the bombings worsened the underground was thrown open and only much later did the city provide latrines, bunks, and catering facilities.

Work began on deep-level shelters, which were constructed parallel to the underground train tubes. These were serious, thoughtful engineering projects that took into account not only protection against bombing but the more important and more expensive requirements for dealing with an extended stay.

The deep shelters, of which ten were planned, were commenced around 1940. Only eight were brought into service as water invaded one site and another, which was to have run deep under St. Paul's Cathedral, was abandoned a year later out of fear that the shelters might undermine the foundation of the cathedral.

Since London is built essentially on the clay that had been laid down over millennia by the Thames River, the actual digging was quick. Beyond the digging the finishing was not as fast as each shelter was composed of two 1,400-foot-long double deck tunnels lined with concrete. They were expensively provided with access to air and water. Personnel used two widely separated double helix staircases, an unconscious anticipation perhaps of the discovery a decade later of the structure of DNA. These efficiently carried up and down staircases in a single tube. Air intake vents were fitted with poison gas filters and provision was made for disposal of toilet wastes. Curiously there were only two toilet facilities, one for men and one for women located at one end of the tunnel, which could involve as much as a half mile walk for many of the ten thousand people housed in the shelter.

The deep shelters, thanks to the speed at which concrete could be poured, took only about year and a half to complete. Each shelter had medical and catering facilities and much care was given to changing the air and sealing the system in the event of a poison gas attack. Should the water supply be cut off from the surface there was a reserve tank of three thousand gallons on hand. Electricity was supplied from two widely separated sources lest one source be cut off.

The deep shelters were complicated and difficult systems to manage and shortly after they were completed, in spite of the enormous expenditure of labor and materials, the government closed them down because of the very high cost of maintenance.

It was not until the Germans started pelting London with V1 and then the larger and more deadly V2 rockets that the shelters were reopened. The only continuing use of one of the shelters throughout the war was as General Eisenhower's London headquarters. Other shelters were used as billets for troops in transit but, in the end, the whole deep shelter program was ineffectual, as were so many other grand defensive plans of this and so many other wars.

KELVEDON HATCH

The Parrish family, who now conserve Kelvedon Hatch, the English bunker designed for the continuation of a curiously named Devolved (read, blown apart) Central Government, describe the aftermath thus:

> There would have been only three or four million people who would have survived (in England). There would have been temperatures of minus 20 to minus 40 degrees. There'd be no harvest for at least three years. The first one would have been burnt off by the flash or the cold would have killed it. For the second you'd be too lethargic and in any case the radiation levels would have been too high. And for the third harvest you'd have to scrape away three or four inches of contaminated soil and sow by hand any seeds that you hadn't already eaten. All this time you'd be contending with marauding gangs of people who have radiation sickness. They're not being fed, have a limited life span and what they want is your food. There's not much of a sanction if you have somebody with a limited life span. In effect, in all respects, you'd be going back to medieval times. Einstein summed it up pretty well when he said that if the next war is fought with the atom bomb then the one after that would be fought with bows and arrows.

Kelvedon Hatch was built in 1952 by a panicky English government, which was convinced that the Russians, frustrated and themselves panicked, would simply wipe out London, and as much of the rest of Britain as they could reach, with atomic weapons. This was before the days of retaliatory missile warfare when Mutual Assured Destruction, the peculiar insanity of the moment, could be delivered from America. Britain was left naked of deterrence. The United States, flush with its initial exclusivity in the nuclear club and thus its implied dominance of the world, was not prepared to share its weapons with even its closest ally.

With offense not possible and with no conceivable defense, the British political elite built Kelvedon Hatch, a bunker that might guarantee governance by standing as an impenetrable bulwark against their own desperately sick and hungry Englishmen, whom they intended to continue to govern. Lewis Carroll's words still best describe the world of the mid-twentieth century, which is almost indescribable.

> "But I don't want to go among mad people," Alice remarked.

> "Oh, you can't help that," said the Cat, "we're all mad here. I'm mad, you're mad."

> "How do you know I'm mad?" said Alice.

> "You must be," said the Cat, "or you wouldn't have come here."

The Kelvedon Hatch bunker, described by one of its constructors as "built not to keep the Russians out, but the likes of you and me in," was constructed in deepest secrecy. The innocent-looking cottage that hid the entrance had reinforced concrete roofs and walls and steel shutters and doors. The bunker itself had walls of ten-feet-thick concrete reinforced by a full inch of tungsten-enhanced steel bars placed every six inches. A mesh cage, called a faraday cage, was placed around the entire structure to deflect electrical impulses generated by atomic blasts, which were capable of wiping out all things electronic. All of this would have been useless against nuclear attack, which would have sealed off the hatch and all within but would have been a cozy place for the ruling class to exclude the sick and desperate hordes that would have roamed the charred remnants of civilization above them.

As with all other mountains of defensive concrete poured in World War II, Kelvedon Hatch ended up serving no purpose. When the cold war petered out it fell into disuse and finally was bought back by the Parrish family, the very folk who were forced to sell this same property to the Air Ministry in the fifties.

Today it is a tourist attraction wherein visitors can view the paranoid detritus of a nuclear war that never happened. Had war come and had the bunker functioned and survived, its existence would have represented the final battle between the elite inheritors of power and the mass of the disinherited.

THE GREENBRIER SPA

The most famous American bunker is one that was kept secret from the public for forty years. It was built underneath and along-side the famous Greenbrier Hotel and Spa, which had been the favorite watering hole for Washington, D.C., elite for generations. Greenbrier hosted all of our recent presidents and most of Congress and the Senate at one time or another. When the time came to consider how to maintain governance in the aftermath of a nuclear holocaust the comforts and the amenities of Greenbrier were an easy choice to guarantee the survival of the power structure of America. Greenbrier itself was big enough to hide a major undertaking as was the use of its commercial function as a screen. It is located about forty miles outside the heart of Washington from which an otherwise useless small rail line was built. Greenbrier had always been viewed as a rather nice way to pass a weekend. The political elite was seriously looking to its own continuance.

By 1960 we were deep into a holocaustic confrontation with the Soviet Union. The construction began then with an unceasing string of concrete Ready Mix trucks hauling endless truckloads of concrete. There was no issue concerning cost. The only issue was speed. Randy Wickline, one of the contractors, remembers that workers were urged to ignore load limits in the rush to get the job done. Wickline was no fool and in spite of being told that the project was an expansion of Greenbrier he quickly got to the heart of the matter.

"Nobody came out and said it was a bomb shelter, but you could pretty well look and see the way they was setting it up there that they wasn't building it to keep the rain off of them. I mean a fool would have known. There would have been enough room to get a few dignitaries in there, *but us poor folks would be left standing outside.* It kind of made me think about it—and hope it never happens."

While schoolchildren were being advised to hide fecklessly under their desks in the event of an atom bomb attack, those in power, concerned more for their own lives than the lives of unprotected millions, were pouring tons of concrete for something under which to hide from their own citizens. By guaranteeing, or seeming to guarantee, their own survival with elaborate hideaways such as Greenbrier, it is possible to argue that the power elite was enabled to act much more aggressively than they might have if they had been exposed, like the rest of us, to a nuclear horror with no protection at all. Perhaps without the putative protection of a shelter of concrete, World War II might have ended sooner and more civilly.

The bunker under Greenbrier was enormous. It covered 113,000 square feet and descended 800 feet into the earth. The walls were reinforced concrete two feet thick. In the dark and gloomy days of the early cold war all the world was going to earth. Even common folk, indeed my own father-in-law, built hapless concrete rooms below their homes to shield their families from the effects of a nuclear attack. Save for stacking up a few canned goods and some meager gallons of water, very little was planned for how to exist during the extended chaos of the aftermath of the attack.

The construction under Greenbrier that took place at a furious pace was blandly explained away as an expansion of the hotel's facilities. In two and half years 50,000 tons—tons not yards—of concrete reinforced by steel were poured in a ceaseless operation.

When the Washington bigwigs started planning their continuity of government scheme the primary concern was for the six hundred or so legislators and executives of the Washington inner circle. The Greenbrier bunker was cynically designed to keep desperate survivors out and protect the favored few within. The great steel doors, designed by the Mosler Safe company, weighing twenty-eight tons each, were designed to be opened only from the inside.

The bunker was stocked to remain sealed off from the world for a minimum of three months. Two-story-high generators with huge tanks of diesel oil provided power. There was a meeting chamber for the Senate and one for the House and even a greater hall for joint sessions. There were decontamination chambers, operating rooms, dormitories for six hundred, and even a crematorium since some of the six hundred, mostly old white men, would be expected to die during the sealed-off period. There were more than a hundred urinals and a like number of toilets. Wastes were pumped deep into the earth and water was to be had from deep wells. Should the wells become contaminated with nuclear fallout, a not unlikely event against which the survivors above had no defense, there was enough drinking water storage, strictly rationed, to last almost indefinitely. There were television and radio transmitting studios with antennas sited far away at the top of a hill designed to effect continued governance over what was left of the nation.

The Greenbrier bunker became obsolete, as did all concrete defensive projects, as a result of the power of the burgeoning technologies of offensive weaponry. It was never designed to survive a direct hit. The builders depended on the inability of bombs to find an exact target. With the subsequent development in the technology of aiming systems and their pinpoint accuracy the Greenbrier, and whatever foolishly conceived defensive burrows that might evolve in the future, would not be able to withstand a proliferated nuclear attack.

Mankind will always devise more efficient ways to kill than ways to prevent killing. "Bunker mentality" was raised to a high art by the availability of concrete. As we have seen in the century just passed, however, the abortive attempts to pour more and more defensive concrete simply did not work as planned. We just may as well settle for living in peace.

Among the recondite uses of concrete in the twentieth century the strangest of all is that which was suggested to the British High Command in 1940. Two British experimenters demonstrated the production of a cementitious product without the addition of cement. Concrete was for the first, and perhaps the last, time made only with aggregate and water, a feat that is reminiscent of the children's tale of the chef who claimed to his king that he could make soup using only a stone.[4]

The story begins with Geoffrey Pyke, an eccentric British genius whose personal history is as strange as the material that came to be known as Pykrete. Pyke was first noticed in 1914 when, bored with university and eager to get into the action of the First World War, he wangled a job as a foreign correspondent while still under voting age. He procured a false passport and upon arrival in Germany he was summarily tossed in jail as an enemy alien.

After the war, and after a daring daytime escape from the German jail, he entered into commerce and managed to corner the market for tin. In those wild, speculative days he made a fortune, which he quickly lost in the financial debacle of 1929. Undeterred, he spent much of the interwar years inveighing against the rising threat of Hitlerian Germany.

When World War II broke out in 1939 he again wanted to get into the action. Pyke appeared at the office of the chief of combined operations in London, disreputably dressed, announcing, "You need me on your staff because I'm a man who thinks."

The luminary to whom this statement was addressed was no less than Lord Mountbatten. Pyke, with the assistance of Martin Perutz, Mountbatten's science adviser and, in some accounts, no less quirky than Pyke, managed to get past a battalion of minions. This alone was a testament to Pyke's persistence and to his ability for creative innovation.

Pyke convinced Mountbatten (who must have had a number of other things to think about at that moment) and landed among that strange coterie of weirdos, geniuses, and English eccentrics called by their puzzled peers the Boffins. These were the oddballs who, almost more than any others, won the war for England by inventing radar and the degaussing of Allied shipping that was being decimated by the magnetic torpedoes of the German U-boats.

Fast-forward to 1942. The scene is Churchill's bathroom in Chequers where the great man was relaxing with cigar and brandy glass at hand. Lord Mountbatten appeared breathless at Chequers and demanded to see Churchill at once. When told that the supreme leader of the British empire was in his bath, Mountbatten ran upstairs shouting, "That's exactly where I want him to be." When he burst into the bathroom Mountbatten announced that he had something to show Churchill and, unwrapping a parcel, he produced a block of dirty ice, which he threw into the steaming tub.

Deferring to Mountbatten's excitement, Churchill waited for the ice to melt. It did not. More minutes passed and the dirty ice, which should have long been reduced to water, continued to bob about between Churchill's legs. The ice that continued not to melt was indeed not ordinary ice at all. The bobbing, unmelting block was eventually to be called Pykrete in honor of Geoffrey Pyke, one of the strangest of the backroom boys.

Pyke discovered that a mixture of about 10 percent cellulose, ordinary wood chips or sawdust, and freezing water produced a hitherto unknown material. The material, best described as dirty ice, not only resisted melting but was immensely strong compared to ordinary ice. Wood chips were cheap and water was essentially free. The addition of artificial, or indeed natural, refrigeration produced a concrete-like material with science fiction–like properties. The process by which water and wood becomes a solid material is identical to the process that uses Portland cement and stone aggregate. In both, the cementitious material crystalizes and crystals reach out and bind together the aggregate. Water plus Portland cement produces these crystals in the same manner as does water plus freezing. The chemistry of Pykrete and its path of discovery are shrouded in mystery and just as mysterious is the lack of commercial or industrial interest in Pykrete. The statement "I don't really know why it has languished in obscurity" by Professor Erland Schulson, director of the Ice Research Laboratory at Dartmouth College, hints at the existence of this and other arcane technologies that have failed in the marketplace of technical ideas.[5]

There are recurring tales, some perhaps apocryphal, of well-researched technologies, such as alternatives to fuel for internal combustion engines, that have been suppressed in the interest of competing commercial interests. In the case of Pykrete there were no competing interests. The use of this startling material simply faded quietly away.

The story of Pykrete is not unlike the larger history of concrete, which, in its long journey from the deserts of pharaonic Egypt, suffered from repeated lapses of industrial memory. Pykrete, in spite of a brief wartime spike of interest, has been totally forgotten and to this day is yet to be recalled to the service of science and industry.

To Churchill, fighting for the life of the British empire, this strange material and the even more strange man who brought it offered some intriguing prospects. Churchill, with his back to the wall, was expert at grasping at whatever straw could help in the war effort. When he was informed that this dirty ice multiplied the strength of ordinary ice by a factor of ten, Churchill, characteristically, leaped into action. The very next day he memoed his staff, "I attach the greatest importance to the prompt examination of these ideas. The advantages of a floating island or islands, even if only used as refueling depots for aircraft, are so dazzling that they do not need at the moment to be discussed."

What had so impressed Churchill was the concept of the "floating island," which had been offered by Pyke when he first brought the concept to Mountbatten. Pyke had envisioned vast floating airfields of the new ice, which were more impervious to attack than icebergs themselves. At one point it was suggested that these islands could be used as enormous rafts to transport as many as eight Liberty ships at one time. The fantastical process would involve the "icing in" of the Liberties in America and towing the entire unsinkable mass of superstrong ice, impervious to the torpedoes of U-boats, to England. Wilder wartime schemes were suggested and some, like the Manhattan Project, succeeded.

Churchill, fighting the Battle of Britain in the air, was more taken with Pyke's seemingly wild suggestion that an immense, ice aircraft carrier be built, which he named H.M.S. *Habbakuk*.[6] This ice island would not only act as an airfield to accommodate the heavily armored Spitfires but also bring Britain's long-range bombers closer to the enemy.

Pyke's ship was to be some two thousand feet in length, long enough for landing any aircraft in use at the time. It would be three hundred feet wide and have walls of the new ice forty feet thick. He estimated that the interior would easily hold several hundred Spitfires and bombers. The audacity of this concept is best brought home when it is remembered that while the largest ship ever built at that time was the H.M.S. *Queen Mary*, which displaced 82,000 tons, the H.M.S. *Habbakuk*[7] would weigh in at 2 million tons!

Mountbatten directed Pyke, and his partner Martin Perutz, to produce some examples of this "super ice," which they did in a meat locker in Smithfield market in London. Mountbatten brought a block of the material to the Allied Chief of Staff's conference in the Château Frontenac Hotel in Quebec in 1943. With the chiefs assembled in secret conclave, Mountbatten laid out a block of ordinary ice and a block of the super ice. He pulled out a pistol and, careless of the consequences, shot at both of the ice blocks. The normal ice shattered, the super ice did not, and the ricochet from one of the two shots grazed the leg of Fleet Admiral Ernest King.

British Air Marshal Sir William Welch was waiting outside the private meeting room. Everyone was very aware of the continuing tensions between the Brits and the Yanks and, in a panic, he rushed into the room shouting, "My God, the Americans are shooting the British." Guards rushed in to find shattered ice, much confusion, and a furious Admiral King. When the hubbub died down and the outraged Admiral King was mollified, all agreed that Mountbatten's demonstration strongly suggested that the matter must be further investigated. Thus was born Operation Habbakuk on the shores of Patricia Lake near Jasper, Alberta, in far-off Canada.

The purpose of Operation Habbakuk was to test four propositions in the construction of a vessel made of a concretion of ice and sawdust that could be used as a weapon of war. First, it had to float. Then it had to demonstrate its ability to bear enormous loads. Next, it had to be impervious to attack by explosives. Lastly, and perhaps most important, it must not melt.

As with so many undertakings of the time Operation Habbakuk was top secret. To achieve this level of privacy Pyke and his crew built what appeared to be an ordinary boathouse with a tin roof in Patricia Lake. From afar there was nothing amiss, but for the special few who ever boarded her the *Habbakuk* was a floating marvel.

She was sixty feet long and thirty feet wide with an enormously thick hull of Pykrete. She weighed a thousand tons, while a similar vessel of its size might weigh a mere fifty tons, if that. But her most astounding quality was that *Habbakuk* did not melt. She was kept intact and frozen with a *one-horsepower* gasoline engine! While she was predictably slow and easily seen by an enemy, she was close to indestructible and, if attacked, was self-healing since, if pieces were knocked off her, she floated in a sea of repair material.

Mountbatten, demonstrating again his affection for firearms, tried to blow a hole in the hull of the prototype. True to Pyke's predictions, the attempt made barely an impression on the icy hull.

By this time land-based aircraft had been developed with greater range and the impending use of the atom bomb marked *finis* to the great ice ship experiment. The low-tech underpinnings of the *Habbakuk* could hardly compete with the spate of blindingly seductive high-tech products of war that World War II had germinated.

The one-horsepower engine was at last turned off in the fall of 1944 and *Habbakuk*, unrefrigerated to the end, did not melt until the end of the next summer.

By that time no one noticed and no one cared.

·　·　·　·

In the advent of the twenty-first century at least two logical uses for Pykrete can be envisioned. One such proposal tries to deal with the problem of proliferation of the ability to produce fissionable material. Peaceful and warlike uses intersect in any nuclear plant so the problem of making needed electrical power available to possibly renegade nations while avoiding proliferation to those nations has become a serious challenge.

Some years ago, rising to this challenge, engineer Joel Rosenblatt of Key West, Florida, proposed the use of floating nuclear plants to supply power to underdeveloped nations. Siting nuclear plants on indestructible Pykrete islands would seem desirable and possible.

Pykrete islands could be used in place of the expensive and technologically complicated steel oil-drilling platforms now in use. Million-ton islands, cheaply built, anchored in place, and as large as would be needed to ensure stability, Pykrete could serve our ravenous demand for oil.

With nuclear power plants unwelcome in almost any location in America, plants could be anchored miles off our shores thus offending no one. Pykrete could handle the enormous problem of the heat produced by these plants and, most important, it could be towed about to wherever it might be most needed at the moment.

Further afield in the future is the looming problem of the unequal distribution of fresh water around the world. Vast quantities of water are even now being shifted about via pipelines. As the sources of these lines begin to be exhausted we may find it necessary to move water over great distances over which pipelines are not possible. It is not too far-fetched to envision the creation of vast, slow-melting Pykrete islands, which could be floated about the world to wherever they are needed most. It would take remarkably little power to do so as Pykrete is kept frozen with small refrigeration units and the sea would allow great masses of anything that floats to become weightless and thus relatively easy to move. If properly utilized Pykrete could make enormous contributions to our crucial need for sustainability.

Murder is messy. Gunshots are noisy and splatter bloody evidence around the scene. Baseball bats need too much room. Knives are much too personal and survival rate is, from the point of view of the murderer, depressingly high. Throttling requires strength and leaves indisputable marks on the neck and poison takes much too long. After the victim is dispatched, whether by gun or by club or by knife or by hand, the most important, the most crucial, and certainly the safest job, again from the point of view of the dispatcher, still remains undone. The disposal of the inconvenient remains.

Sometime during the 1920s a criminally inclined genius solved all of these problems. Up to this time the gentlemen who had been whacked ended up in shallow graves in, say, the dunes of north Jersey. There was an impermanence about this method as any stray dog, or on rare occasions sometimes even the police, would disinter the whackee, which would lead to no end of fuss. This original thinker, whose family were probably hardworking, honest concrete masons, invented the most efficient way to dispose of a human being, with little effort and little chance of attracting the attention of the law. The "concrete boot," as it came to be known, made no noise, left no blood, and forever hid the body from accidental discovery by prying eyes or scavenging animals. The concrete boot was also an extremely cruel and slow death, which was intended to send a message to possible future enemies.

Then there was the interesting advantage that no one actually committed a personal act of murder. No one had to pull a trigger or plunge a knife. The killers did not even have to watch him die as that sad event occurred on the bottom of the sea. All that was needed was a boat, a body of water, a large bucket, ten cents worth of cement, and a handful of sand.

The disposal, undertaken at night far from shore, was unlikely to have any witnesses and all possible incriminating evidence went down with the bucket. The victim, who was restrained but not killed, had his feet immersed in the bucket filled with

THE BOOT BY TONY AUTH

"A Hard Lesson to Learn": A Short Story by Betty Overocker*

*PERMISSION TO REPRINT GRANTED BY THE AUTHOR

"Hey you! Let's go for a walk," said a gruff voice behind me as I sat on a concrete park bench. Without question, I stood up and walked along the concrete sidewalk in the direction the dark suited man pointed to. The heat of the day was intense as it radiated off the concrete building that lined the concrete street we were walking beside. I paused momentarily to lean against a concrete lamppost and concentrate my slurry of thoughts into a more rigid mass. The men in dark suits continued to move me along this set journey.

At a large concrete archway, the men told me to enter. The entrance was very steep, and contained two concrete statues of vicious-looking

dogs guarding the way. The door opened into a large room. The walls were made of concrete blocks arranged in an offset pattern. My mind tried to trace an escape route in the mortar trails between the bricks, but I kept running into dead ends much like the situation I was in. There were no concrete answers.

The room was arranged in a court hall formation consisting of massive poured concrete chairs and benches. A man of questionable character sat in the front of the room, in the largest of the concrete thrones. The men in dark suits motioned for me to approach the front. Being tired from the long walk, I leaned against

the concrete pillars that outlined the path that I least wanted to travel.

I approached the domineering godfather. He told me to place my legs into a cylindrical container that came up to my knees.

The two goons that had been watching me headed to a concrete box nearby. One of the goons carried a bag of premix concrete. The other, a container of water. As they began to mix these ingredients, I began to realize what was about to occur. I broke the code of silence and asked the godfather if I could have one last request. He nodded. I surveyed the scene. Knowing that this long look of the tall concrete skyscrapers may quick-drying wet concrete. Then, still conscious, he was eased overboard and all record of his life and his death was swiftly pulled to the bottom where he remained, standing like a bowling pin, as the local fauna chewed him down to his soles. The floors of various waters are no doubt dotted with these strange monuments from which the washbasin has rusted away leaving only the negative image of feet and ankles in a short, neat column of silent concrete.

THE SICILIAN VESPERS

Late in the thirteenth century around the time that the Vitruvius papers, describing the formula for Roman waterproof concrete, were discovered in a remote monastery in Switzerland, a revolt broke out in Sicily that was to throw a long and violent shadow over the history of the next five hundred years.

On Easter Tuesday, March 31, 1282, the people of Palermo rose against the oppressive domination of Charles of Anjou. Bartolomeo de Neocastro records[8] that "amid cries of Death to the French," there was an outbreak "of fury consequent upon injuries and annoyances of all kinds inflicted on the people by French Barons and officers of Charles of Anjou."

be one of my last, I asked for a large soda and a large cotton candy. Not bad, I thought, for a diabetic on his supposed last binge.

As my last requests arrived, the goons transferred the contents of the concrete mix into the bucket. I could feel the weight of the wet mass entering my shoes. I squirmed just as the deliverer was handing me the food. In the shuffle, the large soda slipped out of his hand and spilled into the bucket in which I was standing. The cotton candy also was lost to the mess on my feet. They thought nothing of the new additives in the mixture. I, on the other hand, was pleased that my plan had worked.

What followed was the usual take-and-get-rid-of-the-guy routine. The goons were not too bright in the ways of concrete. They just followed directions. As for me, the training I received in a high school module on concrete had taught me all about the effects of admixtures on the curing processes of concrete. The sugar in the candy and the soda would prevent the concrete from setting. As the assistants carried me and my "hardened" boots to the water's edge, I hoped that all that modular information was accurate because my life now depended on it. The buckets and I were set on a dolly for ease of movement. The dolly was rolled to the edge of the drop-off and I was released into the water.

Due to the retardation effect of sugar on the setting of concrete, I managed to wiggle my legs out of the fresh concrete anchor and rise to the surface. No one was in sight and I decided to learn more about other industrial materials so I could save my life again some other time.

This spontaneous uprising against an oppressive foreign ruler eventually took on the name the "Sicilian Vespers" and became the root of insurrectional activity that has come down to our own time. It is fascinating to note that the ultimate insult to the Sicilians was Charles's attempt to deprive the people of the right to bear arms. The violent origins of the Sicilian Vespers were demonstrated when, in the ensuing weeks, eight thousand French were massacred.

The movement, initially a public and popular success, was shortly to be driven underground by a resurgent Charles of Anjou. It remained a popular insurgency and, over the years, it morphed into the secret Sicilian society the Cosa Nostra that became the violent shadow government, if not the actual governance, of the island of Sicily.

Early in the twentieth century a substantial Italian, mostly Sicilian, immigration flowed into the United States. The immigrants, desperately poor and ignorant of the laws and folkways of their new home, brought with them to the new world the Mafia that had imposed order and internal justice on folk otherwise at the mercy of unfeeling and often antagonistic governments.

The Mafia, newly reborn in America, was organized around a tight-knit clan from the village of Corleone, the home of the Morello and Terranova brothers, Antonio and Giuseppe Morello and half brothers Vincenzo and Ciro Terranova. It was established in New York City and became known as the 107th Street Mob, the murdering precursor of the equally violent New York Mafia. The Mafia became the protectors and, at the same time, the oppressors of the immigrant Italian community. The Volstead Act prohibited alcohol and thereby created a flood of smuggling money for the Mafia. The organization became rich and powerful and insinuated itself, by way of murder, extortion, the corruption of public officials, and a high degree of organization, into nearly every facet of the life of New York.

By 1980 the Mafia had easily taken over the concrete industry in New York since most of the workers and the owners in concrete making were Italian masons from the old country. The penetration of the Mafia into the construction industry, abetted by its control of the manufacture and, more important, the control of concrete distribution by Ready Mix truckers, added a significant cost to every construction project in the city. These costs imposed by the Mafia on the city of New York amounted to a staggering nongovernmental sales tax. The Mafia had evolved an extortionate process whereby the accounting was specific, was easily collected, and was almost cost free to the extorters.

Enforcement was simple and did not even require much of the strong-arm tactics applied in other Mafia pursuits. If a contractor resisted payment, his Ready Mix delivery did not show up in time. It was not even necessary to actually cut off supplies; the havoc that could be caused to complicated construction schedules by even a delayed delivery was enough to keep contractors in line. The fact that the construction was in the heart of a busy and crowded city made adherence to tight construction and delivery schedules mandatory. The Mafia, in essence, held a veto on the growth of New York City by way of control of the flow of concrete.

There was a kickback of 1 percent levied against all concrete pourings valued at up to $2 million. This went directly to the Columbo crime family. For pourings of from $2 to $15 million the kickback doubled to 2 percent, which was collected from a list of commission-approved contractors called the Club. Not only was the Mafia able to control the pricing of contracts but, by enforcing that only designated contractors in New York City could pour concrete at all, the entire profile of the construction industry in New York was firmly in the hands of a criminal cartel. Almost all construction activity during the period when the Club was active was thereby concentrated into a monopoly of willing builders cemented together by a criminal commission in control of the tap through which all concrete flowed.

The four "commission families" would split the kickbacks more or less equally among themselves. The payments were thoughtfully scaled to the risk undertaken by the builders. In a big project the threat of delay was much more of a danger to the contractors and, as a result, the commission was able to demand higher kickbacks on large jobs to ensure that no disastrous work stoppages or delays would occur. This lucrative and sophisticated pattern of extortion earned the New York crime families, headed by Paul Castellano of the Gambino family, hundreds of millions of dollars.

It was an intolerable situation but one that, because of the mutual advantage to all insiders, was exempt from prosecution. Designated manufacturers and distributors, the Mafia and the easily corrupted police and city officials profited and no one talked. The burden fell entirely on the public in the resulting increase in construction costs.

Frustrated, New York City, in 1986 under the leadership of Mayor Koch, took the unprecedented step of going into business in competition with the Mafia. It was a revolutionary idea. The concept of controlling criminal activity essentially by joining in the marketplace with the criminals was an impressive new approach. It was a de facto admission that traditional law enforcement was unable to match the power of the Mafia. New York City used its financial might and its control over city contracts by subsidizing a private concrete supplier to be set up in competition with the Mafia. A private firm was to be designated and, in addition to $3 million in direct subsidies and the gift of a valuable piece of real estate, it was guaranteed that the city would buy 25,000 cubic yards a year at an agreed-upon fixed price of about $10 a yard cheaper than the price imposed by the Mafia.

Considering that there would be little capital investment, a choice three-acre rent-free location on 57th Street, and a guaranteed sale of product, it seemed like the ultimate sweetheart deal. It was a deal, the city thought, that could not be refused.

A request for proposal was sent out that generated only ten responders. Most were curiosity seekers, a few did not meet the requirements, and only two offers survived the initial winnowing. One of the two, a New Jersey firm, abruptly and mysteriously withdrew its offer. One can only wonder that the paucity of responses and the retraction of the only viable firm might well have had something to do with the dangers inherent in confronting the powerful New York Mafia, however attractive conditions might be.

There was only one man left standing and a more unlikely partner could hardly have been imagined. His name was Mustapha Ally, a self-proclaimed tycoon, a citizen of the tiny country of Guyana. Ally claimed, without proof, to have been a many-termed mayor of a Guyanese district with 250,000 people, a landowner, a master builder, a rice miller, a cattle rancher, and a warehouse operator. That he was a man with absolutely no history of involvement with the production of concrete did little to raise the suspicions of the officials of New York desperate to find a partner. When Ally offered to finance his end of the deal with "a half ton of gold" located in Guyana that he claimed he owned, the titter of suspicion should have burst its pipette.

In the event, it did not, and the city, in a moment of breathtaking municipal denial, signed up with Mustapha Ally who, while admittedly a man of little industrial experience, must have been one hell of a salesman. As matters evolved, Ally never succeeded in producing much concrete and the firm he formed went down into deepest, dismal bankruptcy. A bit too late, the city discovered that the claims of Ally, excepting only that he had no experience in making concrete, not only proved false but could have been detected by an iota of research prior to the deal. Due diligence had not entered into the negotiations.

His claim that he was mayor of a section of Guyana turned out to be a sliver of the Guyanese capital with a tiny population. It further devolved that he had been convicted of a larceny count by the government of Guyana. And the claim of the half ton of gold dissipated when the Guyanese questioned his claim to ownership and would not approve Ally's access to it.

Perhaps the most bizarre red flag that has ever been flown occurred in an interview with Ally when he announced his interest long before the deal was signed. Mustapha, in a moment of crystalline honesty, when asked why he, as a man with little experience in the making and delivery of concrete, chose to bid on the deal, said, "Because I was bored."

A *New York Times* article, reporting on the deal at the time, revealed the following: "Although city officials were unable to verify three of the four U.S. bank accounts Ally claimed to hold, the Board of Estimate approved a five-year contract after a city background check revealed 'no substantial derogatory information.' Under the agreement, signed in August 1986, Ally agreed to build a concrete plant on a city-owned pier at 57th Street and to furnish a fleet of twenty mixer trucks for delivery. In return, Ally would be designated the city's sole concrete supplier, at a price to be determined when the plant was ready to produce. Mayor Koch announced the agreement at a highly publicized city hall ceremony, hailing it as a breakthrough in the city's war against organized crime that would reduce concrete prices in the bargain."

Such was the man with whom the city of New York teamed up to fight the Mafia. A more inept partnership could hardly have been imagined.

The battle with the Mafia cartel was joined and not only was the battle lost but the whole war was won by the criminal conspiracy it was designed to oppose. Not until years later, when the full force of the federal government was arrayed against the New York Mafia, was the total control over the production of concrete weakened, though never entirely dissipated.

This adventure in the disruption of the delivery of concrete points up the fact that concrete had become an uninterruptible resource much like energy and oil and food itself.

CHAPTER 8

THE WIZARD OF MENLO PARK

"There ain't no rules around here. We're trying to accomplish something!"
—Thomas Edison

Thomas Alva Edison, long revered in the scientific mythology of America as the Wizard of Menlo Park, had a staff of hundreds in his laboratories. The staff, if not their leader, referred to themselves as "muckers," a term applied in the past to those who removed manure from stables. In more recent parlance, a mucker is a bungler who bangs around in a state of confusion.

It is interesting that those who knew Edison best, his close laboratory assistants and self-named "elves," were aware that Edison's scientific method was that of mucking about until something wonderful happened.

A case in point is his experimentation that led up to the refinements that made the electric bulb a reality. Starting in 1870 Edison set his elves to work experimenting with thousands of materials in search of a filament that, when exposed to an electric current, would glow for a while before burning up. He even tried a human hair. He spent half a decade mucking about in every possible combination of materials that could be made to produce a light.

A more reasonable use of his people and his time might have been to first ascertain the *reason* why materials burned up and then seek those materials that had a *reasonable* chance of surviving the electrical current. The reason why his earlier filaments failed was because the material had a low melting point. Instead of limiting his researches to those relatively few materials with high melting points the wizard, relying on perseverance and perspiration, mucked about till one of his elves sent a charge through a strand of carbon and produced a glow.

Although reason did not seem to be Edison's strong point, we are the richer for his lack of system no matter how much time and energy it cost. Edison's most endearing quality was his unbridled enthusiasm linked to an energetic impetuosity. While fully involved in the fascinating new world of electricity, Edison charged full bore ahead into the equally fascinating world of concrete. In his mucking about in concrete he envisioned its future while his peers learned from his failures.

If nothing else the wizard was indeed a visionary. As early as 1902, years before the Edison Portland Cement Company produced its first bucket of cement, he opined to a group of reporters that concrete was undoubtedly the construction material of the future. He argued that the forests that built the cities of America were fast disappearing and that, as a result, the price of wood would rise to a level that precluded its use for construction.

VERTICAL KILNS, LEHIGH VALLEY, PENNSYLVANIA

LIBRARY OF CONGRESS

A hundred years later his prediction is proving true. Wood is scarce and expensive though it is a long way from disappearing due to some responsible corporate cultivation and regeneration of fast growing trees.

Since it is just as bad being too early as being too late, Edison's productive detour into a cement making plant and his counterproductive attempts at making concrete homes for the masses both succeeded and failed. However, both his successes and his failures helped to hasten his predictions.

When I was a child, around 1930, my family would borrow a friend's great Packard motor car and take the long journey from Atlantic City to Baltimore where my grandparents lived. In those days one had to motor up the rutted roads of the Black Horse Pike to Camden, take a ferryboat to Philadelphia, and then drive down what was to become U.S. 1 to Baltimore.

About ten miles outside of Atlantic City there was a railroad spur that crossed the highway. Once, as we crossed a set of rails in the predawn dark, one of the wheels of the Packard simply eased itself off and rolled down the highway ahead of us.

Upon alighting we found ourselves in the middle of a scene out of Dante. Surrounding our car were a score of forty-foot-high, bottle-shaped behemoths belching smoke and flame. We had landed in the middle of a plant making "natural" cement. The monster bottles were enormous kilns fired by wood upon which the broken chunks of the limestone from the area were laid and burned from rock to the powder that was to become cement.

It was the most wasteful of processes. Each vertical kiln produced at most two hundred barrels of cement a day as compared to the millions being demanded for a nation explosively building dams and canals. As a result, America was blotted with thousands of such kilns, fouling the air with smoke and the countryside with black soot while trying vainly to keep up with the demand. It was an industry desperately in need of innovation.

Edison's Stewartsville cement plant, in one stroke of engineering insight, increased output from two hundred barrels a day per kiln to eleven hundred barrels a day. By the simple expedient of turning the kiln on its side, tilting it slightly and causing it to rotate and heating it from its outside, Edison was able to produce a continuing supply from a kiln that never needed cooling.

Limestone was dumped into his kiln at the high end, the kiln was rotated and heated, and, with the aid of gravity, the clinker was spilled out of the lower end in a continuous stream. Output continued for twenty-four hours a day and, since the process was soon taken up by other cement producers, America and then the world were able to get on with their grandiose constructions. It was a genuine revolutionary development that addressed the need for predictable deliveries of huge quantities of cement at lower prices.

In the thirty years of its operation the plant produced the concrete that built Yankee Stadium, the Moorish towers and domes of the Marlborough Blenheim Hotel in Atlantic City, and most of the concrete poured in New York City. Additionally, by providing free concrete for a test strip of concrete roadway on Route 57 in Warren County, Edison's Portland Cement Company helped urge forward the use of concrete in the Interstate Highway System.

In his flailing about in a hundred directions, Edison was often able to snatch victory from the jaws of self-made failures. The forty thousandth failure to produce a lightbulb resulted in the forty thousandth and one success. In a like manner Edison's very expensive failure of an attempt to increase the efficiency of iron ore plants to adjust to the decreasingly less rich output of the iron mines along the East Coast, which came to naught, led indirectly to the spectacular success of his cement plant. Edison had believed that the solution to depleting resources lay in the development of more sophisticated means of dealing with the less rich ore that the mines were producing. He developed giant rolling mills to take advantage of the lesser ore just at the moment when

the rich iron mountains of the West were beginning to spew out a seemingly endless supply of cheap high-grade ore.

Stuck with the draining expenditure of capital required to construct the giant rolling mills of the failed iron ore plant, Edison simply converted what was now useless rolling mills to the rolling kilns for the grinding of limestone clinker. It remains moot whether, had Edison not failed at grinding of low-grade iron ore, he would have hit on the concept of a rolling kiln. His failures continued throughout his life to be hidden behind the serendipity of his successes.

His Stewartsville plants themselves were poured concrete reinforced by iron rods inserted into the molds while the concrete was being poured. The process was invented in France fifty years earlier by a nurseryman who required very large, strong pots with which to transfer his plants. In a manner reminiscent of much of the history of concrete, this improvement, the internal reinforcement of concrete resulting in an increase in the strength of concrete, was simply forgotten about for half a century. Concrete is essentially a brittle material that is able to withstand enormous pressures but, unreinforced, fails when cast as supporting beams or columns. The addition of a few pounds of iron, now known as and universally used as rebars, changed the architectural landscape of the uses of concrete and Edison was one of the pioneers in this method.

In 1906 Edison announced the following to an adoring America: "I am going to live to see the day when a working man's house can be built of concrete in a week. If I succeed it will take from the city slums everybody who is worth taking."

Edison, with the audacity of Napoleon's marshals linked to an unattractive hint of elitism, was proposing an urban revolution not incidental to the fact that he had just incorporated the Edison Portland Cement Company.[1]

As he was building his cement company he, typically, concentrated all of his attention on the potentials of concrete. He was fascinated by the seeming simplicity of the process. Build a hollow mold and fill it with this magical slush that quickly hardened into any desired shape. He was intrigued by this emerging technology that suggested he could replicate complicated forms endlessly and perfectly and cheaply.

The cost of labor in America at the turn of the century was beginning to be a serious consideration. Wages were rising and the flood of cheap immigrant labor was peaking. To further limn the future of the cost of labor in industry, Henry Ford was offering the absolutely unheard-of sum of *five dollars a day* in an economy that had just become comfortable with one dollar a day.

Edison reckoned, early on, that the key to future productivity and future profits would be dependent on reducing the amount of labor a project required. His experience with the quick construction of this Stewartsville plant confirmed his belief in the efficient applicability of concrete in the realization of large construction projects. But Edison also was aware that the construction of homes, at the time, was the engine that pushed the economy, and it was dependent on a high concentration of increasingly expensive human labor. In his enthusiasm he intended, as we shall see, to do something about that problem.

And such was the reputation of Edison that others were swept along in his visions. In a biography of Edison published in 1908, Francis Arthur Jones writes, "The time will most certainly come when whole houses will be turned out in one piece, though each part is now separately molded. These metallic moulds may be ornate or plain as the fancy of the householder dictated and it will be no dearer to have that latter than the former. It only requires some smart architects to draw up designs for a few houses of different patterns and of about the size to suit the family of an average mechanic."

Yet this early enthusiasm for quick and cheap housing designed for the lower classes never lived up to the visions of Edison and his admirers. Even today a concrete house is more a luxury than an economy as the cost of construction of small sophisticated concrete homes is still well ahead of the cost of more traditional methods in the developed world.[2]

In developments Edison could hardly have foreseen, concrete construction has become the mainstay of large-scale modern building technology. Starting in the 1950s, the use of precast and cast on-site concrete elements has become commonplace in the skyscrapers that loom about us.

In spite of all of this progress, however, housing for the slum dweller and for the lower middle classes remains not much advanced from the conditions that existed when Edison made his brave new predictions.

In planning for his Stewartsville cement plant, Edison's choice of concrete, at the time an essentially experimental mate-

rial, was motivated in no small part by the threat of fire. Ever the businessman, and dealing with rolling kilns dependent on perpetual burning, the cost of fire insurance had become a serious factor in his decisions. But whatever motivated his choice he soon became a devotee and a prophet in a world that knew little about the breadth and the potential ubiquity of the material.

Never one to be limited by custom he poured the most unlikely of objects in concrete. Unconcerned about the acoustic qualities he might be violating, he proposed a concrete piano. It is unclear whether that instrument was ever produced or whether, having been made, it could ever have been moved and used effectively in a private home. As he had always been at the forefront of recorded sound, he produced and offered for sale the most exotic object that had ever been, or might well ever be, made of concrete: a Victrola complete with scrollwork.

EDISON'S CONCRETE MODULAR HOUSES

"Edison developed the idea that a concrete house should have concrete furniture. He proposed making concrete refrigerators and concrete pianos, and did, in fact, cast several concrete phonograph cabinets. To mark the final resting place of the inhabitants of the concrete world, he devised a concrete tombstone."

—Michael Petersen, "Edison's Concrete Homes"

Edison's entry into home building for the masses was by way of an offhand remark during an after-dinner speech in New York City in 1906. It was typical of Edison who believed that anything that could be thought of could, in this modern age, be accomplished. Especially if thought of by him.

His logic was as modern as tomorrow. Concrete cut the cost of labor, had an endless supply of cheap and ubiquitous raw material, was fireproof and insectproof, would never rot, and was resistant to flooding and winds. The wizard had made a seductive argument to a country that had a profound belief in his ability to pull rabbits out of a hat. In addition the capitalists of the time were beginning to realize that their new industrial centers were attracting hordes of workers who needed housing. Edison had come up with an alluring, futuristic American solution that spoke loudly to the diverse needs of the whole range of the country's economy. He had struck a nerve.

As he was deep in the new and complex problems of the Stewartsville plant, the concrete housing project so rashly announced had to be put on a back burner. But the publicity and the enormous response fed the hunger for more news and, when there was nothing forthcoming, his competitors, engineers, and journalists began to raise questions. Edison had himself engendered public doubt in his abilities and his statements. This was anathema to him and in 1908 he began a series of experiments the challenges of which he had not foreseen.

EDISON'S CONCRETE HOUSES
LIBRARY OF CONGRESS

The technical problems of multiple identical concrete housing were horrendous.[3] Edison was breaking new ground in a new industry and it took time and the oxlike stubbornness of a man who could not allow himself to fail. Ultimately, a full decade after the announcement in New York, the building of the first of Edison's houses was commenced in Union, New Jersey. Forty houses were proposed. Eleven were built and that was all. Eleven houses were all that ever became of Edison's grandiose scheme to reinvent housing for the American lower classes.

The problem that buried the project, in spite of the initial enormous rush of interest, was that nobody wanted to live in them. Edison's houses raised two unsurmountable aesthetic objections. They were ugly and no one wanted to live in a house that had been nationally touted as "the salvation of the slum dweller."

In his evangelical visions of housing for all, Edison was unmindful of the fact that Americans then, as Americans now, considered themselves as middle—neither high nor low—class. Reduction to lower-class slum dwellers was intolerable and after a month only one house had been sold.

> Ten of the original houses remain standing on Ingersoll Terrace (one was demolished to make way for a highway exit), so the technology of the process has certainly shown itself to be durable. The original owners are long gone but new owners have generally positive opinions of the little houses. According to Mrs. Joseph Fila, who occupied an Edison house for half a century, "The twenty-four-inch walls keep out the summer heat and provide good winter insulation." Joe Kearny says that the maintenance cost of his house is "zero." Dolores Chumsky is less enthusiastic; her house is plagued by an elusive leak that defies detection. She adds that any prospects for renovation or improvements are doomed. "Just try to get someone to come and make repairs," she says. "They come in once, but they never come back."[4]

The problems were not all aesthetic. The seemingly simple concept of quickly pouring a structure eventually ran into an untested technology of mold building and usage. Today in India concrete dome houses are being digitally designed on computers. It took a century to get from Edison's visions to today's fact. Had Edison been granted the time he might well, in his inimitable style, have mucked about and changed housing in America.

CHAPTER 9

WHAT IS ART?

With the dismal business of the First World War completed, concrete began to spread like a benevolent plague and not only across the physical landscape. It began to leave its ineradicable mark on every facet of the busy life of twentieth-century aesthetics.

Many uses of concrete had been predicted in the centuries preceding our time but concrete quite suddenly became important in areas that had not been anticipated. Though it was no surprise that concrete would become the preeminent material in construction, there was little evidence to indicate concrete would sweep into the world of fine art.

It was inevitable that home building for folk of all the economic classes would slowly emerge, yet it was unthinkable that these homes would accept the concept of concrete furniture and furnishings. Early in the century Edison had tried but failed to market the idea that this essentially rough and cumbersome material would be suitable for houses.

It took the talents of artists and designers, always reaching out for new materials, to bring it into our homes as furniture and into our galleries as art. The perception that concrete was exclusively an outdoor material, native to walls and dams and the sheathing of buildings, gave way by the end of the century to a realization that concrete was acceptable for even the most intimate of objects in our daily lives. In private homes, bathtubs and countertops and windows and tables accommodated themselves to a material that, by the end of the century, was becoming as smoothly tactile as marble, as light as oak, as maleable as the silver in a necklace, and as translucent as a roll-down window shade.

As usual, it was the artists, "the unacknowledged legislators of the future," who started to make their own "stones" poured in the shapes they desired. It has overtaken steel and stone in establishing an outdoor iconography unknown before our generation. Leonardo da Vinci was able, in an instant, to see the transcendent forms that lay within a block of marble but needed years to chip them out of their hiding places. Today's concrete artists can turn their dreams into reality in the time it takes to mix a batch of concrete in a bucket. When the period between concept and completion is a matter of hours, as it is with concrete and, indeed, in other media such as photography, the discussion about what is art and what is not art widens.

Ars longa, vita brevis no longer shortened the creative lives of sculptors. Art in the twentieth century, first riding piggyback on industrial technologies and then leaping ahead of them, has joined science and the marketplace as the three defining cultural forces of our frantic and impact-driven times.

To those of us bemused by the problem of differentiating between art and everything else, concrete simply added to the confusion. In response, two answers emerged. The first, which seems too simple but which, upon reflection, is not, is the statement that "anything an artist says is art is art." While that requires a precedent definition of what is an artist, it goes a long way to developing an understanding of the diversity that we have experienced in the present-day making of art.

The second definition of art, one that requires no precedent definitions and one that best includes all of the forms of modern art, was offered by Salvador de Mariaga. "Art," he posited, "is the conveyance of Spirit by means of Matter."

If we accept de Mariaga's observation, then every piece of sculpture that speaks to the spirit and that comes from the hand of man is a work of art.

To some, this explication of what is art is blindingly clear and logical. To others it perhaps only deepens the mystery, which once again proves that the amphibology of art is as broad as the differences that define each one of us.

CIRCLE FISH BY STUART PETERMAN

COURTESY OF THE ARTIST

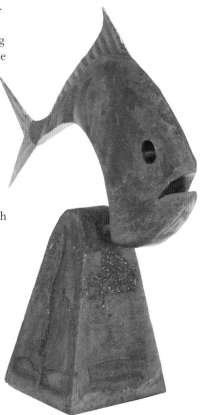

FLIGHTS OF CONCRETE FANCY

For almost a thousand years art has been defined and judged by two criteria: image and technique. Image defined the quality of the mind of the artist and what set him apart from his peers. The ability of the artist to convert thought to image by way of hard won technique and skill in the handling of his materials was the requisite half of reputation.

Thought *sans* skill was anathema until the latter half of the nineteenth century when the idea, the personal way that an artist looked at reality, could be presented with only enough technical ability to make the work that would last through time.

This divorce between the idea and the execution, produced progressively more works of art that depended less and less on the ability of the artist to master difficult and demanding media. The least demanding media appeared on the horizon of the arts around 1900 when the Grassroots movement emerged in middle America. The ease of use of concrete combined with its immediate permanence has, since that time, opened the floodgates of creativity among sculptors.

The result is a panoply of work stretching from the monumental of Picasso and Whiteread to the tiny necklace made of concrete by Andrew Goss of Canada in which is enclosed and hidden forever a small diamond.

Picasso waited decades until he discovered a process that would preserve forever his painterly images scored onto concrete. Goss conjured with a much more subtle concept by burying the most pure and the most rare substance known to man, a diamond, within the most rough and most common substance. The existence of the diamond hidden in the solidified concrete depended entirely on Goss's statement that it was there. And then Goss made a matching concrete necklace without a diamond so that neither he nor a client could ever be sure that it was or was not present in either example. Goss was

PEELED ORCHID **BY BOROTON**

COURTESY OF THE ARTIST

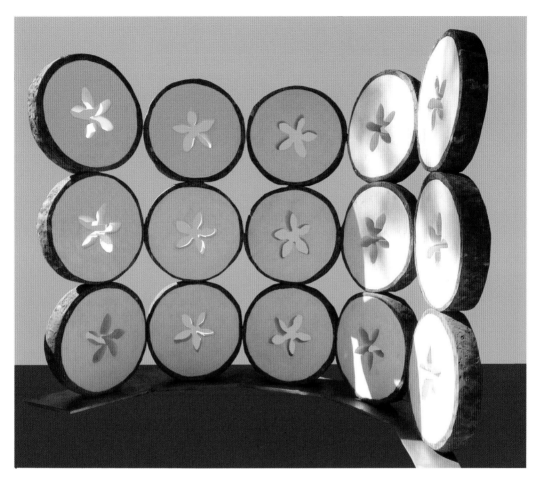

commenting on reality since the very existence of the diamond in the stone was unknowable.

It is impossible to record the breadth of the spate of art that is emerging from the use of concrete. Illustrated is a collection of works that have accidentally hove up over the horizon of this book. Since anybody working with concrete can do anything he can think of, a definition of randomness, the works lie on a bell curve of excellence with the vast majority entirely forgettable. What will be remembered as great concrete art lies in the fog of the future.

SLICED WALL BY BOROTON
COURTESY OF THE ARTIST

"KARLEY'S MARKER" FROM
DIASPORA **BY LORI NOZICK**

COURTESY OF THE ARTIST

GENESIS **BY LORI NOZICK**

COURTESY OF THE ARTIST

CONCRETE BRACELET BY
ANDREW GOSS

COURTESY OF THE ARTIST

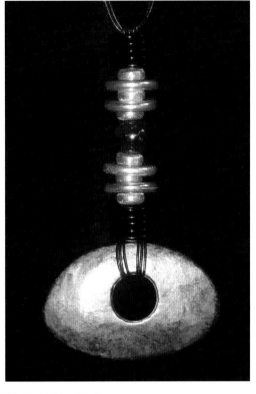

CONCRETE TOTEM #18 BY
MARILYN ARNOLD PALLEY,
CONCRETE, AMBER, SILVER,
VERMEIL, AND ONYX

COURTESY OF THE ARTIST

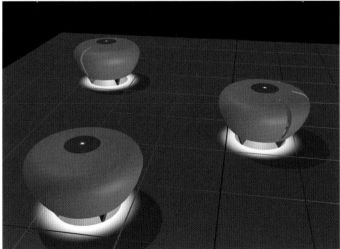

LIGHT SEATS, CONCRETE
SITABLE ART BY ANJA BACHE

COURTESY OF THE ARTIST

ROOTS OF GRASS

After 1900, as the industrial world grew rich, ever more people were relieved from the daily necessity of putting bread on the table. Freed of this constraint, some millions turned from matters material to matters of the spirit and sought to reinvent the world in their own images; "imagined image" is a pretty good way to think about art especially when a million newly disenthralled artists are turned loose on an entirely new medium.

Perhaps the progression most useful for looking at the complicated impact of concrete on art would be from the least to the most sophisticated. By this measure the starting point is the Grassroots movement of the American Midwest. The Grassroots movement is variously called outsider art or naive and was produced by a disorganized group of autodidact artists one of whom, Ed Root, came into art by way of an auto accident and others by way of retirement and boredom.

However the movement arose, it was born in the opening years of the twentieth century and limited, in America, mostly to the agricultural Midwest. Available, malleable, and cheap, it requires little handcraft and minimal skill and, because it arrives in heftable bags, it speaks to the solitary eccentric doing his thing

SAMUEL PERRY DINSMOOR,
GARDEN OF EDEN

on his own. These artists, mostly men, driven by the need for spiritual self-expression in a culture that was conjuring with more material matters, were still able to achieve impressive constructions. They were artists who, to a man, uninformed of the long history and theories of art were, nevertheless, making serious art. Without concrete their works would never have been realized.

These homegrown "outsiders" are all wildly individualistic and unconstrained by the formality of an art education. Their medium is rough as they themselves are but the works have a vitality that raised the commonplace to art.

The doyen, the earliest of all the Grassroots artists, was Samuel Perry Dinsmoor, schoolteacher, Civil War veteran, and freethinking politician. Dinsmoor took it in his mind in 1907 to build a limestone and concrete eleven-room log cabin. Taking twenty-two years and a hundred tons of cement, he built his home and draped around it an entire diorama of the Garden of Eden, snake and all, in naturally colored concrete; the apple was painted bright red.

Dinsmoor was born in Coolville, Ohio, in 1843 and died in Lucas, Ohio, in 1932.[1] He married his first wife, Frances, on horseback in 1870. When she died in 1917 at the age of eighty-one, he married twenty-year-old Emilie Brozek and in spite of his age produced two children. Dinsmoor was the archetypical rugged individualist characteristic of the pioneer families who opened the American West. His politics were populist, his instincts were iconoclastic, and his personal life was as unique as his art.

His *Garden of Eden*, which surrounds his limestone cabin, features a concrete Adam and Eve. Eve is in the act of offering Adam the apple of carnal knowledge while the snake looks on. Above them, on tall concrete pillars, stand the Devil, assorted children, and two storks. To the left, high in the air, an all-seeing concrete eye, a tip of the hat perhaps to the freethinking Masons, watches over the garden.

In the spirit of William Jennings Bryan, labor in Dinsmoor's garden is being crucified by a banker, a lawyer, a preacher, and a doctor who look on approvingly. On one pillar, an octopus representing monopolies and trusts grabs at the world. A soldier and a child are trapped in two of its tentacles. In another tree Lady Liberty drives a spear through the head of another trust octopus, as ordinary folk cut off the limb that it rests upon.

Dinsmoor was a man who set in concrete his moral and political beliefs. Few so clearly limned in stone the sure conviction of who the enemies of the people were.

"GODDESS OF LIBERTY" IN DINSMOOR'S *GARDEN OF EDEN*

NATHAN ED GALLOWAY, a carver of a thousand fiddles, was attracted to this new and wondrous material that could be mixed in a bucket and hardened into rock. A close student of the Indian nations, he chose to build his gigantic totem pole to memorialize their culture in stone.

The pole, a structure of concrete poured over a frame of scrap iron, rose to ninety feet in height and was forty feet at the base. It is the largest such totem pole in the world and when asked why he took eleven years to build a huge monument in concrete after a lifetime of the finicky making of fiddles, Ed, as he was known to his friends, said somewhat impatiently, "I can whittle out a fiddle while my wife gets breakfast!" He apparently required a greater challenge.

•   •   •   •

FRED SMITH was born to German immigrants in 1886 in northern Wisconsin and made his living as a logger in the great virgin forests of middle America among the local Indians, whose images he preserved in concrete.

While still logging in the forest he built and operated the Rock Garden tavern. Like many other of the Grassroots artists, Fred was self-taught in fiddle making and wood carving and eventually discovered the new mysteries of pouring concrete. His tavern became a platform for his skill as a fiddler and, as Smith sought ever more areas in which to express his boundless creative energy, his dabbling in concrete.

•   •   •   •

GLENN STARK is a whittler who turned to concrete early in his career. In many of his concrete works, Stark exhibited the same sort of wry humor as his personal idol, Will Rogers. Of the Grassroots artists Stark was one of the few who was able, like

NATHAN ED GALLOWAY,
TOTEM POLE

GLENN STARK, *DINOSAUR* AND *GOOD OLD DAYS*

IMAGES COURTESY ROADSIDE AMERICA

Rogers, to deftly express his creativity by making quiet fun in concrete. The dinosaur with a foot in his mouth could well be a political comment, a shot at popular culture, and, best of all, a concrete diorama of the "good old days," which says in concrete, with a snicker, that the good old days were, after all, not all that good.

While he made less sly concrete sculptures and hundreds of serious figures whittled out of cottonwood, these few examples define a man who, unlike so many artists, chose not to take himself very seriously. Art in our self-conscious century can be a very serious business, especially concrete art, which, because concrete can quickly become monumental, rarely descends to caprice. Whimsy is not likely to be expressed by the ton.

•   •   •   •

Another artist, **ED ROOT**, also Grass Root, managed to combine whimsy with the monumental. His enormous sculpture of a bison is at once friendly, fierce, and funny.

Ed Root farmed in Kansas until, around 1940, an auto accident forced his retirement. Physically limited he turned his skills to sculpture although there is no record of why he turned to concrete or where he learned the necessary skills. His great bison sculpture was, in all probability, a memorial to the fiercely supported local team the Lake Wilson Bisons. For twenty years until his death in 1960 Root turned out hundreds of concrete sculptures scattered about his farm.

The American Grassroots artists were among the first to realize the potential of concrete as a medium for the making of art. They emerged, surprisingly, from a primitive, almost hand-to-mouth society, in which a man's measure was his ability to wrest usable product from an unyielding wilderness. Churches fed their spiritual lives and there was little room for the making of art and even less for its uses.

The wonder of these artists was not that there were so few of them but that there were any at all.

RACHEL WHITEREAD

Between the work of the Grassroots artists and Pablo Picasso, there are tens of thousands of sculptings in concrete that could have, and eventually should be, recorded in any history of concrete. Like the multiplicity of concrete buildings, the panoply of concrete sculpture in the twentieth century is vast. In this history of concrete we are limited to that which is impactful or which defines an era in the development of concrete. As a result we are forced to leave, scattered by the side of the road of history, a boundless cemetery of great art that, while important as art, had little impact on the flow of the river of concrete.

In surveying concrete art in this century it is necessary to record those works that could be realized only in concrete. Most concrete artworks could have been laboriously chiseled out of stone or carved from wood or poured from metal. But a very few exist because the artist saw concrete as the only solution to an almost impossible problem.

Such an artist is Rachel Whiteread. She was born in London in 1963. Between 1982 and 1987 she trained at Brighton Poly-technic and the Slade School of Art. She won the important Turner Prize for sculpture in 1993, even before she completed her most important and original work. Whiteread's work deals with cast-ings of familiar objects. Her inversion of these objects twists real-ity so that what was familiar suddenly becomes strange. Her work *House* is a cast of the interior of the last remaining house of a late-nineteenth-century terrace in the East End of London. It is beyond reality because she cast it not as a house itself. She cast

RACHEL WHITEREAD,
***HOUSE*, 1993**

PHOTOGRAPH SUE ORMEROD,
COURTESY GAGOSIAN GALLERY,
NEW YORK

it as the spaces above, below, or inside it, making solid the apparently empty spaces of the house. Due to its monumental scale and its near impossible technical requirements, it is a rare work of art that depends for its existence on the material from which it is formed. Whiteread is the conceiver, yet *House* exists only because of concrete's liquid ability to fill spaces with hard rock.

The British newspaper the *Independent* has characterized *House* as "a strange and fantastical object which also amounts to one of the most extraordinary and imaginative sculptures created by an English artist this century. Denatured by transformation, things turn strange here. Fireplaces bulge outwards from the walls of House, doorknobs are rounded hollows. Architraves have become chiselled incisions running around the monument, forms as mysterious as the hieroglyphs on Egyptian tombs."

PICASSO

Pablo Picasso, the quintessential explorer of media, was the first among the leading artists of the century to recognize the monumental possibilities of concrete art. The concept came to him neither quickly nor easily as monumental-sized works of art require long and complicated periods of gestation. In Picasso's case the concept was brought to him in a most circuitous and serendipitous way.

For years Picasso had generated inches-high cardboard and metal maquettes folded into images that he envisioned in his mind as *plein air*, monumental sculptures. Because they were derived, as was almost all art he made, from his line sketches it seemed impossible to him to produce them in a very large scale on a medium that would survive the abuse of unprotected exposure to the elements. The concrete would last, but the painted lines, the core of his creativity, would dim and fade away. In spite of the fecklessness of the pursuit of a problem he considered impossible of solution, he continued, year after year, to pile up and squirrel away endless variations of folded maquettes.

The maquettes bore painted lines on three-dimensional surfaces, which, on wood or iron or even on concrete, were too temporary to suit Picasso's insistence that his work not be subject to weathering. Without the free, hand-drawn lines that are his signature, enormous forms would become anonymous and loose their Picasso-ness.

The story of how his massive concrete sculptures came to be begins with a sailing voyage across the Pacific Ocean. Thor Heyerdahl had built a raft of balsa logs with which he intended to sail from South America to the Society Islands. Heyerdahl wanted to prove that the vast Pacific Ocean was the pathway between that continent and the islands of Polynesia so he built a raft, designed to the primitive technology of the past, in which he planned to drift across the Pacific.

In gathering a crew for the *Kon-Tiki* adventure, Heyerdahl sought out an old friend from his hometown of Larvik in Norway. The friend was Erik Hesselberg, a man of enormous energy and talent, who combined his knowledge of the stars as a navigator with his skills as a carpenter and craftsman. Hesselberg was just the man that Heyerdahl needed.

Hesselberg, a born adventurer, accepted at once and made the famous Pacific crossing, which supported Heyerdahl's thesis as his vessel piled up on a reef in Polynesia at the end of the voyage. Hesselberg returned to Larvik and bought an old wooden tender with the intent of sailing throughout the Mediterranean to document the early passages of the Vikings.

Another Norwegian friend, Carl Nesjar, an artist and, like Hesselberg, a craftsman of all trades, was lured to join in the reconstruction of the old boat. Nesjar also wanted to document the early voyages and settlements of his Viking ancestors in the Med. The two happily spent years working on Hesselberg's wooden boat and dreaming of great adventures to come.

Nesjar's dream was interrupted by a letter from the French government offering him a scholarship for an academic year of study in Paris. The scholarship included funds for living and travel in France and proved too much of an opportunity to resist. Nesjar's dream had to wait.

As it turned out, a new and larger dream that was to swallow up the rest of his life emerged from the scholarship grant and from his friendship with Hesselberg. Nesjar set out on his scholarship and Hesselberg completed his vessel, christened her *Tiki*, and sailed down the waterways of Europe, ending up near Marseilles around 1956.

Nesjar, traveling in France on his scholarship at the time, arranged to meet Hesselberg on the *Tiki* in the Golfe Juan on the Mediterranean coast of France, where Hesselberg had invited him to stay aboard. There was to be a party celebrating the new year to which a few friends had been invited. Among the friends was Eugene Fidler, a painter and ceramist with a substantial artistic reputation.

Aboard the *Tiki* one evening Nesjar told the group that the reason he had come south was to try to complete a mission he had been entrusted with by the Workers Party of Norway.

The party, and the associated Aktuell Kunst Society of Oslo, conceived of a plan to bring good contemporary art to the masses at affordable prices. They were recruiting artists who, for very little or no pay, would produce lithographs in editions of 250. The first non-Scandinavian artist to be included was Picasso. But how to reach him? Phones were awkward, and the committee felt that a simple letter of request, of which Picasso received thousands, might be ignored. It was decided that a courier would be most likely to gain Picasso's attention and they cast about for someone, with a reputation in the arts, to personally carry the missive.

Nesjar, in Paris studying lithography, was sent a letter from the society, addressed to Picasso, with the invitation to participate in this socially progressive project. Nesjar was to contact Picasso and present the offer in person. Nesjar tried to reach Picasso but was unsuccessful so he and his wife simply headed south in the faint hope of somehow making a direct contact. He told Fidler that he had been unsuccessful and he was disappointed by his failure.

At times the universe conspires to assist improbabilities rather than resist them and so it was with this tortured tale of Picasso and his monumental concrete sculptures. With stunning unlikeliness Fidler and his wife were close friends of Picasso and were planning to visit him at Picasso's villa, La Californie, just a short distance away from where Hesselberg's *Tiki* was moored. The purpose of the visit was to show off their newborn baby. Fidler phoned Jacqueline, Picasso's then wife, who was usually very protective of Picasso's privacy. In this case she agreed, out of their friendship with Fidler, to allow Nesjar to come along.

Earlier, in the course of their work on the *Tiki*, Fidler had asked Hesselberg about a Norwegian architect, Erling Viksjo, who had been working on developing a concrete that would be suitable for major works of art. Nesjar had joined Viksjo in perfecting a process called Betograve, which made possible the drawing of ineradicable lines on concrete by the use of a high-pressure water gun.

The strands of Nesjar's past and future were thus being drawn together on Hesseberg's little yacht by this series of accidental and unlikely meetings...all serendipitously focused on Picasso.

The meeting at La Californie between the Fidlers, the Nesjars, and Jacqueline and Pablo Picasso was a great success. Picasso was enchanted by the baby and, as the afternoon wore on, a relationship was forged that would run from that moment in 1957 to the realization of the monumental *Bust of Sylvette* a decade later.

When Nesjar mentioned to Picasso Viksjo's process by which lines could be incised on concrete, Picasso was immediately intrigued and suddenly realized that this could be exactly the means to incise his images permanently onto Brobdingnagian concrete structures that would resist weathering and fading. The hundreds of folded maquettes that Picasso had idled with for decades suddenly took on a new meaning. A marriage of the tiny maquettes with the Betograve technique was the engine for which Picasso had so long waited.

At one point in 1962, with a number of successful but small concrete sculptures under construction, Nesjar was at La Californie to show Picasso some pictures of a proposed installation of a decorated concrete wall on the estate of Picasso's great French dealer Daniel-Henry Kahnweiler. Suddenly, that afternoon, Picasso said, "Let's drive over to Vallauris."

PLAQUE FOR *BUST OF SYLVETTE*

Picasso's connection to the potteries in Vallauris dated from two decades earlier when he had become interested in clay and pottery as a medium. He moved to Vallauris, bought a small, undistinguished cottage, and, for the better part of four years, churned out his remarkable ceramic works. When he left Vallauris he closed up the cottage and returned to it only decades later when he drove down to Vallauris with Nesjar in 1962.

When Picasso threw open the door of the cottage the rooms, covered in the dust of years, were strewn with an array of urns, plates, and vases that a profligate Picasso had completed and abandoned there.

Picasso rooted about and emerged with a small maquette of the head of a neighbor who, during the years at Vallauris, had moved in across the road. Her name was Sylvette David and Picasso was struck with her clean, strong profile, highlighted by her severely pulled back dark hair. Picasso proposed to Nesjar that this maquette be expanded into a sculpture. Since Picasso was loath to part with the maquette he asked Nesjar to trace the outlines of the piece. This hastily scribbled pattern on a tattered piece of parchment that Nesjar had found amid the debris was the beginning of a historic concrete sculpture. However, for years nothing came of the project.

Five years later, with the project for the *Bust of Sylvette* long put aside in the rush of new work, Nesjar received two drawings from Picasso that were to be incised onto the Government Building in Oslo. Nesjar was in Paris at a restaurant excitedly displaying the drawings to a friend. A stranger at a nearby table took note of their wild delight in the papers being passed back and forth. This went on for a time with much conversation and gesticulation until the stranger could no longer contain his curiosity. He approached the two men and was told of the concrete incision process that was at the heart of all Picasso's great sculptures-to-be.

The stranger became immediately entranced by the possibilities of the process and, on his next trip to Europe, he looked up Nesjar to see for himself a finished project.

The stranger then announced, "I have long thought about monumental sculpture in scale with modern architecture and I recognize the possibilities of the concrete technique. Here and now I am beginning a one man crusade to have a monumental Picasso work for one of my projects." The accidental stranger was I. M. Pei.

Such is the lovely serendipity of the random universe that a chance encounter at a table in a Paris bistro could place one of Picasso's major works in the heart of a great city at the center of a great university. After this long line of fortuity and accident, New York University became the home of Picasso's most important concrete sculpture, the thirty-foot-high *Bust of Sylvette*.

Alfred H. Barr Jr., the driving force behind the Museum of Modern Art in New York, was quoted in the *New York Times* as follows, "Forty years ago Picasso began to dream of colossal sculptures. As models he made a series of fantastic figure drawings unlike anything he or anyone else had imagined. But no one stepped forward to make the dream come true until the 1950s. Now, in our city, we shall have a monument sprung from a two-foot-high painted sheet metal, the head of a girl with ponytail hair, as big as the Giant Sphinx of Egypt."

PICASSO'S *BUST OF SYLVETTE*

PHOTOGRAPHS MARILYN ARNOLD PALLEY

ARCHITECTURE

When one of our low-browed progenitors first crept into a cave to escape a wet, windy, cold, dangerous environment, he found a place that was dry and warm and, most important, defensible. At that moment the human race experienced a leap forward in creature comforts that was not to be exceeded until, eons later, someone invented the door.

The cave home was one of man's first tentative steps toward our hegemony over nature. A cave is a far cry from the Guggenheim Museum in Bilbao, Spain, yet both serve man's need to escape from the outdoors. The great and magical structures that leap up about us today are essentially hollow places, as were caves, in which men can more comfortably go about the living of their lives.

For most of man's existence our nakedness to nature was protected first by sod and wood and only much later by steel and stone. Construction involved the placing of one rock on top of another. With the minor exceptions of adobe and ice, and stillborn detours into concrete by Egyptians and Romans, there was little progress in the concept of pouring rock rather than piling it up to create a hollow place into which to crawl.

Concrete entered our recent centuries as a singularity that was about to experience a big bang. This explosion in the use of concrete in the course of barely more than two lifetimes was to change, unalterably, the way we live.

Our cities grew vertically as concrete was married to steel. This compacting of population ended the very culture of the village, which, heretofore, had been the measure of human life. Social changes characterized in part by buildings designed for the concentration of industry and trade forced the working populations of cities farther away from the centers of commerce. This led to the explosive increase of private vehicles and, thence, directly to the furious race to build roads and highways.

Art, architecture, the relation of man to his work, family structure, government, and the governed all responded to the emergence of a universal material that could make real any fantasy we could imagine.

In the beginning of the twentieth century concrete was recruited simply to improve the roofed boxes, some with domes and most without. A multitude of small buildings went up but, since the material was known to have low tensile strength, nothing very high was attempted.

Around 1902 a Cincinnati investor named Melville Ingalls

teamed up with Henry N. Cooper, a structural engineer with a long memory. Ingalls proposed to build a sixteen-story "skyscraper." The popular engineering opinion at the time was that anything over six stories would collapse of its own weight. They labeled the proposal dangerous and audacious.

Cooper knew that in the previous century various small buildings and objects were being formed of concrete supported by implanting metal rods or wire into the structure. Around 1850 Jean-Louis Lambot built two small rowboats by reinforcing the hulls with iron bars and wire mesh. Lambot had larger plans afoot as his application for a patent in 1865 proves: "An Improved Building Material to be used as a Substitute for Wood in Naval and Architectural Constructions and also for Domestic Purposes where Dampness is to be Avoided."

Across the Channel, in 1854, an English plasterer named William B. Wilkinson had already erected a small servant's cottage using iron reinforcement in the floor and the roof. He is credited with constructing the world's first reinforced concrete building. But the first widespread use of reinforcement in buildings occurred under the direction of the French builder François Coignet. He built several large houses of reinforced concrete in England and France in the period from 1850 to 1880, using iron rods as the stiffening elements.

As with so many other developments and discoveries that pepper the history of concrete, these early attempts to meld iron and concrete lay fallow for half a century until, after the turn of the twentieth, Cooper conjured with the conceit of taking a building higher than had yet been attempted.

He was aware of the work of Ernest R. Ransome in reinforcing concrete blocks, which had already been successfully used in low-rise buildings in California, Pennsylvania, and New Jersey. Reasoning that success in reinforcing a small block of concrete was limited in size only by the imagination of builders, Cooper undertook to expand Ransome's work in the construction of the world's tallest reinforced concrete "skyscraper." Rather than taking a safe, incremental approach and building first an eight- or ten-story building, Cooper and Ingalls developed plans for a breathtaking 210-foot structure of sixteen stories.

The construction of the Ingalls building is described on Wikipedia: "Cooper designed a monolithic concrete box of eight-inch (200 mm) walls, with concrete floors and roof, concrete beams, concrete columns, concrete stairs—no steel. It consists merely of bars embedded in concrete, with the ends interlaced.

"The amount of concrete produced during construction—

INGALLS BUILDING, CINCINNATI

COURTESY AMERICAN SOCIETY OF CIVIL ENGINEERS

100 cubic yards (76 m≥) in each ten-hour shift—was limited by the rate at which the builders could place it. An extra wet mix was used to ensure uniform density in the columns and complete contact with iron reinforcing bars, later called rebars. Floor slabs were poured without joints. Columns measured 30 by 34 inches (760 by 860 mm) for the first ten floors and 12 inches (300 mm) square for the rest. Three sets of forms were used, rotating from the bottom to the top of the building when the concrete had cured. Completed in eight months, the finished building measures 50 by 100 feet (15 by 30 m) at its base and 210 feet (64 m) tall."

The Beaux Arts classical exterior is covered on the first three stories with white marble, on the next eleven stories with glazed gray brick, and on the top floor and cornice with glazed white terra-cotta.

As the building rose at the impressive rate of three stories a month, the engineering community and the general population in Cincinnati eagerly awaited the moment when, Icarus-like, the building would rise too high and collapse of its own folly. Indeed, one convinced reporter sat up all night prior to the building's dedication, hoping to be the first to report its demise. There was, and is, in America a hunger for great disasters.

The Ingalls building remains in use as a distinguished address for important corporations in Cincinnati. It was designated in 1975 as a historic building in the National Register of Historic Places. In the several decades after its completion the race for ever higher skyscrapers involving concrete was capped when the Empire State Building was opened in 1931. It was only after the century turned that this height began to be exceeded routinely by oil-rich emirates.

SAN SIMEON

It is instructive to remember, too, that concrete made counterfeiting of the past possible at reasonable cost.

To replicate the romantic pastiches of Venice and Spain and other rococo palaces that dotted southern Europe by employing the original modes of construction was out of the reach of even the greatest fortunes. Money aside, the skilled army of stone workers that created the masterpieces of three hundred years of European architecture no longer existed.

The hunger of commercial moguls of the time for the edificial trappings of royalty was fulfilled, at least in one case, by importation rather than by re-creation. Newspaper publisher William Randolph Hearst had purchased a fourteenth-century French Augustinian monastery in the 1920s. He had it laboriously dismantled, each stone carefully numbered, and shipped to the United States. Having finally lost interest in his acquisition, the monastery lay in storage for almost half a century until it was purchased from Hearst by Huntington Hartford. When the time came for Hearst to build rather than import his own monument he used a material of the future to make a forgery of the past in the construction of San Simeon, which has come to be known as Hearst's Castle.

Hearst lacked even the good taste to consistently ape only one architectural period. The buildings are, as a result, a melange of Greco-Roman and Moorish images, all badly sited and badly conceived. From the outdoor reflecting pool surrounded by an awkwardly scaled Greek temple to the indoor swimming pool that is so jumbled in styles it cannot be easily named, the inadequacies of Julia Morgan, Hearst's architect on the job, are evident.

In spite of the efficiency of pouring concrete, San Simeon took twenty years to build and cost $4 million at a time when a million meant something. Interspersed with cast concrete imitations of the past, Hearst gathered "four carloads of objects" from Europe, which he scattered indiscriminately about the project.

HEARST'S CASTLE AND HEARST'S POOL

PHOTOGRAPHS NORMAN ALLEN

In a letter to Julia Morgan, Hearst lays out his confusion.

The San Diego Exposition is the best source for Spanish in California.
The alternative is to build this group of buildings in the Renaissance
style of Southern Spain. We picked out the towers of the Church at
Ronda. I suppose they are Renaissance or else transitional, and they
have some Gothic feelings; but a Renaissance decoration, particularly
that of the very southern part of Spain, could harmonize well with
them. I would very much like to have your views on what we should
do in regard to this group of buildings, what style of architecture we
should select....I am not very sure about my architecture...but after
all, would it not be better to do something a little different than other
people are doing out in California as long as we do not do anything
incongruous? I do not want you to do anything you do not like.

There was a moment in 1922 when the kind of energy and
money that were poured into this retrograde structure could have
defined architecture for the twentieth century. Instead, San
Simeon stands merely as an architecturally confusing and insignificant monument to a megalomaniacal personality.

Constructed of the best of materials, sand from the beach
carefully washed with sweet water for his concrete, and created by
the most sophisticated of craftsmen, San Simeon stands today
as an example of how the advantages of poured concrete can be
so misused.

· · · · ·

As architects less intimidated by overbearing clients grew more
familiar with concrete, the use of this material changed in the
latter half of the twentieth century. Because of the developing
sophistication of engineering science, what could be sketched in
two dimensions on paper could be easily realized in soaring three
dimensions. Architect's plans became manifest as the potential
of the ultimate building material was plumbed.

The quintessential works of mankind—shelters, amphithe-
aters, bridges, dams—turned away from materials that had to be
held together, such as cut stone and bricks, to concrete, which
had the unique ability to hold itself together. It is this single and
unique capability of concrete that has changed our world.

SHELTERS

It is manifestly impossible, and perhaps ultimately uninteresting,
to attempt to catalogue any representative number of the astounding concrete buildings of the past half century. There are thousands
of profoundly interesting structures that deserve to be mentioned
in any record that presumes to be historically inclusive.

For the purposes of this book two shelters, both seminal and iconic, will have to suffice. They are the unforgettable Sydney Opera House of Jørn Utzon and the equally unforgettable Fallingwater of Frank Lloyd Wright. In addition to setting out a visual feast for all architects to come, both are products of men of unyielding opinions.

Since the late 1930s, Denmark has quietly re-created itself as inventor and arbiter of what is known as the International style. In every field of design, from furniture to furbelows, Danish architects and engineers have made their contributions. This tiny country, whose total population of only about five million, no larger in population than the city of Baghdad, has had as large a role in the shaping of things we use and the places we live in than almost any other country in the world.

It is no surprise, then, that the Danes' use of concrete should parallel their imaginative use of more familiar materials. From the huge and influential shells of Jørn Utzon's masterpiece in Australia to the modest little outdoor lighting seats of Anja Bache, concrete has flowed from the drawing boards of Danish architects and designers. As Utzon, the unfortunate Hamlet of architecture, has said of the use of concrete in the Sydney Opera House, "The contrast of forms and the constantly changing heights between…two elements result in spaces of great architectural force made possible by the modern structural approach to concrete construction, which has given so many beautiful tools into the hands of the architect."

The story of the Sydney Opera House is a tale of soaring triumph, unimaginable tragedy, and pettiness by a world-class nation, which is hard to conceive in the realization of the great structure that was to become one of the iconic images of the late twentieth century.

Jørn Utzon was the son of an accomplished naval engineer and was considering a career as an officer in the Royal Danish Navy. By an extraordinary concatenation of events, Utzon was led away from a life that would have denied the world the glorious opera house. On a summer vacation he fell in with a group of artists who introduced him to the wider world of contemporary fine art. One of the group was Einar Utzon-Frank, a cousin of Jørn's father, who was a professor at the Royal Academy of Fine Art. It was due to this meeting that the seeds of Sydney were planted in Copenhagen since the professor urged Utzon to stand for admission to the Royal Academy. Utzon was not a particularly good student. His poor marks generally, and especially in mathematics, should have been more than sufficient to deny him entrance. Yet, one would surmise, he gained admission to this august institution due to the influence of Professor Utzon and benefiting also from the high reputation of his accomplished family.

It was at the academy that Utzon's gifts in architecture began to emerge. He graduated in 1942, a war year that was not kind to young architects. At the end of the war he went to Finland to study under Alvar Aalto whose influence was to shape his professional life. Parallel with Aalto was Utzon's interest in Frank Lloyd Wright, a curious set of mentors since their end products and their philosophies were antipodal. Indeed, of the two major projects of Utzon's professional life, one, the Kingo houses, could have come from the drawing table of Wright while the Sydney Opera House was clearly from the intellectual loins of Aalto.

In 1955 there was an entirely anonymous worldwide call to architects to design an opera house for the capital of Australia. The specs called for two concert halls holding up to three thousand people each and the call strongly emphasized that the resulting project "must be beautiful."

Utzon's submission was certainly beautiful. It was to be roofed with enormous upward soaring concrete shells that appear as if the entire construction has raised sails and is setting out to sea. Utzon, with the skimpiest of professional bona fides and no firm to back him, won the competition against submissions from vastly more experienced firms. His lack of background, and the fact that his submission was little more than a working sketch, should have eliminated him in the first round, but the leading judge of the competition was the giant of modern architecture Eero Saarinen, who called Utzon's submission an act of genius. Perhaps the submissions were not all that anonymous and perhaps Saarinen and his peer and countryman Aalto, under whom Utzon studied in Finland, might conceivably have lent weight to their interest in the young architect from Denmark. It is from such fragile accidents of association that the Sydney Opera House, which under less serendipitous and more strict circumstances could never have risen, was given life.

It took several years for Utzon's sketches to be developed into constructable blueprints. When complete, as Utzon himself reported, the ultimate design of the shells was based on sections of a sphere. Indeed, the fourteen shells if brought together would form a perfect sphere, an unlikely yet impressive accomplishment for a young man who had a lifelong struggle with mathematics.

At this point the tale that should have been the peak career experience for any architect turned into a professional nightmare, a tragedy for Utzon that shut down his enthusiasm for major projects and denied the world of his visions of "what might have been."

In 1965, in an election in Australia that shifted power to the Liberal government, Utzon found himself at the mercy of second-guessers who had political axes to grind. Motivated by Utzon's budget, which ballooned to a cost overrun of 1,400 percent, the government, in the person of Minister of Works Davis Hughes, would not accept Utzon's cost estimates. He simply cut off payments to Utzon and forced him to resign as chief architect. Utzon, a proud and private man, found this interference with his creation intolerable and, in 1966, fearing the legal wrath of the government, he secretly fled Australia. Utzon was never to return and he was fated never to view the realization of his design.

The Australian government, in childish revenge to Utzon's fleeing the country, sought to excise the facts, and even the memory, of Utzon's creation of the opera house. In 1973 the great building was opened to an admiring world by the English queen, who traveled to Australia for the occasion. In an act of egregiously shameful pettiness, Utzon was not invited to the ceremony and, more astoundingly, his contribution was ignored. Utzon's name was not even mentioned as the man whose vision created this landmark building.

It has been suggested that the revenge suffered by Utzon was the result of the Liberal government's desire to make political hay of its opponents' handling of the original contracts. These contracts, and their cost estimates, had been obviously lowballed by the preceding government in its rush to get the building on track. That previous government believed that if the true costs of the building were revealed the project would have been a nonstarter. It would be interesting to know from whence came this enormous pressure to build in the face of unannounced, hidden costs. One can only surmise that interested parties in government had a stake in the construction, either political or financial. Stranger things have happened in Australia.

The true and abiding tragedy of the Sydney Opera House is that the events surrounding Utzon's rejection, none of which had much, if anything, to do with him personally, destroyed his professional life. The great buildings that might have come from his rare ability to turn architecture into enduring works of art never emerged from what became a self-imposed alienation.

The Sydney Opera House, as easy to recognize as it is difficult to describe, can be read as either a heroic image of frozen music or an audience straining to hear the music of the sea. Or, more likely, it is a work of art distinct from the need to describe it.

As Frank Gehry wrote in commenting on the Pritzker Prize awarded to Utzon almost too late in 2003, "Utzon made a building well ahead of its time, far ahead of available technology, and he persevered through extraordinary malicious publicity and negative criticism to build a building that changed the image of an entire country. It is the first time in our lifetime that an epic piece of architecture has gained such universal presence."

The building, and its use of concrete, also expanded forever the architectural sense of what a public building should be. Horizontals and verticals, roof lines and boxes became abstract, sculptural expressions rather than elements of construction. It is to this building, completing a process only hinted at by Hundertwasser and Gaudí, that we owe our gradually dawning understanding that there may be no architecture separate from art.

The high quality of design responsible for so much beauty and excitement in our great cities is also responsible for buildings that are mere pastiche and parody, far removed from any permanent contribution to the culture of great works. Because of the explosive leaps in economic activity, especially in China and the oil-rich Mideast, there are scores of buildings that, from haste and inexperience and the desire to exceed the West at all costs, have been designed more to shock than to rationally inform or efficiently contain. Only one example is needed to make the case that extreme freedom in the use of construction materials contains the seeds of both beauty and disarray. Such a building is the Burj al Arab Hotel in Dubai. Its garish exterior is matched by luxury gone wild.

Much of the building being done today as a result of the permissiveness of concrete pays homage only to the school of "shock and awe." Novelty, by its own definition and meaning, is mere novelty and quickly becomes tawdry and embarrassing.

There are masterpieces of shelter that owe much to the grandiosity of their vision. Such was the Sydney Opera House. At the other end of the scale there are architectural masterpieces that can best be described as *multum in parvo,* an entire universe of originality jammed into the smallest of spaces. Such is the breathtaking Fallingwater of Frank Lloyd Wright. Even after half a century Fallingwater still has the smell of tomorrow. On site it is

SYDNEY OPERA HOUSE
PHOTOGRAPH NORMAN ALLEN PALLEY

BURJ AL ARAB HOTEL, DUBAI
COURTESY DUBAI TOURISM

a series of unending sensual surprises. Even in photographs, inadequate and out of scale, the building instantly alters our long-held convictions of what is beauty in architecture. Fallingwater is a place with no margin for improvement. Its progeny rarely, if ever, equal let alone surpass it. It burst full blown and complete, nonpareil and ultimate, from the mind of one man.

In 1934, Edgar Kaufmann visited his son who was apprenticing as an architect under Wright at Taliesin. Wright and Kaufmann, client and architect, were a perfect match at the moment when a new architecture was about to emerge in America. During that visit the two men, a wealthy department store owner and a yet to be widely appreciated architect, agreed to join in building a country retreat for the Kaufmann family.

The site is spectacular. It includes a waterfall that runs down a rock ledge into the stream called Bear Run. The concept of integrating the rushing fall of water as a central design of the house must have been well formed in Wright's mind when, in 1935, he received a call from Kaufmann asking to see the results of a year's work.

FALLINGWATER, MILL RUN, PENNSYLVANIA

COPYRIGHT ISTOCKPHOTO

Answering his hand-cranked telephone, Wright boomed, "Come along, E. J. We're ready for you." Edgar Tafel, who had joined Wright as an apprentice in 1932, reacted with horror on overhearing the conversation. "Ready?" Tafel recalls. "There wasn't one line drawn."

To Wright, a project was complete on conception. He had already envisioned not only the lines but also the details of the house and its interiors. He had even thought through the direction of the grain of the veneers that he wanted in the furniture he was yet to design. Kaufmann, the perfect client, had given Wright carte blanche for every element of and in the house. Fallingwater, uncomplicated by any conceptions save his own, was to become one of Wright's many masterpieces. It has remained so to this day.

Wright was asked in the fifties to recall his impressions upon seeing the site for the first time. He said, "There in a beautiful forest was a solid high rock-ledge rising beside a waterfall and the natural thing seemed to be to cantilever the house from that rock-bank over the falling water. You see, in the Bear Run House, the first house where I came into possession of concrete and steel with which to build, of course the grammar of that house cleared up on that basis. Then came, of course, Mr. Kaufmann's love for the beautiful site. He loved the site where the house was built and liked to listen to the waterfall. So that was a prime motive in the design. I think you can hear the waterfall when you look at the design."

At a later date Wright mused, "Fallingwater is a great blessing—one of the great blessings to be experienced here on earth. I think nothing yet ever equaled the coordination, sympathetic expression of the great principle of repose where forest and stream and rock and all the elements of structure are combined so quietly that really you listen not to any noise whatsoever although the music of the stream is there. But you listen to Fallingwater the way you listen to the quiet of the country."

IDIOSYNCHRONICITY

Because concrete is immensely strong and can be made into a remarkably lightweight construction material for smaller structures, the conventional architectural and engineering concerns of large industrial and commercial buildings can be ignored. A small home, carefully poured, will have sufficient inherent strength to deny, over very long periods of time, the engineering stresses of large constructions. Additionally, it is in the general nature of concrete to mature through time toward strength and hardness rather than toward decay as do most other construction materials.

In the less developed world, where construction skills and oversight regulation is less intense and more haphazard, there have been some interesting experiments in low-income housing.

CONCRETE DOME HOUSES, INDIA
PHOTOGRAPH CATALYTIC INDUSTRIES

The clusters of small dome houses that are being industrially produced in India are a most economical and rational solution to a housing shortage that is pandemic across the third world.

With the coming of modern concrete an unskilled worker with a bucket and a mold is able to do in an hour what the skilled stonemason building a cathedral with his hammer and chisel would need a month to accomplish. Gaudí was a man with a bucket. Both he and the old stonemason dealt in excess. Gaudí's Barcelona buildings are a tour de force of excess but, unlike the cathedral builders, Gaudí's superfluity is limited to his surfaces and has little to do with the underlying architecture.

Much of what we see on the surface of a cathedral deals with the support and structure of the building. What we see of a Gaudí building has nothing to do with structure. His beams and columns do not waver or lean. His great contribution is trompe l'oeil in stone. The architecture beneath the surface is straightforward, unimaginative, and dull. Over this traditional box Gaudí becomes entirely an artist, painting with concrete and violating the linear understructure of his buildings.

Infrequently, but it does occur, a genre in art is born, lives, and dies in the creative mind of a single artist. Gaudí said everything that can be said of an image and said it so brilliantly that there was no room for improvement. What followed Gaudí was imitation without the possibility of improvement. He said it all in any one of his many works.

But Gaudí's vision combined with concrete gave rise to a different sort of movement, essentially a phalanx of amateur

GAUDÍ'S LA SAGRADA FAMILIA, BARCELONA

COPYRIGHT © ISTOCKPHOTO

GAUDÍ'S CASA BATLLO, PASSEIG DE GRACIA, BARCELONA

41 KORNHER HOUSE, SAN MIGUEL DE ALLENDE, MEXICO

PHOTOGRAPHS STEVE KORNHER

builders who have dotted the world with homemade homes that are "little Gaudís." Not much new has been added to his heritage except that he released a spate of creativity among the fold who wanted something different and wanted to do it themselves.

Not a small achievement.

Most are equally fantastical but one is perhaps more outré than the rest. That is the small handmade home of Steve Kornher in old Mexico near the ancient town of San Miguel de Allende.

There have been thousands of homemade, idiosyncratic dwellings that have sprung up like mushrooms, which, by the way, because of the nature of poured materials, they curiously resemble. In the United States these homes avoid the scrutiny of city codes as they dot the emptier areas of the United States and slip under the radar of regulation.

It is precisely because they are essentially unregulated that the design and the details are so fresh. The lack of the need for rigid standards and materials testing in small concrete construction has led to most aesthetically intriguing developments of the use of concrete, especially in self-built homes. In the hands of imaginative amateurs, concrete has developed into a minor picturesque branch of home architecture. Concrete has become an artistic, rather than architectural, medium that runs along the wilder shores of design. It is limited, as is clay in the hands of a sculptor, only by the imagination and the audacity of do-it-yourself builders.

Few of these structures are built commercially for an organized housing market. Most are an expression of a raging need to be different, as different as possible, from the organized, melded iconics of conventional architecture. It is in the plastic nature of concrete, a material that has an infinite range of aggregation as well as a Gaudian abhorrence of straight lines, that these rebels have found their medium

America, and the rest of the world, is speckled by these unrepeatable personal structures. In the United States many of these builders are concentrated in the arid and warm states of the Southwest, where the tradition of building your own home was commonplace a mere generation ago. In states such as Arizona and New Mexico the use of adobe, an antecedent of concrete construction, is indelibly part of the culture. Just as bricks of sand held together by straw preceded the use of concrete by the Egyptians, the use of concrete, mostly lightweight concrete, was preceded by adobe, which is simply packing mud into brick-sized forms and allowing the hot sun to do the rest.

The construction of small dwellings requires minimal concern with the eventual strength of the material. Like modern

Dacron made of overly strong fiber ropes, concrete in its original format of heavy, immensely strong aggregates far exceeds the structural requirements of its use in small buildings. Since the self-builder's back and muscles were the main engines of his work, the search for lighter concrete was motivated as much by the physical limitations of one man as by engineering or aesthetics.

Concrete can be made of almost anything. Mix cement with any ground-up material and a concrete of varying density, weight, strength, and finish is easily accomplished. In small-scale construction the making of concrete is hardly rocket science; indeed, it is rarely science at all. When science intrudes, standardization sets in, necessary for industrial construction but death to the wild flights of imagination of small-scale, amateur builders.

By mid-twentieth century, when materials control and standardization of mixture content had taken firm hold in the concrete industry, small builders in the American Southwest began to destandardize the content of concrete in response to very personal needs for the homes they were building for their families. Every mixture was tried and almost everything worked. Papercrete, in which the aggregate could be your daily newspaper, remains a successful medium for a lightweight material that also has great insulation capabilities. Concrete made from trash works as well, and the confluence of ancient adobe techniques with the new lightweight concrete created an entirely new way to build small homes. One raw material, lightweight natural volcanic ash or man-made fly ash, a by-product of all things that burn, is available almost anywhere in the world. These mixtures make a concrete half the weight and adequately close to the same strength as that made from stone aggregates. And the mixtures require only a man with a bucket and a strong back.

The self-made concrete industry filled a need of these experimenters to escape from deadening standardization, a chance to have the room to swing their aesthetic cats. Architects in our century are dominated in design by the mass production construction elements as well as windows, doors, sinks, and other rigidly standardized elements. Even colors are limited in the interest of economical production. Henry Ford, at the turn of the century, encapsulated this drive to reduce diversity in favor of cost coherence in his famous declaration reminiscent of Hobson's choice, "You can have my Model T in any color of the rainbow so long as it is black." This dead hand of design central to industrial regulation profoundly limited experimentation and personal preference not only in architecture but also throughout the economy. It had its most effective limitation in home construction where the personal preferences of the ultimate user, the home owner, were submerged in a sea of sameness.

When Levittown, one of America's first planned communities, was built just after World War II this obeisance to regularity and efficiency was decried in a folk song of the time.

> And they're all made out of ticky-tacky
> And they all look just the same.[2]

This seemingly innocent little ditty can be read as a prophetic vision suggesting that such housing itself leads to an undesirable roteness in our lives and in our culture.

It was in revolt against this narcotically bland landscape that the amateur builders rebelled. And it was concrete, in its simplicity and its liquidness, that made the revolt easy and possible. Ordinary, nonprofessional folk found in concrete a ubiquitous material that they could make themselves, form into fantastical shapes with their own hands, and color and decorate the surfaces with as much imagination as a Picasso. Concrete was their genie, which would do all of their biddings and would last "four hundred years." Concrete was the ultimate people's material, which liberated them as had the little auto "'bug" of a related name. The death of rectilinearity was at hand, at least for a brave and energetic few.

Yet "few" is a relative term. As the historian seeks to synthesize this rampant surge of variety into some sort of systematic presentation there is an early recognition that, except for the use of concrete, there are no phylae or species into which these self-propelled home builders neatly fit. Indeed, neatness itself is anathema to them. Image-wise one example of these idiosyncratic creations is as good as any other and, at the same time, any one is as different from any other. As a result the only selection process is to reach blindly into this embarrassment of riches and pluck one with which to tell the tale of all the others.

Steve Kornher was our choice. His photographs and his own words tell an eloquent tale for tens of thousands of his compatriots.

"My wife, Emila, and I live on a two-acre ranchito about twenty-five minutes from San Miguel de Allende in the mountains of central Mexico. Our home is a work in progress, built Mexican-style pay as you go and leave the rebar sticking out for future additions. We built the house and large warehouse over a period of two years using one or two local workmen. Building slowly is a lot more enjoyable and you can be more creative, since you can think things over and make changes.

"The house has about 1,200 square feet of interior space with plenty of terraces for outdoor living. Most of the first floor is of adobe construction. Later additions and roofs are lightweight volcanic aggregate. South-facing windows and overhand provide passive solar heat in the wintertime. All roofs are masonry— concrete—vaults with shell motifs. Mexico has some great masons and I owe a lot to the knowledgeable maestros who have helped me figure out how to do this wild and crazy stuff.

"One of my main goals is low-cost building construction that lasts four hundred years. To accomplish that in this climate you need to build self-supporting structures and use masonry construction—adobe, lightweight concrete block, reinforced concrete columns, etc. The roof is the key to long building life, so it needs to be self-supporting, roundie-curvie and not flat. Self-supporting vertical walls by nature want to be roundie-curvie. You go on from there and pretty soon everything is roundie-curvie. When you start to think about a long-lasting house, it's best to build so that remodeling is possible, probable. With adobe and/or lightweight concrete construction, you can hack out a doorway later on. With hard concrete this is an almost impossible project."

Finally, in the words of Christopher Alexander, architect, philosopher, futurist, who writes in his book *A Pattern Language*: "There exists a whole range of lightweight concretes which have a density and compressive strength very similar to wood. They are easy to work, can be nailed with ordinary nails, cut with a saw, drilled with woodworking tools and easily repaired. We believe that ultra-lightweight concrete is one of the fundamental building materials of the future."

· · · · ·

The author of this book recently found a fault in his seawall. With a registered contractor what was essentially a small repair gradually grew into a project that involved master craftsmen, helpers, trucks, equipment, and overhead. The cost became prohibitive to shore up a wall that might, or just as likely might not, become a victim of the next hurricane. The inclination in such a situation is simply to put it off and hope that the hurricane gods would be merciful.

The elderly father of a neighbor wandered by and offered to do the job for a wage and supplies. No charge for equipment, helpers, or overhead. With some trepidation his offer was accepted.

The next day the old man showed up with an assortment of cinder blocks and bags of concrete. He slowly but steadily unloaded the materials, which included a hammer, some nails, a long-handled homemade wooden "smoother," and a "tamper" he had made himself the previous day. He had also gathered some scraps of lumber that had been lying about in his yard.

Then he started working, all alone and at the slow and steady pace of the tortoise abjuring the dashing about, ostensibly to save time, that is characteristic of contracted workmen. He lifted and placed the blocks, mixed his concrete in an old wheelbarrow, and shoveled the setting material into place. This took a day or so. The next day, with the concrete setting nicely, he brought his tamper and smoother to work and in another day the job was quietly, efficiently, and aesthetically completed.

I watched this lone and no longer young man proceed at a solemn and productive pace without tools other than those he had made himself create a structure that would last for ages. From him I learned more about the relationship of man to material than from all of my researches. In fact, watching earth and water turn into useful rock may have been the inspiration for at least part of this book.

DIEGO REPAIRING SEAWALL
PHOTOGRAPH REESE PALLEY

LITURGY IN STONE

The designs of Christian churches, until very recent times, were a mind-numbing iteration of the Middle Ages. The ideal, even for parish churches, were the great cathedrals, slightly varied in design between the continent's north and south, that grace the face of Europe. The designs of these soaring structures were constrained by the limitations of piling one stone upon the other, the classic architectural methodology handed down from the Egyptians.

As in all other matters erectable, the twentieth century changed all. While wonderful and imaginative, churches thrusting up across the land, though well into the twentieth century, were still slavishly imitating the past.

The bellwether change, in the form of a trickle down of fluidic stone, appeared at the top of a hill in northern France. Le Corbusier, in 1954, built the chapel of Notre Dame du Haut at Ronchamp, a concrete building too perfect to have imitators and one that broke the restricting bonds of traditional church architecture.

However, change came with the dulling pace of drying concrete. The illuminating lessons of Ronchamp were so missed that by 1965, while other architects were undertaking riveting adventures in concrete, one concrete church, typical of the Gothic, premodern genre, was erected that managed to combine an inapplicable architectural past to a profoundly misunderstood architectural present.

That building is Prince of Peace Church in South Carolina and it was not alone in its violation of the modernist spirit of the times. But the Prince of Peace Church exceeds all of its dolorous imitators in its lack of understanding of how to respectfully accommodate theology to an entirely new technology.

A glance at the interior tells the story of slavish imitation of the Gothic in church architecture. The shapes of the precast concrete walls, considering that they are of cast concrete, could have been anything other than a repeat of the shallow arches that in the past were used to sustain height and weight. In appearance the nave seems wedged in between two looming nineteenth-century factory walls and entirely misses the vertically inspiring thrust of the great cathedrals.

There is an uncomfortable fragility to the walls of the nave, held together as they are by beams that are themselves imitations of Henry VIII's House of Parliament. The ceiling beams are the visually fragile support that prevents the flat, unbuttressed walls from falling in on the praying congregation.

The architects, responding to an ancient yearn for the time when the function of cathedrals was to awe brutish peasantry of the power of the God, designed a dull and insecure shell that, with the addition of two floors and some buttressing, would make a perfectly good factory.

While there are, even in this century, solemn parodies of the past still being cobbled together, there have emerged from the bellies of Ready Mix trucks lyrical houses of worship that, in their beauty and audacity, have redefined liturgical architecture.

As with everything architectural in America, the work of Frank Lloyd Wright becomes the starting point. Wright, in around 1905, was a member of a Unitarian Universalist congregation in Oak Park, Illinois. The wooden building that housed the congregation burned down in a storm and Wright was asked to design a new church. It took a mere two years for the new church, or temple, as Wright insisted, to rise from the ashes. Wright, like most Unitarians, was only lightly connected to God and the temple he built, inside and out, was dedicated only marginally to God's service. In Wright's own words it was dedicated equally to "the service of man," or, "a modern meeting house and a good time place." In his artful and cunning underground attack on organized religion, Wright eliminated two iconic elements of almost all Christian churches, the tower and

the heavenly reaching spire. He considered them to be too sug-
gestive of transcendence. Wright's credo was always, "I believe in
God, only I spell it Nature."

This marvelous building, stolid in poured concrete, rejects
in design the welcoming openness of traditional houses of
worship. It turns its back to the noisy hustle of the street with
stark concrete walls that evoke an ancient Hebrew temple.
Entrance and exit are from the rear where congregants pass the
altar on the way to the pews, a subtle miscegenation between
priest and laity. More significantly, almost as much space in a
separate but connected building is dedicated not to the worship
of God but to furthering the social and recreational needs of the
congregation.

Unitarianism, in Wright's understanding, was and remains
an essentially unorganized religion. Indeed as Wright was often
heard to complain, if "religion is good,why does anyone have to
organize it?" This 1905 building leaves the spirit of God in the
dust. It was Wright's testament in concrete to the ascendency of
the spirit of man.

Dr. Rodney Johonnot, a religious leader of the Unitarian
congregation of Oak Park who advocated in 1905 for Wright's
design, sounds as fresh as tomorrow on the benefactions of
concrete. "Concrete is much less expensive than stone, yet
treated in this way gives an equally dignified and substantial
structure. Walls, floors and roof will be built out of it, thus
involving little skilled labor and the employment of but one set
of workmen. This construction also gives a building absolute

fireproof…Thus the problem of a dignified and substantial building at a comparatively small cost is met."

If a turn-of-the-century architecturally untutored churchman could be so clear in his grasp of the beauty of concrete construction, it is a wonderment that, in the nine subsequent decades, so little of his clarity was absorbed by earnest and dedicated "building committees."

LE CORBUSIER

There is little in the literature that touches on the reasons that drove Charles-Édouard Jeanneret to drop his patronym and assume his mother's maiden name. The move to Le Corbusier might have been a simple matter of dislike perhaps for an insensitive father or more likely it emerged from Corbu's desire to cut from the past, create himself anew as an example for the rest of the world that re-creation was possible on the largest scale. However, as history has shown too many times, resocialization is a rare bird to catch.

NOTRE DAME DU HAUT, RONCHAMP, FRANCE

PHOTOGRAPH BIGSTOCK PHOTO

Le Corbusier, the purist, nursed and nurtured the Bauhaus movement. In almost all of his buildings straight lines, unadorned surfaces, and Cartesian logic defined his divorce from the past just as the name change defined his personal deliverance from accepted family forms. He built rigidly to his image of clarity in and rationality in architecture. He was a utopian of perhaps the most dangerous kind, a messianic utopian.

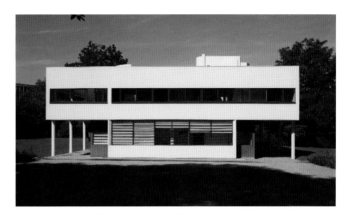

He was quoted in a radio broadcast as declaring that "people lived in the wrong places and people worked in the wrong places" and he set out, using the bulldozer of architecture, to put the world on the right path.

He was a master builder, addicted to giganticity, peppering the world with his image of beehive habitations close to beehive workplaces. This, at least in America, led to the "Projects" that were built for low-income blacks and which had such a terrible social impact on the people who inhabited them that most of the huge and expensive structures simply had to be torn down. The projects designed in Corbu's vast image of a new society to be utopian retreats for the poor turned quickly into hells of gangs and dope and murder. The projects were a cancer with no possible cure. They had to be radiated away.

When, in his early years, Corbu was not impassioned and consumed with society's change, his addiction to Bauhaus produced at least one superb example of what can be done when rationalism and modernity are married to concrete. The Villa Savoye built in 1928 was the high example of modernist, Bauhaus architecture. Its power emerged from its purity of line and rejection of any ounce of adornment. It taught the basic Corbusian theory that a house is a simple machine for living and there was no trace in this lovely construct of the didacticistic utopianism of his later compacted, urban structures. In measuring this jewel against the later gargantuan habitations Corbu, in contrast to his own later instincts, proved that there is indeed much in little.

Then for a quarter of a century Le Corbusier dedicated himself to ever larger urban colossi in all the variations of industrial forms of concrete. Each potential curve of his habitations was straightened as if by a hot iron on hair. Diversity was banished and repetition ruled. His buildings, his "machines for living," took little account of the chaotic diverseness of the lives of the folk who peopled them. They were imitated and uglified as workers' paradises by the Soviet Union and prepared the world for the triumphs of Corbu's United Nations Secretariat building in New York, Mies van der Rohe's Seagram's building, and, later, the stark verticalities of I. M. Pei.[3]

Descartes, Kant, Spinoza, and Le Corbusier were the triumphant master builders of the mid-twentieth century. Supported philosophically by these giants and driven by his own messianic passions and imitated by Corbusians the world over, Corbu remade the faces of cities but left untouched the delicious and attractive chaos of homegrown urbanism.

In 1954 Corbu turned his back for a brief moment on all of his beliefs and instructions and built the most irrational concrete structure one could ever have imagined coming from his pen. All curvy and wavering the Notre Dame du Haut, the magical chapel at Ronchamp, seems to plump up out of the empty hill in the heart of France.

Ronchamp transcends church architecture. It has become, along with Utzon's Opera House in Australia and Wright's Fallingwater in the United States, one of the iconic structures of the twentieth century.

THE CHURCH OF THE POET

For four hundred years, from the sixteenth through the nineteenth century, Icelanders lived in the most abject poverty, both material and spiritual. There was little margin for art as their main concern, down the centuries, was the pursuit of sustenance. Iceland, a land of long winters and short summers, scraped a pauper's living out of its hardscrabble land. The only connection with the distant, outside world was by sailing ships from Norway and Denmark. The fecund sea, showering Iceland with fish, was the only dependable source of food as importation was slow and expensive and Icelanders had little with which to pay for what the outside world might want to sell.

Aside from fish, the people sought the comforting well of religion. It was free, it apologized for their present wretchedness, and it supplied a spiritual warmth much like the hot springs that dot the length of the land. For centuries Icelanders sustained themselves on a diet of fish and faith…and the poetry of Hallgrímur Pétursson.

Pétursson was a cleric of the people. He was born in 1614 and died, oddly enough, of leprosy, a disease more usually associated with the hot countries, in 1674. His secular writings attacked the wealth and excesses of the upper classes. But his religious poetry, his fifty hymns of passion that traced the life and death of Jesus, struck deeply into the hearts of the Icelandic people. Three hundred years after Hallgrímur's death architect Gudjon Samuelsson commenced the thirty-six-year process that terminated in one of the most remarkable poured concrete buildings in the history of church architecture. Unique in design, the Church of Hallgrímur is even more astonishing because of the bleak and desolate imagery of the land from which it springs.

The Hallgrímur is a parish church that, in its scope and spirituality, surpasses many of the cathedrals of Christendom. It is entirely of poured concrete, the aggregate of which was dug from indigenous rocks. The cement was imported, as was the five-thousand-pipe organ,[4] but the fabric, design, and spirit are pure Iceland.

From the exterior the nave is like a powerful, long, and hunchy caterpillar that rockets upward two hundred feet at the steeple. This steeple, the highest structure in Iceland, has two outstretched buttressing arms descending from the tower as if to gather in all of the congregants. The arms are a dramatic, modernist iteration of the colonnade in front of the Vatican but, as they emerge not from the rich fabric of imperial Rome but from the visual paucity of Reykjavík, they are, by far, the more awesome.

Attempts to quantify and compare the architectural achievements of a society must account for the starting point of the work. The modern liturgical architecture of the West was built on the inspired history of two thousand years of Christianity. The modern liturgical architecture of Iceland, in contrast, commenced at the end of the nineteenth century from ground zero.

By this measure Iceland's stride is, by far, the longest.

Another concrete surprise from this small country[5] is another entirely remarkable church that was built not in the center of a populous city but in the pastorage region of the East Skaftakellsysle region, one of the most isolated areas in all of Iceland, disconnected from the rest of the island by fast-running rivers and glaciers.

HALLGRÍMSKIRKJA (THE CHURCH OF HALLGRÍMUR), LUTHERAN PARISH CHURCH, REYKJAVÍK, ICELAND

PHOTOGRAPH PÁLL STEFÁNSSON

BJARNARNES CHURCH, HÖFN,
ICELAND

PHOTOGRAPH PÁLL STEFÁNSSON

Bjarnarnes village, a center of small farms, has had a
church as long as records tell. In 1911 a new concrete church was
built that did not stand the test of time and in 1956 the farmers
of Bjarnarnes decided to build a new church.

At the time the reigning reverend Rognvaldur Finnbogason
was something of a radical who objected to the dominance
of the state church authorities. He turned to Reykjavík architect
Hannes Kr. Davidsson whom he remembered from Davidsson's
summers spent in Bjarnarnes. The reverend was also attracted
to Davidsson because he had voiced critical opinions of the tendency of the established state leaders to build bad replicas of
traditional forms.

In the end Finnbogason became disenchanted by his choice
since Davidsson chose to build in concrete rather than in wood
in a radical design. Remarkably the congregation, in spite of its
reflection of the essentially conservative cant of Iceland, opted
for the most revisionist of images for their new church.

The Bjarnarnes Church is constructed of unfinished and
unpainted poured concrete. Since there is no insulation, the
imprint of the wooden forms used in its construction can be seen
on both the inner and outer surfaces. The use of a pure pyramid
design was a worldwide departure in church design and the
marriage of the pyramid to the vault is an architectural triumph.
It is, in the stark landscape of far east Iceland, an otherworldly
structure and remains one more monument to the startling gutsi-
ness of this small nation.

Not surprisingly the extreme design proved controversial. So intense was the opposition that the bare concrete vault of the church was abandoned in the 1950s and left open and empty for seventeen years. Because it was entirely of concrete it had suffered not at all when in 1974 it was decided to complete the project.

The other side of the story of houses of worship is the boon that concrete has been for small and poor local parishes. Countries that were not industrialized were the first to recognize the economy of small concrete construction. South America, eastern Europe, India, and the poorer parts of the Middle East, unable to afford steel and bereft of wood, were busily building small parish churches from concrete.

Many of these were raised by the congregations that were to populate them. Volunteer labor and shared skills made many small constructions possible. Mostly one-story, single-room designs they required little architectural skill. The skills of local masons were more than adequate to the job and, along with the enabling lack of enforcement of building codes, this allowed for fast and cheap and, essentially, amateur construction. Extensive research into the thousands of these small concrete churches is beyond the scope of this book. One example is the naive, small parish church in Nicoya, Mexico.

PARISH CHURCH, NICOYA, MEXICO

CHAPTER 10

FLAGLER'S FOLLY

In the early 1930s, as poverty was descending on most of an unsuspecting America, the richest man in the world celebrated his eleemosynary instincts by tossing dimes to children as he was pushed down the Atlantic City boardwalk in a rolling chair. John D. Rockefeller, then an old man, took his pleasure from his wealth by investing the dollars and giving away the dimes.

His partner in Standard Oil, a man whom he'd met in his youth by the accident of renting rooms on the same street, took his pleasure in his wealth not by accumulating it but by disbursing it, often with little hope for gain.

By the beginning of the twentieth century, Henry M. Flagler, the lesser-known partner of John D. in the oil business, became bored with accumulation and actively sought a satisfactory means of spending his burgeoning wealth. It was a race of dispersion that Flagler lost since, in spite of lavishing millions on projects considered "Flagler's follies," he still managed to die a very rich man.

Of all the economic royalists of the period who piled up unimaginable fortunes, Henry Flagler stands out as the one who converted rampant wealth to personal delight and satisfaction while accomplishing generally beneficial national projects.

In the course of the few years between 1900 and 1913, Henry Flagler invented Florida. The process started when he entrained south with an ill and infirm wife to seek relief from the rigors of a Northeast winter. His party traveled to the last stop on the rail line in a private and luxurious railway car on a railroad that he himself had helped to build. He landed in Jacksonville, Florida, a small city second in population only to the distant and remote town of Key West, a thousand miles farther south.

Finding insufficient accommodations, and realizing that his railroad needed an attractive destination, he built an extravagant hotel in the hope that the rich and stylish folk up north would be encouraged to seek the balm of Florida via his East Coast Railway. It was an instant success and began the process that converted Florida from a scrubby subtropical wasteland into the concreted wasteland that we know today.

The most publicized and audacious construction project of the new century up to that time had been the proposed canal to be cut across the isthmus of Panama. The second, less known but perhaps as audacious, was the Great Ocean Railway, an extension of Flagler's East Coast Railway, which would involve the laying of tracks across marsh and marl and shifting tidal sands and ultimately across the open sea itself.

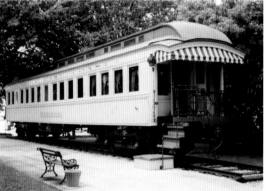

FLAGLER'S PRIVATE CAR
COURTESY MONROE COUNTY LIBRARY, KEY WEST, FLORIDA

Flagler, with his piled-up wealth, had found an expensive, attractive, and exciting way to spend it. Starting in Jacksonville he extended the rail line down the east coast of Florida, stopping to build luxurious watering holes for the rich every few hundred miles. With relative ease he reached and founded the tiny settlements of Palm Beach and Miami. From here on the prospect of extending his railroad the 150 miles to Key West looked impossible. The roadway would have to cross dozens of tiny marl-based keys, some no bigger than a few hundred square yards, and in the process would require the construction of a score of bridges where the scant and discontinuous land of the Keys gave out.

In spite of the daunting problems Flagler decided on extending the rail line to Key West. He called in his engineers. He characteristically asked them not how much it would cost but whether it could it be done. When J. R. Parrott, head of the Florida East Coast Railway, met with Flagler in 1903, the following conversation took place:

"Is the railway to the Keys possible?" asked Flagler.
"It is," affirmed Parrott.
"Then get busy and build it."

The decision was Flagler's but the near impossible task of throwing more than a hundred miles of track, much of it across open ocean out of sight of land, fell to a group of engineers just beginning to be comfortable with a relatively new material. They realized that the only possible solution to much of the construction would be the extensive use of waterproof concrete. Thus was knitted together the discontinuous string of tiny patches of land by the Florida East Coast Railway Key West Extension, better known as the Great Ocean Railway.

When the rail line left Homestead, situated on the last dry land in the Keys, it was faced with dozens of marl-based and marshy tiny isles, separated by long and short stretches of open ocean. Great machines had to be invented to mix and pour concrete from barges where the width of single rails was the measure of the only dry land available.

Concrete requires an aggregate (rocks, sand, etc.), cement, and fresh water, none of which could be found along a hundred miles of the Keys over which the rails were to be laid. The initial inclination was to mine the marl that underlies the Keys, the remnant of dead coral, for use as the aggregate. For decades prior and even decades after the railway was built the easily accessible marl was the aggregate of choice for speculative builders. But Flagler's engineers, in spite of the absence of any proof through time, were suspicious of the salt content in the marl. Their expensive solution was to haul every pound of aggregate for a hundred miles by ship or, as the rails proceeded, along the single track they were building.

The same was true of water of which not one dependable ounce of fresh could be found in the Keys. They built huge wooden vats mounted on flatcars, containing thousands of gallons of water drawn from aquifers in the north. These flatcars were themselves mounted on barges or on the completed sections of the line. The huge vats were marched endlessly between the

aquifers of the mainland and the places to which the rail line had advanced.

Finally, dissatisfied with the quality and uniformity of American-made waterproof Portland cement, engineers imported the megatons required all the way from Belgium. At one point there was so much Belgian cement being imported for the project that it caused a serious shortage of maritime transport capacity across the North Atlantic.

There were four unique elements in the construction of the railway that were not characteristic of any other large construction project. The first was the absence of land for staging. Major engineering projects require considerable contiguous spaces and, in some areas of the Keys, there was barely enough land for the rails let alone for service areas. As a result service areas had to be created on floating barges anchored in open ocean. Changes of wind and tide and other vagaries of nature in the course of construction opened up new problems daily that had to be solved.

The second problem involved the actual machines and equipment needed. In ordinary construction wheeled trucks and machinery for construction and excavation and for mixing and delivery of concrete were easily at hand. In the absence of land all needed to be mounted on floating barges. No project prior to this railway had faced the problem of building for miles directly from the sea.

The most serious problem was the actual mixing of concrete, which had to be accomplished simultaneously with all of the other activities going on. Cement and water and aggregate, all brought from distant parts, had be brought together at the proper moment and in the proper quantities on these floating barges.

Today one picks up the phone and orders his precise mixture, which arrives on site in a ready-mix-truck at the precise moment and the precise condition for pouring. Imagine accomplishing that from large barges in a location that was often out of sight of land.

Also there simply were no machines specific to the terrible conditions facing the builders. Single-purpose machinery had to be designed and built on the spot.

In addition, no other major construction project had ever had to endure and continue work under the threat of fifteen seasons of hurricanes. The entire length of the Keys lay in the path of most of the weather that bedevils Florida. However, since the Keys were essentially unpopulated in those early decades, except for Key West, which, at the time, was Florida's most populous city, little hurricane damage was done to the Keys other than to vegetation and the few people thinly strung along them.

With the coming of the railway all of this changed. Within a few years buildings and workmen appeared along the entire length of the Keys. It became a certainty that men and the works of men would eventually cross paths with unpredictable hurricanes. Today we have detailed warnings as much as five to ten days prior to a strike. In the early 1900s all observers had was their own experience of the changes in sky and cloud that presaged storms by a day or less.

Four major and innumerable minor windstorms roared across the Keys during the period of construction. On October 17, 1906, with construction barely commenced, a hurricane of only moderate intensity struck at Long Key. At that time the workmen lived in quarters boats, which slept up to 150 men. The quarters boat at Long Key was moored to pilings sunk for the construction of the Long Key viaduct. The eighty-mile-an-hour wind, the lowest speed at which a storm could be labeled a hurricane, tore the quarters boat from its moorings and swept it out to sea. More than a hundred died in what was only the mildest of hurricanes but which resulted in the highest loss of life for the project. Some were killed as the boat was being torn apart and most died by drowning as the hull was swept off its

AFTER THE HURRICANE OF 1909

BUILD AS YOU GO MACHINE

The marl (coral rocks) in front of train will be moved.

DESTRUCTION AFTER MILD HURRICANE, 1909

mooring. Some survivors clung to pieces of the boat and were rescued by passing steamers well out into the Gulf Stream. Many were saved by the warmth of the Gulf Stream waters as most deaths from immersion are caused by hypothermia. While the quarters boat was destroyed none of the freshly poured concrete at the Long Key viaduct was affected.

On the afternoon of January 21, 1912, one day ahead of schedule, a record rarely achieved by today's standard of major project construction, the Overseas Extension of the Florida East Coast Railway was declared complete. On the very next day, January 22, the actual date scheduled for completion some fifteen years earlier, a five-car train departed in the morning from Miami and rumbled into Key West with Car 90, Henry Flagler's private car, attached. Flagler and all sorts of luminaries, diplomatic, political, and industrial, were packed into the train. But not one of the rail workers, many of whom were World War I veterans, and of whom hundreds had been lost in the construction of the road, were on the train.

PADDLE WHEEL STEAMBOAT PULLING AN OPEN OCEAN DREDGE AND A QUARTERS BOAT FOR WORKERS

COURTESY MONROE COUNTY LIBRARY, KEY WEST, FLORIDA

This engineering miracle, which had cost $27 million to build, almost all of Flagler's own money, never made a dime but made engineering history. That day in January was the beginning of a long celebration attended by almost the entire population of Key West, most of whom had never seen a railroad train. And it was the beginning of the short history of the Overseas Railway, which ceased operations after the great hurricane of 1935.

Barely a year and a half after that triumphal entrance into Key West in January of 1912, Henry Flagler, who had seen his dream come true, was dead.

The great hurricane of 1935 was one of the two most powerful storms ever to hit the U.S. mainland up to that time. Wind speed was estimated at two hundred miles an hour and the storm surge along the central portion of the Keys on which the furious winds were concentrated was recorded at eighteen feet above normal levels. The highest point of land in that area was a mere sixteen feet, with in most places only a foot or two above normal tidal levels.

There were upwards of a thousand workmen scattered along the path of the storm. Most were World War I veterans, supported by the WPA as part of the response to the Depression of the 1930s. These were the workmen who bore the brunt of the storm. The stories of survival were terrifying and miraculous as there was so little land in the Keys on which to hunker down.

Some of the steel bridges suffered minor damages and some roadways were washed out, but the hundreds of concrete piers including those that crossed the seven miles of open ocean between Little Duck Key and Pigeons Key were virtually untouched. All sorts of barges and boats and land-based structures were washed away, but all concrete construction remained intact. Drive down the Keys today and cross the Seven Mile Bridge and a few hundred yards off to your left are the 180 concrete pilings standing in perfect condition. Well built, out of the best of materials and with the best of engineering talent, they have remained intact for a hundred years. It is unlikely that much will affect these great concrete supports in the next hundred years.

It has been mistakenly argued that the great hurricane of 1935 destroyed the Great Ocean Railway. The startling fact is that, after the fury of a major hurricane, the railroad managers brought the line back to full operation in a few weeks and at extremely modest cost. The truth is that the Key West extension, along with the entire Florida East Coast Railway, was bankrupt by 1935. The impetus to rebuild a financially failed line that was losing money simply did not exist. It was not the two-hundred-mile-per-hour winds of the 1935 hurricane that destroyed the line; it was the winds of the deepening depression that ended Flagler's great "folly."

Had the old man still been alive the story may well have had a different ending.

SHIPS

Buckminster Fuller called the shape of seagoing vessels among the loveliest inventions of man. From the beginning of time, yearners for horizons have sought all sorts of materials to achieve a hull that is strong, efficient, and pleasing to the eye, a hull that would bring sailors home safely.

Reeds were used by the earliest seafarers. Thor Heyerdahl on the raft *Kon-Tiki* proved that a reed boat could survive the months of a Pacific crossing. American Indians stitched together the slightest of fabrics, the bark of trees, into canoes the shapes of which have hardly been altered to this day. Then came wood, and then came steel, and then came plastic.

And then *almost* came concrete.

In 1917 the Norwegian N. K. Fougner designed and built the first oceangoing concrete ship, the eighty-four-foot-long *Namsenfjord*, which proved to be both an engineering and a financial success. Another, the *Violette*, also built in 1917, is in current use as a floating clubhouse on the Medway River in England. The *Violette*, now nearing one hundred years old, the oldest concrete vessel still afloat, is still as good, and in some ways better now than a century ago when it was built.

The problem is that in shipbuilding, as in most human endeavors, perception often surmounts truth and, although the truth is that concrete in certain configurations floats, the common perception is that that statement is ridiculous. The popular image of a chunk of concrete plunging to the bottom put concrete ships low on the list of believability.

Luckily, also as in most human endeavors, economic realities eventually surmount perception and in 1917, when the Allies were losing more steel vessels to the German U-boats than they could build, the unlikely idea of concrete freighters suddenly became not so unlikely.[1]

In 1917 steel, the preferred armor of modern warfare, became scarce and expensive. The successes of Fougner attracted the belated attention of the U.S. Navy, which hired him to investigate the possibility of constructing concrete ships for use in war. Thus began our short-lived experiment in "ships of stone."

The very first effort was made not by the United States Shipping Board, the agency responsible for wartime shipbuilding, but by a private person, Leslie Comyn, who, turned down by that board, started pouring concrete for *Faith* in late 1917. The ship was poured in six weeks and set out on its maiden voyage in May of 1918, bound from San Francisco to Vancouver.

She was suspect from the beginning. Concrete was well known for being brittle and, in the days before standardization of concrete formulae, almost anything could come out of a mix. What came out of the concrete mix in the case of the *Faith* was a remarkably ugly but tough vessel with straight lines and little sheer who, on her maiden voyage, confounded all the naysayers.

The *Washington State Star* reported, "In the course of a trip to Vancouver she encountered 80 knot gales and 35 foot waves. During this storm she made a speed of between 4 and 5 knots, considered an excellent performance under the circumstances... in addition she carried more cargo than steel ships of her size."[2]

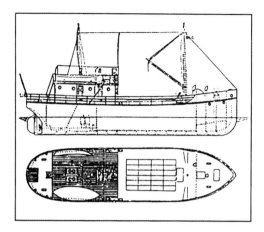

NAMSENFJORD

SKETCH BY AUTHOR AFTER
ANONYMOUS DRAWING

She carried freight for the next four years between major Pacific and Atlantic ports and ended up in 1921 being sold to Cuba where she still serves as an indestructible breakwater. Even in death a concrete ship serves better, and with less of an environmental impact, than any rust bucket could.

Still the wheels of the USSB ground slowly. It was already late in the war before President Wilson approved the construction of twenty-four concrete ships of which only twelve were ever built.

The stories of these twelve ships, how they served and how they ended up, are lessons that should have led to economically viable concrete fleets. However, the war ended, the price of steel dropped, and builders, naturally conservative as all who conjure with the sea should be, fell back into old and familiar habits.

Most of the ships came down the way long after peace broke out. All did serve one way or another, some pointing toward new and improved concrete vessels; only one had the ill fortune to back up the naysayers.

The S.S. *Atlantis*, launched in 1918 as the first of the concrete fleet, was too late for the war. She was first used as a ferry landing for a short time off of Cape May, New Jersey, commencing and ending in 1926.

It was a curiously inept plan in which fifty feet of the stern of *Atlantis*, facing seaward, was cut off. A hinged door was installed that would drop as a ramp to the ferries. The ferries were to back up to this door to unload their vehicles. The vehicles would then run along a lower deck of the moored *Atlantis* to a hundred-foot ramp, which finally would lead them ashore.

A more Rube Goldbergian arrangement could not be imagined. Nor one more ill-conceived since the small matter of the tides and the very rough weather of Cape May had been considerably underestimated. After a few months of service a classic nor'easter struck and *Atlantis* broke her moorings and grounded in a sandbar still in good condition. It was impossible to move her so there she sat, upright, concrete essentially intact, in good form, almost afloat.

To attest to the strength of her concrete construction, she remained intact under the relentless pounding of Cape seas for thirty-one years until, in 1957, a seam finally opened in her hull. Even after this event, which would have immediately destroyed a conventionally built vessel, it took four more years for her to break in two and sink back into the sea.

The concrete S.S. *Cape Fear* was involved in an accident that might well have instituted a whole new theory of design for concrete ships. She collided with a cargo ship in Narragansett Bay in Rhode Island and, because she and all other concrete ships were built in imitation of steel designs, she broke "like a teacup" and went quickly to the bottom. Had the demand for concrete vessels not disappeared someone might well have recognized that when a material is changed, design must change with it. If subsequent designs had run to fat, egg-shaped boats, the impact instead of shattering the hull would, as in an egg, have transferred throughout the structure of the hull, possibly resulting in very little damage. As we shall see, when we talk of even more unlikely uses, this is the very design theory that suggests concrete submarines may be vastly superior to steel subs.

The other concrete vessels also served in various capacities. The S.S. *Cuyamaca* became a floating barge in New Orleans. The

S.S. *PRELATE* IN USE AS A BREAKWATER

S. S. *Denser* became a breakwater in Texas. The S. S. *Lithium* and
the S. S. *Miff* became floating oil platforms. The S. S. *Palo Alto* was
turned into a dance club and restaurant at Sea Cliff Beach, California, and then became its fishing pier. The S. S. *Prelate* was used as
a fish cannery and then became a breakwater in British Columbia.
The S. S. *Polias* hit an underwater ledge off Maine and sank.

The S. S. *San Pasquale* has had the most interesting history
of all the World War I concrete boats. She ran aground off Cuba
and was first used as a depot for the storage of molasses. Then
decades later, in World War II, she was fitted with cannon and
machine guns as a guard post against German U-boat attacks.
During the Cuban revolution, when the dictator Batista was being
attacked by Castro, the government used the ship as a prison. Her
most famous prisoner was Che Guevara until he was released by
the advancing partisans. Today, almost a century since she was
built, the tough old veteran serves as a small but elegant ten-room
hotel aground off the beach resort town of Cayo Las Brujas, which
has grown up round her. She is probably the most unique hotel
in all of the Americas and will likely be entertaining guests for her
second hundred years. The variety of uses and the hundred years
she has lain in tidal waters attest once again to the incredible ability of concrete to survive at sea.

The S. S. *Sapona* also ended up in a contrary use. During
Prohibition she was anchored just outside the three-mile limit off
the coast of Florida and was used as a liquor warehouse for the
slim and speedy rumrunners who would make pickups of illegal
liquor from her and run them into shore. It was an extremely
efficient arrangement since the three miles into the Miami area
could be quickly covered many times a day. Few of the rumrunners
were ever interdicted. Even after being driven ashore by a hurricane she still serves as a popular dive site.

The last of the twelve, the S. S. *Selma*, known, for some
reason, as the Flagship of Texas, was scrapped and grounded off
the Texas coast.

It has been said, and generally agreed upon, that generals
and admirals are most likely to fight the previous war than the
one they find themselves in. Or, as Barbara Tuchman succinctly
said, "War is the unfolding of miscalculations." So it is no surprise
that the great military minds of the 1930s, in preparing for
World War II, committed the same mistakes of their military
elders. At least when it came to concrete ships.

England, standing alone against the Nazi juggernaut, existed
by virtue of a tenuous line of shipping that stretched from London
to the East Coast of America. The United States, which came

reluctantly into this most moral of all wars, sorely underestimated the deadly efficiency of the German U-boats, especially when they were organized into the infamous and efficient wolf packs. Early in the war, but almost too late to do anything about it, the Allies realized they were losing the war in the cold seas of the North Atlantic. Many more ships were being lost than they had estimated could be rebuilt. It was only by an enormous last-ditch effort by American industrial might, and, not incidentally, by the fortuitous inventions of radar and ship degaussing by the British, that England survived as a base for the successful Allied invasion of Hitler's *Festung Europa*.

A glance backward from the thirties should have lighted a fire under the limekiln oasts of America's shipbuilders. In 1918 concrete hulls were being poured in weeks, rather than the months required for steel. Additionally, the critical shortage of steel, and delays in delivery, made the shipbuilding effort a bit touch and go. Meanwhile, concrete was in easy and cheap supply and there it remained until, in those sad and universal words, almost too late.

The Allies' "miscalculations unfolded" and it was not until a year after the United States entered the war, with tonnage going to the bottom of seas at a terrifying rate, that America began to act on the construction of concrete vessels.

Things were so bad by this time that the entire course of the war was being metered by the tonnage lost each month. A good month meant that enough ships evaded the wolf packs to allow England to carry on the war in a limited way. A bad month, when more vessels were being lost than could be built, meant that disaster threatened the entire Allied strategy. It was clear by 1942 that the war would be won or lost depending solely on the Allies' ability to keep England supplied and to keep her from being invaded.

In an earlier conflict the course of the war turned on "the want of a nail." In 1942 it turned on the want of a ship.

Finally, in 1942, the United States Maritime Commission contacted the shipbuilding firm McCloskey and Company of Philadelphia. The company was directed to build a fleet of twenty-four concrete vessels, a drop in the bucket of North Atlantic seawater, but it was a start.

McCloskey discovered that thirty years of improvement in concrete technology since the first concrete freighters were constructed enabled them to build ships lighter, stronger, and faster than the experimental vessels of World War I. The company also settled on a warm water port, Tampa, Florida, so that weather would not impede construction.

METHOD OF CONSTRUCTION

Building a concrete hull requires little skilled labor. The hull is poured, rather than built, around a reticule of iron bars of varying diameters. The structural strength comes from the compressive strength of the concrete. The iron rods, rebars, reinforce the concrete and resist cracking or shattering.

As seen in the illustration, the entire framework of the hull is built complete from the keel to the gunwale. When the network is complete the pouring begins. Note the wide, flat members of steel running the length of the ship. These allow the concrete to be poured in progressive tiers.

All of the skilled labor that is required takes place after the concrete hull cures. Engines and machinery are lowered into the open hull and the ship is sealed with the installation of the decks and superstructure. These are built mostly of steel plate but in some of the earlier ships wood was used.

Shipbuilding commenced in July of 1943. McCloskey estimated that construction would take three months but the company, under the desperate pressure of the loss of ships to the U-boats, was able to put a hull in the water in as little as four to six weeks. They were launching a ship a month and, had this program been instituted earlier, the ultimate victory of the Allies

S.S. *PRELATE* UNDER CONSTRUCTION

LIBRARY OF CONGRESS

might well have come much sooner and with much less loss of lives and treasure.

McCloskey built twenty-four ships but only two saw any significant action in their use as blockships sunk along the coast of France during the Allied invasion.

When it became clear, in the postwar years, that an extreme surplus of steel ships was on the market, their prices dropped precipitously. International maritime trade could not absorb all of this tonnage and, since the concrete ships were a bit slower and, more important, unfamiliar, all were decommissioned or lost.

Nine of McCloskey's ships were sunk as a breakwater for a ferry landing in Kiptopeke, Virginia, where they still serve. Two remain as wharves in Yaquina Bay in Oregon and seven are still miraculously afloat in a giant breakwater on the Powell River in Canada.

The twenty-four ships were thoughtfully named after early developments in the history of concrete. The S. S. *John Aspdin*, which proved her mettle when she was caught in a hurricane with sixty- to eighty-foot seas and survived with minimal damage, was named after the man who, in 1824, first patented the formula for Portland cement.

The S. S. *Henry Le Chatelier* was named after the early experimenter in reinforced concrete. Le Chatelier was an engineer noted for his graceful bridges such as the seventy-five-meter Saint-Jean-la-Rivière Bridge.

The S. S. *Edwin Clarence Eckel* was named after a Canadian inventor who patented a silicon-based cement in 1927.

The S. S. *Francois Hennebique* was named after the French engineer who, in 1879, developed a system of construction using reinforced concrete. Some examples of his discoveries are still in use.

The S. S. *Alfred Kahn* was named after a Jewish immigrant who became nationally famous as a designer of reinforced

S. S. *HENRY LE CHATELIER* AS BREAKWATER, POWELL RIVER, CANADA

COURTESY CITY OF POWELL RIVER, BRITISH COLUMBIA

concrete factories. He built the Packard plant in Detroit, which attracted the attention of Henry Ford. Ford evidently did not allow his self-avowed prejudice against Jews to interfere with recognition of a useful talent. Many of Ford's plants were designed by Kahn. At one point Kahn was responsible for 20 percent of all factory construction in the United States.

The S.S. *David O. Saylor* was named after one of the first industrial developers of the Portland cement industry. In 1866 Saylor started Coplay Cement Company in Pennsylvania. After experimenting at his kitchen stove, Saylor created the first Portland cement formulation in the United States. He received a U.S. patent in 1871. As his cement was made with high heat it proved to be stronger and more stable than other cements that had been made in the United States. The Coplay Company became the largest producer of cement in the world. A museum in Pennsylvania is dedicated to his work.

S.S. *John Smeaton* was named after the man who "invented" the profession of civil engineering. His lighthouse on Eddystone rock lasted almost 150 years and had to be taken down only because the rock it was founded on wore away.

S.S. *L.J. Vicat* was named after the early researcher who, in 1835, published a book describing the uses of lime-based cements. The book was immensely important as it was the first in the English language to critically review the use of concrete material. As has been noted Vicat invented the Vicat needle as a test for the hardness of concrete.

S.S. *Vitruvius* carried the most important name in the history of concrete. Vitruvius was a Roman whose important history has been reported earlier.

Details of the other names of the twenty-four ships have been obscured in the shifting fogs of history. The folk whose names graced the vessels all made their contributions in their own time as did the unsung concrete vessels named after them.

POWELL RIVER BREAKWATER

The operators of a logging mill on the Powell River in British Columbia, Canada, accidentally created a virtual museum of the World War II concrete ships. Needing a breakwater to protect its logging operations, the company took advantage of the glut of ships that appeared as the war ended. Steel ships could be had almost for the asking and many breakwaters and wharves using them were built around the world.

However, the Powell River folk, more forward looking than others, wanted a breakwater that would both last longer than steel and require less maintenance than the rusting hulks that dotted rivers and estuaries.

The surviving concrete ships could no longer compete with the steel vessels that were going at knockdown prices. Shippers, who think in terms of a decade as the useful age of a vessel, were buying ships that could be thrown away in a few years and be worth more in scrap than the ships had cost them.

As a result the "longlastedness" of concrete was no asset to shippers but Powell River required neither speed nor efficiency; they needed a breakwater that would last for decades and, perhaps more important, a breakwater that could be reconfigured to accommodate changes in their business operations.

Settling on concrete, they scoured the world for the surviving ships of the few that were built. The U.S. Maritime Commission was charged with getting thousands of vessels out of government yards and, in 1947, it offered six out for bids. They were the *John Smeaton*, *Le Chatelier*, *L. J. Vicat*, *Considere*, *Thaddeus Merriman*, and *Emile N. Vidale*. The economics of the time made all six ships available for $133,000, a price that included ships, anchors, chains, and all consumables, which had been left untouched when the ships were decommissioned. This collection of ships, now virtually a museum of concrete vessels, still stands guard, after half a century, over the waterfront of a no longer operating logging mill.

POWELL RIVER BREAKWATER, CANADA

COURTESY CITY OF POWELL RIVER, BRITISH COLUMBIA

The arrival of the ships at Powell River created a sensation in the small town and the left-aboard consumables were too much of a temptation. Over the months after the ships arrived a conflict developed between the company and the hordes of "private salvagers" who were intent on stripping everything not nailed down and some stuff that was.

A merchant ship, when it is commissioned, is completely outfitted with kitchens and furniture and linens and silver and all of the amenities needed for the comfort of the crew. These went first, over the side into the waiting small boats of the townsfolk that clustered about the great ships. The youngsters of the community quickly discovered that each lifeboat contained survival provisions, which included great blocks of chocolate. Since chocolate had been in short supply during wartime, this was an irresistible treasure and the provisioning kits disappeared as if by magic.

Each ship was filled with the hard operational stuff that made the ship work. Pumps and wheels and gears and compasses, radios and heaters and gauges and even the wood paneling of the crews' quarters created a veritable "cargo cult" for the small town. The company protected much of the wares but it is likely that every home in Powell River had a little piece of the concrete vessels.

Ultimately, the company sold off what was not "salvaged" so the end cost was much less than what they had paid the U.S. government. The company got its permanent breakwater, the townsfolk got their loot, and the maritime world got an irreplaceable museum. A good deal for all.

A few years ago the Concrete Technologies Laboratory of Chicago was hired to check on the viability of the Powell River floating breakwater. Concerns were that the effect of fifty years in the extremely brutal conditions in which they served might have endangered the hulls. The results of both visual inspection and a laboratory test of cores found that "the concrete is of exceptionally good quality and overall is in excellent condition." Steel hulls would have long since rusted away.

Wars are the incubators of technology. Great minds from the Romans through the Renaissance down to Einstein in our own day were all, one way or another, involved in this organized business of mutual killing. Very early on, nations learned that he who has the most left standing is declared winner and earns the right to rewrite history. These histories tend to be exonerative and vast globs of inconvenient events are lost in the "fog of postwar."

Wars have an especially short memory when it comes to technology. At the end of all wars, the expensive, experimental, and sometimes unreliable technologies lose both their spokespeople and their market. The generals are relegated to marble and bronze in the town squares and there develops an understandable revulsion to figuring out more ways to kill more people.

Thus the war-incubated technologies often fail to reach their kindergarten let alone adulthood. They are hung up in a closet of ideas useful to the last war and, when dusted off for the next one, never quite measure up to new circumstances and new and, perforce in their own time, temporary technologies.

That is the way it was with concrete ships. They were overcome by a glut of hastily built steel ships. After World War II there was neither the need nor the curiosity to conjure with concrete, a dull and pedestrian concept when compared to the excitements of atoms and jets.

There were lessons to be learned, and still are, from the fact that the failures of concrete ships, also hastily built and in an unfamiliar technology, were so few. There is only one recorded event that highlighted an inherent weakness of using concrete for hulls—that was the World War I–built S.S. *Cape Fear*, which collided with a cargo ship in Narragansett Bay in Rhode Island harbor. Its flat concrete side shattered and the ship plunged to the bottom in a matter of a few minutes, taking with it nineteen crewmen.

In October of 1943 an American sailor, Richard R. Powers, described maintenance aboard a concrete vessel: "I will never forget the sight of the bosun getting a sack of concrete to patch up the cracks. At an average speed of three knots it took us 33 days to Liverpool."[3]

An unfair comparison, "cracked like an egg," leaps to mind but an egg-shaped hull would have had much more of a chance of survival as the compressive resistance of an egg is well known. Egg-shaped hulls of a more forgiving concrete mixture may yet be in our future as in 1998 when the Russian navy was reported to have been experimenting with, of all things, a concrete submarine.

While the thought is wildly counterintuitive, there is good and reasoned argument that concrete may well be the steel of the future. Heinz Lipschutz patented designs for a concrete submarine in 1957. In the late 1980s the British Royal navy proved uninterested and the Russians picked up on the idea. Lipschutz's designs are based on the compressive strengths of both an egg and the concrete that forms an egg's shape. Everything that displaces less water than its weight will sink. Everything that displaces more water than its weight will float. The ability of ships to float has everything to do with its shape and little to do with the weight of its material. All that is necessary for a functioning concrete sub is that it contain a sufficient volume of air to counter the weight of the concrete.

A concrete submarine, shaped like an egg, would have the ability to submerge to hitherto unreachable depths in the oceans where it could hide and lie in wait for enemies. Steel subs have a depth limit of merely 1,800 feet. A concrete structure could survive five times that. Thus a concrete sub could lie in the depths, targeting all that passes over it, with the additional ability to confound sonar by confusingly mimicking the rock around it, being of the same material.

The ability to resist crushing forces by an ovoid-shaped object is in direct relation to the thickness, that is the weight, of the hull. The heavier the hull, the more space the hull must encompass to maintain weightlessness. There is no theoretical limit to the size of a concrete sub. If a designer determines the size of the vessel to be built and the depths it is constructed to reach then only a sufficient thickness of the sub wall to reach the "weightless" state that would allow the submarine to be operational is required.

Extending the concept, it would be possible to construct not only large and efficient subs but also enormous concrete bubbles that would allow subaqueous human activities in the bottoms of the seas.

At the absolute opposite end of the scale from monster concrete submarines are graceful concrete sailing boats and thin-walled concrete canoes, some of which are light enough to be carried by a single person.

The development of modern lightweight concrete pleasure boats harks back to the earliest uses of concrete in modern times. In southern France in 1848 J. L. Lambot designed and built concrete rowing boats using wire mesh to hold a thin layer of concrete, one of which is still afloat in France. While these boats were a design success they never developed a widespread use and governments, unlikely to take such entrepreneurial risks, did not pick up on this new, economical method of shipbuilding. It was not until half a century and two world wars later that concrete, known in the marine trade as ferro-cement, was first taken seriously in mostly home-built sailing yachts. Even this technology was unceremoniously dropped, aborning with the development of fiberglass sailboats.

A few years after Lambot, in 1850, another Frenchman, a gardener named J. Monier, developed a metal mesh reinforced concrete flowerpot that was the progenitor of what we now call ferro-cement, and later, in 1867, he extended his potting line to include variously shaped garden tubs.

These two early attempts at melding the tensile strength of steel to the compressive strength of concrete to create lightweight waterproof forms are the basis of today's increasingly rare ferro-cement sailing yachts and racing canoes. In Bangladesh, China, India, Indonesia,Thailand, and throughout much of the East, where timber is in short supply and steel is prohibitive for local uses, ferro-cement has taken the place of these materials. Fishing boats, farming structures, and small transport riverboats in ferro-cement are the backbone of near shore activities in lesser developed countries. China alone, as of 2006, has six hundred ferro-cement yards producing 600,000 to 700,000 tons of small boats and barges a year.

The first widespread use of ferro-cement in fisheries development and restocking is taking place in the Philippines. Ferro-cement tanks for prawn broodstock and ferro-cement buoys for a flotation system in the culturing of green mussels have been in successful use for a number of years.

There is nothing man has made that is more lovely in line and concept and less likely to impose a burden, either physical or spiritual, on our planet earth than a sailing vessel. A sailboat, since it derives its impetus directly from nature, must perforce abide without deviation from the laws of nature. Just as the universe creates perfect and elegant orbs of stars and planets so does nature create an immutable, most efficient shape for the hull of a sailboat.

There is nothing less lovely in appearance or in concept than a tub of concrete and yet sailors have formed that tub into vessels of the same beauty and efficiency as those formed from steel or fiberglass. Ferro-cement sailing yachts were first conceived of as do-it-yourself boats, using the cheapest of material and requiring the least technical skills in construction. Since early ferro-cement sailboats were overbuilt by amateurs in an excessive concern for safety and, perhaps, a bit of worry that thin-walled concrete was less strong than other maritime materials, this led to heavy boats that were slow and awkward to sail. As a result the early home-built vessels cast a bad image over the use of concrete.

There is a reference in the literature that the Chinese, prior to 800 BCE, were using a cementitious material reinforced by bamboo in the construction of river boats. Very little documentation has been preserved concerning the use by the Chinese of concrete-like materials. However, it is unlikely that, in the vast and technologically sophisticated history of China, so basic a material as concrete and so ubiquitous a resource as bamboo would not have found a symbiotic use.

It has taken some time for serious naval architects, mindful of safety, weight, and the needs of nature, to replicate in concrete what has been so elegantly contrived in steel, aluminum, and fiberglass. Modern ferro-cement yachts weigh the same as the others, have the same displacement as steel and plastic, and, if the design is good, are just as fast and nimble and vastly less needful of maintenance.

At the other, and simplest, end of pleasure boating are lovely concrete canoes. Concrete canoe racing, especially at our universities, has become a teaching device as well as a sport. Engineering undergraduates strive to design and build canoes that are just a smidgen lighter and fractionally faster than their colleagues in other engineering schools. The results are tough and agile vessels that are not unlike American Indian canoes of earlier times. For

almost twenty years the races have grown from intramural to national competitions. This racing is often referred to as the America's Cup of college civil engineering, and many undergraduate teams spend entire academic years working on their canoes without earning academic credit. A true labor of love.

However, because of the design of canoes, all canoes, having been brought almost to perfection over half a millennium, results of the contests between the university canoe racers are likely to be determined more by the strength of the rowers than by the design and the strength of the crafts they build.

The civil engineering honors class at the University of Illinois, studying under Professor Clyde Kessler, built and paddled the first student concrete canoe in 1970. The next year, civil engineering students from the University of Illinois and Purdue University made history when they staged a concrete canoe race.

The magic of concrete canoes is that they are concrete. Their wonder lies not in design or production but in the popular sense that the whole undertaking is counterintuitive. Concrete boats are *supposed* to sink. The fact that they do not has failed to fully overcome the deep popular belief that concrete boats should go straight to the bottom. Concrete boats float.

CONCRETE CANOE

The University of Alabama in Huntsville's entry in the ASCE/MBT 2001 National Concrete Canoe Competition

COURTESY CLYDE KESSLER, UNIVERSITY OF ILLINOIS

CHAPTER 11

A WOEFUL CENTURY

The Pantheon was constructed around 120 AD, over two thousand years ago. The roof is an unsupported poured concrete span of more than 140 feet. The counterparts of the Pantheon's concrete construction in the United States began to appear belatedly less than a hundred years ago; indeed the greatest volume of concrete laid down in the United States is less than fifty years old. For most of the twentieth century concrete had been considered almost immortal. As a result, our road and bridge and building constructors, along with our politicians, vastly overestimated the ability of this ultimately toughest material to withstand industrially induced wear and tear, erosive pollution, and ever increasing abuse of our roads by ever increasing load levels of truck traffic.

Private concrete buildings, in contrast to public infrastructure, have fared slightly better. Many privately built constructions are still functioning as factories or warehouses or office buildings whereas publicly built roads and dams and airports and other works were and are, at the end of the twentieth century, beginning to fall apart.

The difference may be due to the attitude of private ownership in contrast to public ownership. Privately owned roads, intent upon maximizing profits, would be disinclined to allow abusive truck traffic, for example, or any other abuse, to debase their investments. They would have no outside social or political lobbying to allow destructive use of their investment. Moreover, the need to preserve capital and extend its working life would inevitably lead to constant and careful maintenance.

Public construction, on the other hand, must deal with short-term pressures from, in the case of our nation's roads, a transportation industry with a heavy whack in Washington. Public constructions feel little pressure to be concerned with preservation of capital for future use especially in the face of increasing stringency in budgets for capital improvements. Government-

161

owned facilities, with their access to endless finance, tend to be profligate. We would have been better served as a nation had we not, in our colonial history, viewed private toll roads with disdain. In a complicated industrial society, well-regulated monopolies, such as the provisioning of electrical power, often serve the public interest best.

Two hundred years after we abandoned privately owned toll roads, our ill-maintained concrete infrastructure is falling to pieces around us. Recently there has emerged a growing recognition that privatization of our national networks of roads and highways might well serve our longest-term national interests and provide us with much longer intervals between replacement of heavy infrastructure. In addition, in the private sector, economic models provide for reserves for the replacement of capital.

It was the privately owned rail network of the nineteenth and twentieth centuries that helped foster the growth of America. Easily maintained, a railroad bed lasts for centuries, as is demonstrated by routes laid out two hundred years ago that are still in use. These railroads, alas, are for the most part no longer with us. They have been diminished by the economic lobbying power of the trucking industry, which has become accustomed to heavily subsidized roads. The road transport industry was easily able to demonstrate to politicians the short-term economies of trucking over rail. Short-term arguments are facile, understandable, and convincing compared to the inconvenient and complicated arguments anticipating future needs.

The truckers are not responsible for the roads over which they traverse and this lack of responsibility, the fact that they did not need to pay for the attrition they commit, led in part to the present disarray of the interstate and intrastate systems that had been built with public dollars.

While some concrete civil engineering projects did last a hundred years, as predicted, we are now faced with a vast and expensive deteriorating infrastructure that lacks public funds for adequate maintenance and were being overused by the private sector.

The United States today is pouring 120 million metric tons of concrete a year, soon to increase to 200 million, mostly for new construction. Within a very few years we will need some trillions of dollars just to rebuild dams and bridges and roads and airports and sewer systems and all of the other appurtenances of our comfort. To maintain growth and to rebuild our humongous concrete infrastructure we might well require on the order of 300 million metric tons of concrete a year, which would triple our concrete output, an amount that comes to the astounding figure of one metric ton of concrete for every man, woman, and child in the United States.

Concrete quality has been slowly increasing over the past century. The material being poured today, and the improved techniques for pouring, will result in longer-lasting and more use-resistant concrete than anything in the past. But the lesson must be learned that, like a museum with a permanent endowment, each great concrete undertaking must be accompanied by a sum of capital that will, in perpetuity, guarantee careful maintenance. At the end of the useful life of a construction, its endowment should be intact and directed toward replacement, so that a cycle of build-maintain-build could anticipate crises of infrastructure replacement in the future.

Serious economic damage is being wreaked upon us as we cover boundless acreage of the earth with concrete pavements, roads, and buildings. The normal replenishment process of rainfall is being interdicted. Additionally rainwater can no longer take care of its own dispersal and drainage. Runoff from rain and snow must be collected by huge concrete sewer pipes, which carry water polluted by road use unnaturally down to the sea, completely detouring the aquification process. Not only does this cost us precious, naturally filtered water, it also imposes a dollar cost for the maintenance of the enormous sewer and storm drain systems that underlie our cities.

There is one bright spot in this exigent and looming problem. It is the recent development of pervious concrete. This material, still in its infancy, allows water to pass easily through it, obviating much of the need for storm drains. The wide use of pervious concrete, which imitates soil in its permeability, requires few if any storm drains and thus holds the promise of vastly lower costs of all areas of construction. Pervious concrete, when we finally get around to replacing our unimaginable tonnage of impervious concrete, will diminish the pollution of our rivers and our seas and—no small consideration—add to the natural and endless flow of fresh water.

THE END OF THE ERA OF PROFLIGACY

The inconvenient truths of the twentieth century are, as yet, barely perceived. The most inconvenient of all, only because it is best understood, is the carbonization of our atmospheric envelope.

For half a millennium we have been dumping deleterious gases, 18 percent of which can be traced to the production and use of concrete, into our atmosphere with little concern for the effect of this massive transference. Hastened by the industrial age, the possibility of a fundamental change in the chemistry of the planet we live on has only just pierced the veil of present comfort. We can now project, with fine-tuned certainty, that due to the acts of man the end of the twenty-first century will be so unlike its beginnings as to be virtually unrecognizable.

The warming of the earth cannot be reversed in our lifetime even with the most draconian of industrial changes and restrictions. To even slow down the process so that we may come to terms with the end of profligacy, our industrial and engineering processes will have to undergo wrenching and expensive shrinkage and alteration. The very chemistry by which we make the stuff that eases and enriches our lives will have to be altered from a chemistry of carbon, as it is for concrete, to an alternate chemistry at a profound cost to our ease and riches.

Short-term protection against encroachment by the sea will be possible only with the erection of towering concrete dikes. No other material would be available in the staggering quantities that will be required by the year 2200. New Orleans alone will require thirty-foot-high concrete structures surmounting the existing dikes and extending back toward the mainland by miles. Such an undertaking will raise the question of whether New Orleans can be saved at any cost.

Worse yet would be the fate of southern Florida. With only a seventeen-foot rise in sea level the entire five hundred mile southern end of Florida all the way north to the foothills of Orlando would be gone by 2100. Perhaps thirty-foot concrete dikes could save some of southern Florida but most of its land, and the teeming millions of sun-baked retirees, will have to go.

How much we can save from the rising seas depends on how strong our will is to slow down the melting of Arctic ice. Major diminution of carbonization of the atmosphere will result in minor victories against the sea so long as the production of concrete can be altered from its present chemistry. Even without the concrete that will be needed to protect populations in low-lying coastal areas, the present consumption of cement will increase from two-plus billion tons in less than two decades to four billion tons.

If we factor in the same rate of growth for the next ten decades we will be using the unimaginable total of twenty billion tons by 2200. If we factor in what might be required to build dikes worldwide we would likely need to produce double that, forty to fifty billion tons of cement, just to keep us relatively dry for a hundred years. Such a drain of resources and industrial capacity, combined with the cost of relocating millions, would result in a world-shaking catastrophe.

The twentieth century was a hundred years of reaping the whirlwinds of pollution that spiraled up from dirt devils to global hurricanes. It was a century of the sowing of dragon's teeth with which we must now figure out how, if at all within the allotted time, they can be contained.

That we have the technology and the smarts to survive is not in question. We know the chemistry to reverse global warming. We have the medical miracles to fight the onrushing pandemics. We have avoided a nuclear Armageddon for half a century with a tiptoe détente that seemingly proves the genius of our species. We even have the capability to nudge an earthbound, apocalyptic meteorite away from our fragile home. And ultimately we have concrete, and a new chemistry of concrete, without which any future is unthinkable.

Robert Oppenheimer was once asked if humanity could survive a nuclear holocaust. "It depends," he replied, "on what you define as human."

Nuclear holocausts are the least of the holocausts we face. New cataclysmic events, earthly or unearthly, might well demand a redefinition of what of man survives how he survives and what will be future man's relation to what we now call human.

ALL ABOUT SUSTAINABILITY

If humanity is to survive, the central drive of the twenty-first century must be to discover and implement processes to sustain the resources available to us. "Survive" is a curious word; derived from the Latin it means "to hold from below." It suggests that we must strive to keep what we've got. It bans the biological directive to growth and expansion. It is the modern embodiment of the medieval keep, the last redoubt, the last stand, backs to the wall. For the first time in human consciousness we must deny many of our most profound directives.

The key word of the twenty-first century, barely a decade old as this is being written, is sustainability. The realization that our planet cannot even now sustain us has come upon us, as time is measured historically, in a flash. Sustainability is at the core of most of the industrial research driven by corporations, universities, and trade associations as they slowly are coming to recognize that the prodigal use of resources, which defined the industrial expansion in the previous century, is no longer possible.

Sustainability is being codified and measured much like commodities such as oil or wheat. One measure is that we already require the resources of 1.2 earths to sustain the one earth we live upon. Even worse is the prediction that within a few decades we will require two earths.

There are two paths to sustainability. The first is a net reduction of what we produce and the second is a net reduction in the unused and unwanted by-products of what we produce. Considered from this admittedly narrow view of the problem, the use of concrete in its many new forms significantly and negatively affects our future. However, there are new concretes and new concepts of concrete use that can address many facets of the sustainability issue. Considering that concrete has become the preeminent material in the construction industry, any ecologically economic use of concrete can significantly lighten the load on our stressed planet.

It was not until Portland cement began to dominate the use of concrete at the beginning of the twentieth century that a reliable and repeatable formulation became the basis for development of the expanding uses of concrete. Old habits die hard, and the habit of looking at concrete as a cheaper substitute for steel lasted well into the 1950s. With one exception, not even the Second World War altered conventional usage. That exception was the cheap and easily repaired concrete freighters that grew out of the crucial shortage of steel.

It was not until late in the last quarter of the twentieth century that small-time individual inventors began to grapple with the idea that concrete had a life after steel.

The construction industry's views about concrete had set hard, much like concrete itself. The industry had come to believe that the future of concrete was a repeat of its immediate past. In construction, an industry that was dominated by the use of concrete, there was little thought given to the idea that concrete could be anything except what it had been, a heavy, brittle, incompressible material useful in rough construction.

Change, as is usually the case, had to come from outside and come it did in a rush from the minds of folk who had few preconceptions about the function of this awkward and recalcitrant material. The parade of the weird, unlikely, and, on the surface, implausible suggestions grew, in a matter of decades, into an entirely new universe of concrete.

Among these new directions three can be singled out as revolutionary. They include the impact of concrete on the availability of our water supply, the impact of concrete on ocean travel by which most of the world's goods still are transported, and the use of the vast surfaces of installed concrete as potential scrubbers of the atmosphere.

Of these the preservation of our potable water supply is, by far, the most crucial.

Aquifers underlay almost all life on earth. Prior to the infestation of the globe by too many people the aquifers were stable, unstressed, and undrained. Today, with too many billions of us competing for available potable water, our aquifers are shrinking as too much water is drawn out of them by exploding, prodigal populations.

The aquifers are not being replenished. More and more of the land is being covered with waterproof, impervious concrete, which interdicts the ocean-sky-earth-aquifer cycle. For the past two centuries we have been sheathing our world primarily with concrete and to a diminishing extent with asphalt. As the sheathing continues, the volume of water that reaches the aquifers has diminished. Some aquifers have already disappeared, or are about to disappear, as a result of the double-bladed attack of more out and less in.

The presence of impervious surfaces—roads, highways, sidewalks, parking lots, rooftops—requires that rain, which was meant to filter down naturally into aquifers, is now being diverted and collected. Drainage must be constructed, sewers dug, and retention ponds created, at great cost, to deal with rain and storm water runoff. Most of our sewer systems take this water, now polluted by the passage across industrial surfaces, and dump it directly into a more and more polluted sea.

This unnatural cycle could not be worse. Even without global warming a scary scenario can be written. Not only would the aquifers be denied replenishment but the natural cleansing, depolluting, filtering action of the earth as water is drained through it would no longer be functional. Everything is at risk. The aquifers, our water supply, and the purity of the sea itself are heading toward a tipping point beyond which the only foreseeable result would be a drastic reduction in human and other animal populations.

It has become dramatically evident and immediately crucial that we halt the dumping of millions of tons of carbon dioxide into the atmosphere each year. It is less dramatic, but more crucial, that we stop interfering with the regenerative flow of rainwater into our aquifers, as we could more easily run out of life-sustaining water long before we run out of livable temperatures. These hermetic raincoats must soon be replaced with a more pervious material over which to run our SUVs and minivans. The ultimate and sensible solution would be to rebuild our railroads, which, by all measures, lay a lighter hand on our ecosystems. However, as we are addicted to the freedom of the internal combustion engine this is not an imminent outcome. Ultimately, therefore, an infrastructure valued at some tens of trillions of dollars in the United States alone will have to be replaced by an infrastructure that must return to a more natural cycle of the reuse of the earth's limited and increasingly rare water.

The threat of running short of not only potable but even usable water is immediate and strikes each of us personally and painfully. When contemplating a decrease in the availability of water, the threat hits us where we live—in our private life today, right now, and in our industrial life today, right now. The denigration of our water supply is much more powerful a threat than the increase in, for example, air pollution. We can, and have been, breathing more or less polluted air for centuries. The wondrous capabilities of our bodies have been able to adjust to all of the debris we throw into the air. But as egregious as it is this pollution, which gets worse each year, has a very long way to go before it has an immediate impact on what we do each day and how we do it.

Compare this to an interdiction of water, the basic construct not only of our personal biology as creatures whose bodies are 80 percent water by weight but of the broader industrial biologies that deal with what we eat and how well we live. As the availability of potable, usable water diminishes, an unthinkable reassignment of resources to compensate for centuries of abuse will profoundly change the very quality of our lives.

A substantial part of our ultimate salvation will be somehow to return to the natural cycle of water regeneration via aquifer filtration. Salvation, however, will depend on whether we have the will to wrench ourselves out of the warm cocoon of comfort and recognize that our fool's paradise of plenty is coming to an end.

A significant step toward sustainability of our water supply will be in the worldwide shift to a cementitious material known as pervious concrete. Pervious concrete combines larger than normal aggregates, Portland cement uses somewhat less water than is required for normal concrete. The resulting product has relatively large interstitial spaces, which can pass water through at an average rate of ten gallons per minute per square foot. This is equivalent to about three hundred inches of rain per hour, a level considerably greater than even the highest rates of rainfall we experience.

The advantages of the use of pervious concrete are enormous. The filtering capability of pervious concrete allows the action of soil chemistry and normal biological and bacterial processes to break down the by-product toxins of transportation and industry. With impervious installations these chemicals collect on the surface and are carried in large and concentrated quantities into the surrounding environment and sewer systems. Whenever we interdict the natural flow of water into aquifers it is necessary to build expensive sewer systems. These sewer systems conventionally gather rainwater and direct it into sewers, which eventually run into the sea. While there is a growing tendency toward the reuse of gray water, every gallon of sweet water that ends up in the salt-laden sea is lost, in the short run where it counts, to our biological and industrial lives.

The sealing of the earth's surface, thus emptying the aquifers and resalting sweet water, has as much dire consequence as the terrifying prospect of global warming. The earth will warm slowly, giving a period of some centuries during which an enlightened humanity can adjust to the changing environment. But the earth has been losing its sweet water to an extent that we, each of us individually, are already beginning to feel the costs of the unintended consequences of the sealing.

The conversion to a culture of the pervious is the single most important development of which we are capable to help reverse the cycle of unsustainability. The city of Chicago has made an incremental lurch forward in the use of this material. It has undertaken to transform all of its alleyways into pervious surfaces. Mayor Richard Daley, in a letter introducing the program, wrote, "Green Alley designs showcase innovative environmental technologies to help manage storm water, reduce heat in urban areas, promote recycling and conserve energy." One small step for Chicago, one huge step for pervious concrete.

A great start, but either the surfaces of our world are reversed toward perviousness or we might well be the last generation to know how bountiful our earth can be. Nature's generosity floats tenuously on a shrinking underground lake of sweet water and we are endangering its renewal.

As has been shown, trees and other plantings account for a significant amount of decrease in carbon dioxide dumped into the air. Impervious concrete deprives root systems of water and oxygen, which leads to stunted growth and a shortened life of urban-sited trees. This is especially noted in parking lots and sidewalks where trees, in addition to their positive effect on the atmosphere, are an essential part of shading and the aesthetics of our daily lives.

Pervious concretes have been developed with strengths up to three thousand pounds per square inch. Presently pervious concrete is as yet unsuited for the high speed and heavy traffic loads imposed on our major highways but serious research efforts are under way to increase its carrying strength. The marrying of perviousness and strength will be a major task for our new century as the replacement of aging road systems will become necessary.

The return to a natural process in the handling of rainwater must take its place along with the return to nature of many other prodigal cycles that our juggernaut industrial society has egregiously affected in the past hundred years. In the rainwater matter, pervious concrete promises a doable solution. Other cycles may not be so easily addressed.

When the idea of a concrete submarine is mentioned, the image generated is "sink like a stone." A military submarine, as we know it, is one of the most sophisticated of all of the constructs of man. A submarine operates in the least hospitable environment on earth. It swims about in an unfriendly medium whose weight and pressure disallow a steel submarine to descend much over 600 meters. After that depth its ductile steel envelope, limited in thickness by weight, simply implodes with inrushing tons of water seeking the essential vacuum within.

The development of steel submarines has been a slow and evolutionary search for that next small bit of strength to make an essentially unsafe vehicle a little safer. But with all of the technology that has been brought to bear in a military-supported industry that need not concern itself about costs, that immutable 600 meters of depth remains. Beyond 600 meters there is no future for operational submarines.

In 1994, as has been previously noted, a most unlikely inventor, living a thousand miles from any ocean, actually built a submersible that blew away all of the conceptual limitations

CONCRETE MILITARY SUBMARINE, 75 FEET IN LENGTH

A four-man concrete sub, cheap to build and cheap to operate, can dive to four times the depths of conventional subs. It could wait at depths beyond sonar range and release torpedoes at overpassing vessels.

ADAPTED FROM W. ELLMER

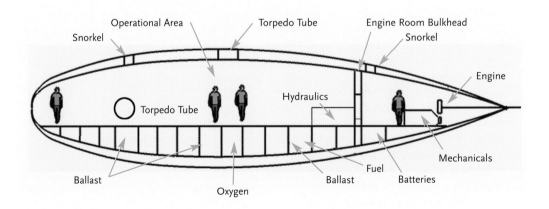

so expensively arrived at by the military. In that year Wilfried Ellmer constructed a diveable, maneuverable concrete sub in the garage under his house in Austria. It was 9 meters long, 2.5 meters in diameter, with an 18 cm thick wall. Its form was that of a blimp, its weight, fully ballasted, was twenty tons. He simply built wooden forms, got some buckets, and poured himself a revolutionary vehicle in which, in his own words, "I personally had a lot of dives and fun in my sub. The fact that I am still writing proves the validity of the concept."

SMALL PRIVATE SUBMARINE
COURTESY WILFRIED ELLMER

The best source of information concerning the ability of concrete to withstand hydrostatic pressures is in the construction of the huge trolls, or "legs," that support the structures that extract gas from beneath the sea. Oil drilling platforms stand on hollow cylinders that reach down about 300 meters and are embedded in the soil of the ocean floor. It is these cylinders, now in use, that give some insight into the depths that a concrete sub might reach. The diameter of the platform legs is 24 meters and the thickness of the concrete wall is 1 meter. The ability to resist pressure lies for the most part in the diameter/wall thickness ratio. This places the implosion depth of troll legs at just over 600 meters, about the same depth as the best of the steel military submarines. When this ratio, 24 meters/1 meter, is adjusted to the 9 meters/18 cm ratio of Ellmer's sub, the sub has almost exactly double the ratio of the legs of the troll, meaning that the theoretical destruction depth of Ellmer's sub, if it were a simple cylinder, is at over 1,200 meters.

When it comes to the resistance of Ellmer's amateur submarine to the enormous pressures of deep sea diving, it is most instructive to use Ellmer's own words: "From the photo you see that my sub floats—without ballast—on the middle line which means that half of the displacement is hull weight. Bringing the concept to an extreme, you could almost double the wall strength and still have positive buoyancy. Which brings us down to over 2,400 meters based on a cylinder shape. Given that my prototype is a spheric curved blimp shape, it could stand—let me guess—3,000 meters—in case of a pure sphere shape even more—probably a lot more—this takes us down to 4,000 meters.

"However, we are still talking about normal concrete. Any special concrete, as those used in the core of certain record seeking buildings, can increase the compression strength of concrete by a factor of four compared to normal concrete. This brings us down to 12,000 meters destruction depth without being limited to the size of the spheres and still with positive buoyancy."

No one has tested actual depths yet with concrete but, if the logic holds, only 10 percent of the ocean floors worldwide would remain inaccessible. An entirely new world would open up at very small cost and the theory and practice of wildly expensive military submersibles would come to an end.

Any process that adds to sustainability and reins in prodigal use of resources, however small, is welcome. Since there are so few military subs afloat and private yachting is a very minor industry, the relative contribution from these industries toward building a sustainable world is very small. More important is how this use of concrete can point the way toward greater gains.

The production, transportation, and consumption of oil is the bête noire of our industrial society and, as such, should be a prime target in the search for sustainability.

There are great costs and damages associated with the production and the consumption of oil, both of which, if altered, would be a positive assist to the ecology, but these alterations would represent huge immediate cost increases to all consumers whether they be the driver of an old (or new) Cadillac and to the fiscal integrity of any firm making anything in the world.

In the ocean transportation of oil, unlike the production and consumption of oil, and as well in other bulk oceangoing commodities, there lies, over not too far a horizon, a real possibility that a change in ocean transportation of all products could effect a sizable and immediate reduction in costs as well as a welcome and measurable reduction in the pollution of our seas and the CO_2 in our air.

A steel supertanker of 500,000 tons requires some $40 million in original construction plus about $5 million a year in maintenance. These monsters deteriorate rapidly as the hulls rust away at the rate of almost a millimeter of steel annually. This limits their safe and useful age to about twenty years, at which time hulls should be scrapped. Instead they are sold to progressively less responsible carriers whose interests lie solely on the immediate bottom line. As a result of this extended use of aging tankers the oil industry itself has recorded that, from the years 1995 to 2001, there have been an average of 408 oil tankers *a year* that have failed and either sunk with the loss of their tankage or released millions of gallons of crude into the sea.

If we carry Ellmer's informed dreams from military submarines into the infinitely broader field of conventional ocean transport the advantages are compelling. Seagoing vessels, tankers as well as all other carriers, are expensively designed to deal with the storms on the surface of seas. Oceangoing vessels cannot be designed to an average of bad sea conditions. All must be able to withstand, as best they can and not always successfully, to the worst of conditions. This obviously puts an enormously inflated cost on the design and construction of ocean carriers and is reflected, somewhere down the line, on an increased burden on our already unsustainable resources.

Most of the dangers of going to sea, whether it be in a sail-powered forty feet of cockleshell fiberglass or a thousand feet of double-hulled steel, have to do with weather and roiling seas, all located where air meets water, at the surface. Bad things happen when violent winds excite watery surfaces. It is at the surface, and only at the surface, that the unending battle between steel and sea takes place. Inevitably, the sea wins both in wrenching apart our heavily wrought steel vessels and, ultimately, in dissolving them in its caustic brew.

Just a few feet below the surface howling winds and breaking seas cease to exist. Below the surface little motion exists, and what movement there is tends to be regular and nonabusive. The hydrostatic tearings and wrenchings at the surface no longer apply. Hundred-ton sea monsters and two-ounce denizens are blithely unaware of the troubles above them. There exist two universes, separated by only a few feet, one violent and unpredictable and the other calm, static, and without surprises. It is this tranquil land of submarine sea that promises an end to the conflict between man and the oceans that began when the first sailor floated out to sea in a hollowed log.

A hollow concrete vessel can float at any reasonable depth. A concrete submersible need only take on a little water ballast, leaving a snorkel above the surface, to ride out the worst storms imaginable in an essentially motionless and quiet environment.

In shallow water a conventional vessel puts an enormous strain on anchors and tackle as the vessel rises and falls to seas that can reach and exceed forty feet at the surface. Underwater there is no change in verticality and the vessel can ride to a very small anchor with little chance of breaking free. Anywhere, in any sea, a safe harbor or a hurricane hole are immediately available to a snorkel-equipped concrete submersible.

On the surface enormous reserve power must be available to counter the effects of wind and seas but under the surface these reserves can be reduced by several orders of magnitude.

Considering the energy efficiency of the blue whale as a case in point, Ellmer writes, "No long distance surface swimming animal exists because this is not energy efficient. On the contrary moving heavy streamlined bodies under water is very energy efficient. The energy expended by a 200 ton whale has been estimated at 20–40 HP, or just over one tenth of a HP per ton, taking into account that little reserve power is required to counter the effect of storms."

Conventional ocean transports weighing half a million tons are usually powered by engines of approximately 45,000 horsepower, most of which is needed for enormous emergency reserves. A concrete submersible, a 500,000-ton freighter, weighing nothing when submerged, would require an engine of essentially insignificant horsepower to push it along. The enormous savings in fuel and the concomitant reduction in CO_2 emissions are desirable sustainability goals. Additional economies and additional contributions to sustainability would be realized by the fact that these concrete submersible transports not only would be cheap to build but, since concrete does not rust and is slow to deteriorate under water, can last far longer than steel. Floating in a three-dimensional medium rather than two dramatically reduces the probability of collisions. For all these reasons, and more, the coming of concrete submersible ocean transportation seems inevitable.

BENDABLE CONCRETE

COURTESY CRC TECHNOLOGY APS, HJALLERUP, DENMARK

CRC AND OTHER NEW CONCRETES

Major life-changing movements most often turn on serendipitous events. The long history of concrete, characterized by the loss and rebirth of the process many times over the centuries, owes much of the present condition of the material to lonely researchers, often working away in obscure kitchens and laboratories. In the feverish scientification of the twentieth century, work outside the great research centers by individual, often autodidact, inventors is often lost for want of the economic power to bring it to the marketplace.

One such example was generated by an accidental series of events in the early 1960s in Denmark, a country smaller than many of our cities. H. H. Bache, trained as a civil engineer, wallowed aimlessly about after coming out of engineering school. He had dreamed of building great dams and bridges but, somehow, found himself reluctant to direct his life's work in those traditional engineering directions.

A friend recommended that he look into a newly formed cement research facility in the north of Jutland. In no hurry to pursue what seemed to Bache to be outside of his core interests, it took three months and continued urging from his friend to set up an appointment with the director of Concrete Research Laboratory in the city of Karlstrup. Like Bache, the laboratory itself was not sure exactly what its brief was and just where it should be heading.

The interview was less than inspiring, except to a young man wandering about in the mists of career confusion. One remark by the director struck Bache as an interesting match to his own indecision. When he asked the newly appointed director of the facility just what he should be working on if he accepted the position, the answer "I don't know" seemed to profile and define his own reluctance to settle in professionally.

It is from just such an offhand remark, "I don't know," that great events often emerge. In Bache's case, in the permissive and nondemanding atmosphere of a concrete research station that had little sense of direction, he began to wonder why, for 150 years, the formulations of concrete had remained essentially unchanged. He wondered why, for those same decades, concrete was being used merely to enhance existing architecture rather than becoming the agent for an entirely new architecture. What he observed was that concrete, as conceived in the early years of the twentieth century, had become popular in making the work of architects easier rather than, confronted by this new and transmutable material, forcing architects to stretch beyond the conventional concept of concrete as a pourable, self-hardening variation of bricks and hewn stone.

By 1970 Hans Bache had published a paper in the *American Journal of Ceramics* that was to become a challenge to established experimenters in concrete. Unlike most who had come before him, Bache was beginning to propose changes in the fundamental physical makeup of concrete rather than just ringing the changes in formulae. He was inventing what he called a "new concrete," and a new technology to accompany it.

Early-twentieth-century concrete was a pedestrian material that attracted plodding and pedestrian researchers. Laboratories all over the world were busily altering the amounts of cement versus aggregate in order to increase the strength, the ductility, and other characteristics of a material that had been developed some thousands of years earlier and had sustained precious little change since then.

Experiments to reach out for high-quality concretes were proving only marginally successful because, Bache believed, the researchers were dedicated merely to "evolving" new mixtures. He felt that the slow evolutionary method was satisfying the marketplace but ignoring the need to dig deeper into the theory of how things, in this case concrete, hold together.

In lay terms, concrete is held together through a process called hydration—in a word, the addition of water. When a mixture of cement and aggregate is wetted the water reacts with the cement to form crystalline matter. These crystals harden and interlock and bind the aggregate together.

Bache reasoned that concrete would be a tougher material if the crystals had more surface of the aggregate to which to adhere. By reducing the size of the aggregate, and of the cement particles, Bache discovered that the strength of the concrete increased dramatically. A convenient formula describing the process is that "the strength of concrete is in an inverse ratio to the size of aggregate and cement particles." Eureka!

He named it CRC, compact reinforced composite. Almost all concrete these days is reinforced by the addition of iron rods but Bache, applying the same thinking to the reinforcing material, that is by reducing the diameter of the iron, sometimes to mere bundles of iron wires, provided the hydrated crystals with more surface by which to more firmly adhere to the reinforcing rods. What worked for cement and aggregate worked as well to increase the efficiency of the iron reinforcements.

In a curious way he was replicating the experience of Mr. Rolls and Mr. Royce whose cars were demonstrably superior to all the rest at the time. This superiority rested on the fact that Rolls-Royces used multiple small bolts to hold things together rather than the few huge bolts, continually increased in size upon failure, of their competitors.

Not only did CRC prove more resistant to compressive forces, which was never a problem with ordinary concrete, but it developed a remarkable ductility. As the photo shows a CRC beam acts more like a steel beam than it does concrete. Under the load illustrated, ordinary concrete would have long since failed while CRC demonstrates bendability near to that of steel. Additionally, as the density of CRC is less than half that of steel, CRC has the more favorable strength/weight ratio. This can in some cases make CRC better suited for long spans, moving structures, or cantilevered structures.

Another impressive result was its resistance to a cannon-shot projectile. CRC is well suited to resisting impact loads as

A CANNON-FIRED PROJECTILE SHOT INTO CRC (COMPACT REINFORCED COMPOSITE)

COURTESY CRC TECHNOLOGY APS, HJALLERUP, DENMARK

the ductile performance of CRC helps distribute local loads to larger parts of the structure. This has been demonstrated in tests with explosives, but it has also been demonstrated for projectiles.

The picture shows CRC slabs after being hit with a twenty-inch-long projectile fired from a cannon at a three-hundred-yard distance. The weight of the projectile was such that the result of the collision in ordinary concrete would have been a room full of flying chunks of concrete. This photo shows the projectile embedded into the concrete and clearly demonstrates that CRC is sufficiently strong and sufficiently ductile to capture the shell in mid-flight.

With advances in concrete technology, ultra-high-performance concretes (UHPC), variations of CRC, have become a new focus for researchers and the concrete industry. UHPC is characterized by high compressive strength and excellent durability, properties that result in lighter structures and longer life. The graceful structures illustrated here are a direct result of the work of H. H. Bache. The mystery behind CRC is that, in spite of its demonstrable superiority, the construction industry continued to pour heavy, oversized elements for a quarter of a century.

After decades of proven research, this capability has not been taken up and expanded into myriad construction profiles. General and widespread use of CRC could halve the volume of material used, reduce the output of pollutants in the production and use of concrete by double that, and, at the same time, realize huge savings in the energy required for direct production of old-fashioned concrete as well as its polluting cost of transport. The single most friendly change that could easily and measurably help to sustain our burdened planet would be the shift now to the many variants of CRC.

The fact is that the current use of the original CRC is a mere spit in the river when China, the Middle East, and the unindustrialized world in general are using concrete at a rate that is demonstrably unsustainable in ecological terms.

Wind farms, hydroelectric dams, nuclear plants, and solar

CONCRETE SPIRAL STAIRCASE

COURTESY CRC TECHNOLOGY APS,
HJALLERUP, DENMARK

installations, all huge consumers of scarce and increasingly expensive capital, are making their own positive contributions to the looming golem of global warming.

Whether concrete production shifts to CRC or not, the fact is that the production of any concrete, like the production of other material, is a burden on the ability of our planet to sustain itself. It can be argued that, considering all environmental negatives, CO_2 production, transport costs, water degeneration, by-product disposal, etc., on the face of it the production of concrete is no more of a burden than the production of any other construction material.

Having said that, the anticipated production of concrete over the coming decades is so huge that its environmental imprint will be unsustainable. The costs of using concrete are not hidden. The present production of greenhouse gases as a result of the production and use of concrete has been estimated to be as much as an astounding 18 percent of the total of all such gases produced throughout the world each year. The ultimate villain is carbon, which is the major by-product of the use of energy. In a world pushing the limits of sustainability, and assuming nothing is done to reverse our prodigality, we will need to double the earth's resources. It is obvious that stringencies must be devised to halt this process, and especially in those areas where enormous waste occurs and where enormous savings can be made.

Scattered investigations leading to reducing the environmental impact of massive quantities of concrete are being pursued around the world. The most logical and least costly method would be to reduce the total tonnage of concrete produced. The relationships between tonnage produced and energy and CO_2 are direct; the less of the former then the less of the latter. As has been argued a simple shift to the use of CRC, representing more strength for less mass of material, would solve some of the problems. But the exponential increase in the use of concrete anticipated in the next decades calls for more complicated and technologically challenging solutions than the mere reduction of tonnage.

Much important work is being done in Denmark by cooperative actions between the Danish government, the Concrete Center of the Danish Technological Institute, and the Aalborg Portland Company, which provides almost all of the cement used in Denmark today.

Cooperation comes naturally to the Danes, especially since, at least in the cement industry, there is no argument that the immediate problem is the reduction of CO_2. The Kyoto Agreement, signed on to by all parties except the United States under the Bush administration, has set achievable but difficult goals to be met before 2012. The Danish goal is a reduction of 21 percent from the 1990 levels along with the use of residual products of other industrial processes in order to reduce the need for landfills.

The abstract of the Danish Centre for Green Concrete[1] states, "The goal of the Centre is to reduce the environmental impacts of concrete through the development of new resource-saving binder systems and increased recycling and energy recovery of waste materials." Having pronounced their goals, the Danes have laid out clear plans for achieving them.

According to the study, the present world consumption of concrete is represented by a cube three miles high by three miles on each side. To attempt to comprehend this inconceivable statistic it is likely that if the cube were situated on the equator it could alter the stability of the earth itself.

In Denmark, as an example, concrete represents 2 percent of its total output of CO_2 and if the curves are allowed to continue as anticipated that could double in a few years. The Danes have decided that the curves shall not continue, but instead of replacing concrete with another construction material that might be more environmentally friendly, if such a magical material can be found, they have embarked on a program of production of green concrete and green buildings. The Danish study anticipates that it is technologically and financially feasible, by going green and by using residual products from other industries such as fly ash, to halve the CO_2 output within the targeted time as well as unburden the ecology of a vast amount of waste materials.

The goals of the Danish study go beyond the production of concrete to defining the parameter of green buildings. By 2012 such a building must:

- Reduce CO_2 emissions by 30 percent.
- 20 percent of the aggregates shall be from residual products.
- Considerably increased use of the concrete industry's own residual products.
- Use of landfill products or products disposed of in other ways.
- The use of at least 10 percent CO_2 neutral waste-derived fuels.

In addition, the Danes decree that a green building must avoid the use of ecologically damaging substances that would reduce its use as recycled material at the end of its useful life.

The Danish study investigates the lengths to which the concrete industry must go to contribute to world sustainability goals. Clinker is the material produced by the burning of limestone in cement kilns. Any reduction in the percentage of clinker in concrete results directly in a saving in energy and thus, in our present oil-based industrial profile, a significant reduction in the release of carbon. A process being tested called mineralization involves the addition of small amounts of minerals to the kiln. The direct result is a 5 percent reduction in the consumption of energy accompanied by an unexpected increase in strength of the resulting concrete by as much as 5 to 10 percent.

The Danish government plans to completely eliminate the production of fly ash, a major by-product in the burning of coal. Although this is a major step forward in the reduction of greenhouse gases it has the unintended consequence of denying to the concrete industry in Denmark one of its main components in the production of a more sustainable cement. This problem is being dealt with by the substitution of sewage sludge for fly ash, a most fortuitous substitution since sewage sludge is a major component in scarce landfills. Thus a change that is forced upon an industry is, in this case, a solution for another element of sustainability.

These two special cases from Denmark limited to the fairly technologically simple concrete industry demonstrate the enormous amount of work that needs to be done throughout the world in order to begin to address sustainability only in this one area of production.

Little Denmark, in the person of its concrete industry, represents but a tiny microcosm compared to the actions and decisions that will have to be made in all industries worldwide. These decisions will fundamentally address the level of personal convenience and comfort in industrialized nations. The time has come to pay the piper.

While the availability of oil remains vital we are already anticipating an endgame in which oil must become progressively less important. However, there is no conceivable endgame in the need for water. The temptation of dealing with the distant future is to posit solutions that seem, on their face, to approach the ridiculous. But the future is a slippery eel and what seems ridiculous now may be essential down the road.

The total quantity of sweet water is the central problem, yet there is an interesting parallel problem in that the distribution of this most precious commodity about the world could not be more uneven. However constricted water supply will become in one part of the world, there will always be another part in which sweet water runs wastefully into the sea.

This raises the possibility that, at some time in the future, there will be a need to transport water over great distance. This is an enormously greater problem in terms of volume than the transport of oil. The transport of gargantuan quantities of water from one part of the globe to another may become necessary to sustain life in increasingly arid areas. Pumping such quantities would require the unreasonable expenditure of energy. The only plausible method of distribution of water on our planet may be by sea, using concrete submersibles built cheaply to unthinkable dimensions.

·　·　·　·　·

In the Italian town of Segrate a street was repaved in 2003 with a concrete that had been developed when the architect Richard Meier urged the Italian firm of Italcementi[2] to find a concrete that would retain a blinding whiteness through decades. Meier had designed a church one feature of which was its white concrete. As a result of Meier's desire for the church to remain white "in perpetuity"' Italcementi turned to titanium dioxide, a chemical that had long been used for making various products, including food, paper, and paint, very white.

A street was repaved with the new very white concrete and residents began to observe that the air quality in the area was improving. When the air was tested, it was discovered that particulate matter, volatile organic compounds and nitrogen oxides, all diminished. Researching the matter, Italian scientists found that concrete, treated with titanium dioxide, was a natural antipollutant photocatalyst.

The solution to the search for whiteness was to incorporate titanium dioxide in the surface of ordinary concrete, which, it turned out, kept both the concrete and the air clean. The now famous *cemento mangiasmog* is a new breed of "transmaterials," trademarked as TXActive, which are endowed with antipollutant properties. Change, both for the worse and occasionally for the better, continually comes upon us with surprise and wonder. According to the company, concrete treated with titanium dioxide[3] speeds up the natural oxidation process of pollutants in the presence of natural or artificial light. The pollutants are converted into innocuous compounds such as water and nitrates. A small amount of deleterious CO_2 is also generated in the process, which points up the complexities inherent in environmental control.

What had started as an aesthetic requirement by a demanding architect has turned out to be a material pregnant with possibilities. Since concrete surfaces will expand exponentially in the coming century, the possibility that concrete can serve sustainability as well as diminishing it has excited the research arm of the industry. Smog control using the familiar concrete barriers that line our roads and highways as well as the highways themselves could deal with much of the emissions of transportation.

Combining this "smog-eating cement" with pervious concrete could develop a context that would point the way to green solutions for the rehabilitation of our deteriorating highway infrastructure over the next decades. Though the concept of a "cleansing concrete" is in its infancy, research studies inevitably will seek out specific chemical combinations of concrete that might well address other serious problems of pollutants.

Concrete has become the omnipresent material for almost every long-lasting construction in our society. As more uncounted billions of tons will be required to shore up our infrastructure and satisfy the soaring needs of developing societies, concrete, in its pervious state combined with these new pollution-eating capabilities, could be one answer to an entire litany of sustainability problems.

·   ·   ·   ·   ·

All of the news about the beneficence of the use of concrete is not good news. Nearly three tons of concrete are now being produced *for each man, woman, and child on earth.* This mind-bending number is expected to double in coming decades and, since the production of concrete has an important carbon footprint, its increased use comes with a carbon price.

Cement production in the United States accounts for a significant 1.5 percent of our emissions; the emissions worldwide account for as much as an unsustainable 18 percent of all carbon emissions. Western industries are considering methods to further control emissions but the most pressing present threat are the newly developing juggernauts China and India. The closer to subsistence levels on which an economy operates, the more difficult it is to reach expensive sustainable goals. Pushed by expanding populations newly introduced to the cornucopias of consumption, these economies generate little incentive to conservation.

The production of cement requires many levels of energy consumption. Ninety-five percent of the energy consumed is used in the burning of limestone at temperatures up to 3,400 F degrees to produce the calcinated substance that becomes cement.

The reduction of carbon emissions from 5 percent to a more sustainable but still deleterious 2 percent, could be accomplished short term worldwide only by heroic acts of crushingly expensive edicts from above. The only, and seemingly impossible, direction is to find a substitute for limestone. Eliminating limestone from cement production would be akin to eliminating water from the production of ice.

In fact this world-changing concept is being looked at in a number of laboratories around the world. A team of researchers at MIT has discovered that the building blocks of cement, calcium-silicate-hydrate particles, have a unique *nanosignature* "indicating that the strength of concrete does not rely on a specific mineral but on the organization of that mineral as packed nano-particles, opening the door for identifying an alternative mineral to be used in cement."[4] This insight indicates that concretes can be envisioned that are made from minerals that, unlike limestone, do not need to be burned before use.

Replacing high-temperature combustion in the production of concrete is far from a vain hope. Professor Franz-Josef Ulm, a civil engineer at the Massachusetts Institute of Technology (MIT), suggests that those minerals that form the ultrastructure of bone could be a model. "Bone consists largely of calcium and achieves a very similar packing density at the nanoscale, is manufactured at mere body temperature with no appreciable release of CO_2. If we can find a way to mimic the process and speed it up, we could replicate it to fashion a new building material."

It is a heady thought, indeed, that curious investigators are on the trail of replacing an earth-damaging process with a natural and harmless process that our own bodies employ every day at a burning temperature of 98.6 degrees rather than 3,400 degrees.

Other hopeful developments involve the dilution of the amount of CO_2 producing cement with the addition of supplementary cementitious materials (SCMs). These materials, slag cement, fly ash, and silica fume, have the additional advantage of being waste products of other industrial processes, thus requiring no additional CO_2 production and as a result reducing the amount of deleterious materials in cement in addition to conserving landfill space, not a small concern.

Some researchers are concentrating on replacement rather than dilution. Civil engineers at Montana State University are using locally available high-calcium fly ash as the sole binder in industrial-use cement. Starting in 2002 they have had success in field trials of small structures using conventional mixing, transporting, and placement equipment.

The resultant concrete "does not have the history of Portland cement" in the area of durability. Little is known about long-term strengths and freeze-thaw performance but these tests are under way, and the old slogan of Dupont, "Better Life Through Chemistry," may well be an important one in a sustainable future.

OUR SENILE INFRASTRUCTURE

We all get old. Everything wears out and, while a concrete structure may appear more ageless than our own frail bodies, the best laid concrete usually shows the pressures of age before we do. Concrete structures begin to age badly at around fifty years while our soft and ductile muscles and tissues sail past half a century with amazing grace. At the age of fifty, assuming the most modest of natural regimens and excepting the self-abuse of ingesting poisons such as alcohol and tobacco and certain foodstuffs, our bodies have been self-repairing from almost the instant of birth.

On the other hand concrete structures tend to live a very long time before they start to die. It is the most rare of such structures that survive in a usable condition beyond a century or so and only the Pantheon, the single intact remnant of the glory that was Rome, has managed the miracle of a continuing life after two thousand years.

We must now begin to duplicate the Roman miracle. It would seem, considering the power of technology and the accumulated knowledge of concrete usage, that this would be a fairly simple and overwhelmingly obvious task. But things are not, certainly in a habituated and resistant concrete industry, always what they logically should be. We are still pouring many millions of tons of concrete that require the same level of care and service as a bed-wetting baby. Indeed, the destructive inclusion of water, a direct result of the inherent hydration process in both bridges and babies, is the seed of their discomforts. Babies eventually learn to control their water: Bridges never do. We are still erecting bridges and buildings and dams that require intense and increasingly expensive maintenance to hold them together for at least the next hundred years, which, as things are progressing, is a date not so far away as it once seemed.

We are designing structures with built-in senility, which we will have to spoon feed for half their lives. The costs of senility increases at an unplanned-for exponential rate. It is entirely predictable that the cost of propping up senile structures toward the end of the twenty-first century will have become so expensive that abandonment of much of our infrastructure may be forced upon us.

The American Waterworks Association, an industry organ that, like others, is more prone to cheerleader optimism than to reality, makes the following lugubrious prediction.

> The importance of safe drinking water to public health and the nation's economic welfare is undisputed. However, as we enter the

21st century, water utilities face significant economic challenges. For the first time, in many of these utilities a significant amount of buried infrastructure—the underground pipes that make safe water available at the turn of a tap—is at or very near the end of its expected life span. The pipes laid down at different times in our history have different life expectancies, and thousands of miles of pipes that were buried over 100 or more years ago will need to be replaced in the next 30 years. Most utilities have not faced the need to replace huge amounts of this infrastructure because it was too young. Today a new age has arrived. We stand at the dawn of the replacement era.

Extrapolating from our analysis of 20 utilities, we project that expenditures on the order of $250 billion over 30 years might be required nationwide for the replacement of worn out drinking water pipes and associated structures.[5]

Another industry estimate is that simply for keeping our aging bridges in a usable condition, and not including the cost of replacement, another couple of hundred of billions will be required. The average life span of a bridge is approximately fifty years and most of the infrastructure in this country was built during the economic boom after World War II. Already, 60 percent of the half million bridges in the United States are showing distress. The prospect of replacing these bridges before the end of the century in this country alone is a scary measure of the impossible.

The final judgment of the state of American infrastructure comes from MIT and deserves to be quoted in full.[6]

Physical infrastructure, once the pride of America and a major contributor to its economic and social growth and success, has in recent years become an acute embarrassment to this nation. Infrastructure failures, ineffectiveness, and the inability to properly plan, construct, manage, and maintain it now pose an acute challenge to America's claims of economic, social, environmental, and technological leadership.

Most of our road, rail, water, sewer, electric power, wired telephone, and other distributed systems infrastructure are old and in need of repair. Our ports, airports, and rail terminals are archaic, ill-designed, badly run, and poorly maintained.

Levees, coastal defenses, and dams often lack effective inspection and maintenance. In New Orleans, the core of many levees had been washed out, causing them to fail—a fact not discovered by simple visual levee surface inspection. Yet seismic measurements would have readily identified the growing problem for timely remedial action.

Similarly, the recent Minnesota highway bridge collapse should have been prevented by proper timely inspection and maintenance. But most of our infrastructure is 50 years old or older, uses outdated designs and engineering, and has experienced little if any maintenance updating or repair. We do not have nor use advanced infrastructure testing, inspection, or maintenance management methods.

Performance of recent infrastructure projects such as Boston's "Big Dig" and its Kenmore Square bus station, New Orleans' levee reconstruction, and various dams, bridges, port and airport projects are a reminder of how far this country has sunk in its public infrastructure development capability.

Taken together we are looking at not billions of dollars but trillions. There is no prediction of just how many trillions of dollars we can pile on a profligate consumerist economy before a contracting economy implodes. Even without the imponderable costs of global warming, the question that remains unanswered is whether our present democratic political structures will be able to survive the cataclysmic expenditures that face us. The answers to this question may well be how we define democracy.

These predictions of the costs of survival are manifestly insupportable in our present economic organization and, if foisted by necessity upon us, will warp our economy beyond recognition and so destroy our self-mandated sense of comfort as to threaten not only the economic basis of American life but perhaps even our political structure. Costs such as these are not likely to be subscribed to by a democratic society even if they are the very costs of survival. Survival, in the face of profound and fundamental change, is most likely to lead to an authoritarian state dominated by very big capital. Unless we are able to beat the sustainability rap complicated by senility, our future may well be a reverse syndicalism in which more and more of the means of production will be transferred from the public to big business. The end of this process may very well be a form of homegrown American fascism in which all economic decisions, and perhaps political ones, are handed down from an authoritarian group of technocrats. All of course for the "good of the people."

COST OF PROFLIGACY

The poster boy who best limns the relationship between mankind and the earth in the coming centuries is the little Dutch boy with his finger in the dike. Our future needs, in this area, will require a finger of Brobdingnagian proportions considering the thousands of miles of waterfront that will need protection from rising seas.

The Dutch have taught us that the sea can be held at bay. For a while. For generations, the efforts of the Hollandish lowlanders, using in early constructions only earthen walls, have been successful in converting vast tracts of "oceanatory" to arable and useful territory. We soon will have to copy the Dutch but on an immensely larger scale. The only weapon that will do the job and is in sufficient supply and can allow a controlled transition not destructive of our economic life may be, of course, concrete.

Burning is the problem. But since burning, oxidization, is the central engine of the biomass on earth it is a problem of exquisite complexity. Even the reader who now holds this book, with each breath exhaled, is dumping another mite of CO_2 into the atmosphere. Multiply that mite by six billion, add to that the billions of consumable animals that we herd for food, and it is possible that, even without the industrial burning of fossil fuels, we could be reaching for a warming scenario.

About 60 percent of the CO_2 that is produced during the making of concrete is produced directly from the burning of limestone to clinker. The balance of the carbon, 40 percent of the total, is created by the use of electrical and fossil fuel consumption in the mining, delivery, and use of the material.

A decrease in the 40 percent can occur if we continue to concentrate on the production of electricity from renewable and nuclear sources. But it will be in the development of a substitute for limestone and the elimination of the need for burned clinker where the greatest savings will occur. Even our present use of concrete is unsustainable, if only in terms of rising sea levels. The natural advantages inherent in the use of concrete, the abundance of local raw materials, the ability to manufacture close to construction sites, and its ability to use recycled aggregates in its production are even now being negated by its insidious by-product. If we are to defeat encroaching seas, an entirely new set of industrial equations will be necessary to balance the deleterious versus the advantageous in our hunger for concrete.

To comprehend the complexity of the challenge, consider that many experts believe that global warming, even at its present unaccelerated rate, will cause sea levels to rise dramatically. Thermal expansion has already raised the oceans four to eight inches.

The Intergovernmental Panel on Climate Change of the UN reported as early as 2001 that the average temperature is likely to increase by between 2.5 and 10.4 degrees Fahrenheit by the year 2100. A recent *Nature* study suggested that Greenland's ice sheet will begin to melt if the temperature there rises by 5.4 degrees Fahrenheit. That is something many scientists think is likely to happen in as little as another hundred years and that is where the bulk of all of the fresh water on the planet is locked up.

"The complete melting of these ice repositories could raise sea levels by 23 feet. But even a partial melting would cause a one-meter (three-foot) rise. Such a rise would have a devastating impact on low-lying island countries, such as the Indian Ocean's Maldives, which would be entirely submerged. Densely populated areas like the Nile Delta and parts of Bangladesh would become uninhabitable, potentially driving hundreds of millions of people from their land."[7]

Even a three-foot rise in sea levels, which would not require the complete melting of the ice caps, would wreak havoc on the Gulf Coast and eastern seaboard of the United States.

"No one will be free from this," says Jonathon Overpeck,[8] whose maps show that every U.S. East Coast city from Boston to Miami would be swamped. "A one-meter sea rise in New Orleans," according to Overpeck, "would mean no more Mardi Gras. Even with a small sea level rise, we're going to destroy whole nations and their cultures that have existed for thousands of years."

Perhaps these are worst-case scenarios but, without a sure knowledge of the future of the planet under changing conditions of which we have no experience, it is the height of imprudence to gamble on just how terrible the changes may be. The odds are further stacked against us when we recognize that not only do we not know what is in store for us but there are some things that we do know that make matters worse.

Some of the processes inherent in global warming are self-reinforcing. This simply means that there is a circularity about global energy transfers, which posits that "the worse things get, the worse things get." Rising global temperatures, which result in the melting of the ice caps, release the volumes of water that raise sea levels. But all of the water released does not go into the oceans. Because of heightened temperature of our atmosphere, the air itself is thus able to carry and contain more of the released water in the form of water vapor.

This would seem to mitigate the situation and lead to a not-so-high ocean level. But just the opposite is the case because increased water vapor means increased cloud cover and cloud cover retains heat as surely as if there was an increase in greenhouse gases. Since increased cloud cover operates exactly like the greenhouse gases in preventing the escape of heat, poor old earth now has two global processes that act in tandem and reinforce each other as the seas lap ever higher at sea walls vainly seeking to preserve borders and lifestyles. How much land we lose and how much of our present cultures and mores we can save depends on a thousand slippery variables, not the least of which just might be our ability to fill future needs with concrete.

As in all materials dedicated to the uses of man, the burden placed on the earth eventually comes down to volume related to available sources. As little as a hundred years ago the pressure of demand on what were considered unlimited resources was of little concern. We now know that our planet, relative to our industrial pressures upon it, is not only fragile but terrifyingly finite. Therefore, any reduction in the simple volume of usage, even a reduction in the rate of increase, must be pursued with vigor. We must first seek to address rampant profligacy and the excess that characterizes our consumer. The reduction of profligacy lays the least penalty on our comfort and may be the least-wrenching change that can be made.

Profligacy in the use of concrete is often difficult to describe as so much of the detail of its use in a particular project is hidden in indecipherable engineering statistics. The overriding instinct of the engineering community is to overbuild. The prospect of a failure of a very big project is so horrendous that "what is necessary" is too often seen as "not enough to protect my rear end." It is too easy just to continue to pour concrete as there is no penalty for overdoing that comes anywhere near to the penalty for underdoing. Besides there is no independent measure of what is enough. "Enough" is the sole purview of the engineers. Public and private communities responsible for paying for very big projects may well question expensive furbelows in design but will never question the possibility of overbuilding. After all, their rear ends are perhaps even more exposed than the engineers'. No one wants to underwrite the risk of incautious use of materials and, since there is no organized way to measure that risk, there is an inbuilt bias toward profligacy that pervades all construction.

It is in the most rare of circumstances that the layman can make the case for the profligate use of materials. The Three Gorges Dam is a project that has poured more concrete than any in history. The concrete was poured for years at the rate of 22,000 cubic meters of concrete *a day*! The concrete mix was made more environmentally supportable by a high percentage of fly ash, but still the design of the structure depended on the

THREE GORGES DAM, YANGTZE RIVER, CHINA

ability of many tons of concrete to hold back the water rather than a design that might well have cut the material consumption by a large percentage.

The Three Gorges design seems unsophisticated in concept for it is simply a straight wall of enormous weight thrown across the gorge. Compared to the Hoover Dam, a dam built almost a century earlier, Three Gorges is primitive indeed.

A glance at the design shape of the Hoover Dam instantly reveals an engineering solution that has been around since Roman times. The Hoover is in the form of a true Roman arch laid on its side. Thus the weight of the water it holds back is thrust not on the simple weight of the dam, but is transmitted to the solid rock on either side. Had the Hoover Dam been built as was the Three Gorges, straight from side to side, it would have required an enormous increase in the weight of concrete to hold back Lake Mead.

Another ultimate symbol of profligacy in architecture is the increasing use of cantilevered elements. A cantilever has almost no rationale in construction other than aesthetic. When Frank Lloyd Wright created the architectural gem Fallingwater he created more a work of art than of architecture. Artists such as Wright must be allowed license in selected buildings but journeymen architects, in imitation of the greats, must not. The use of unnecessary cantilevering for pure aesthetic reasons in major building projects might be excused in economies not under the gun of sustainability but in our present perilous position with regard to our planet home cantilevering is no longer an option. In almost every cantilever application it can easily be demonstrated that a simple addition of a post or two would, without violating the spirit of the building, reduce the total use of materials by a substantial and surprising percentage.

Bridges are gravity personified. The tensions and the pressures of great weights lifted aloft are instantly visual in every bridge, suspension, or arched Roman that help us across our rough geography. While suspension bridges evoke the tensions of gravity contained, the pyramids are like evocations of its pressures kept under solid control. Both bridges and pyramids

HOOVER DAM, COLORADO RIVER, NEVADA–ARIZONA BORDER

are hungry consumers of scarce resources, yet the prime directive in both, indeed in all matters of our vast engines of consumption, must be to demand the minimum consumption of material consonant with effective use and function. But move one small degree away from the perfect pyramidical shape or change the most elegant suspension design by a foot or two and we begin extravagances of architectural design, and of all other objects that we use.

The most extreme examples of wasteful use of resources, in a world no longer consonant with waste, are the arrogant structures of the architect Santiago Calatrava.

His buildings, and his bridges in particular, are prime examples of an architect more intent on making showy art than responding to human needs in a scarcity-dominated economy. We would be better off if Calatrava and architects of his ilk would confine themselves to sketching in order to demonstrate their brilliance rather than laboriously and expensively converting those sketches to concrete and steel. His bridges are simple suspension types contorted into fantastical shapes that add not a whit to function but suck up unnecessary steel and concrete in enormous quantities and profligate cost.

In a world where even the air we breathe and the water we drink are becoming scarce, we must seek in all directions to reduce the burdens of our activities on our dwindling resources. Since concrete consumption is presently epic and growing exponentially, it is one of the most obvious of areas in which we must actively restrict profligate use.

Our architects and our engineers should harken to lessons of elegance that chess teaches us. The very best of master chess games are those that are won in the very least number of moves. The fewer the moves the more elegant. In the crises of scarcity that loom, our solutions, as in chess, must be accomplished with the least amount of resources.

CALATRAVA BRIDGE, PUERTO MADERO, BUENOS AIRES, ARGENTINA

CHAPTER 12

THE INDUSTRY

O n a chilly January morning in 2008 the concrete industry opened its annual trade show in Las Vegas. The show, entitled the World of Concrete, was enormous, filling all of the vast enclosed spaces of the Las Vegas trade center and spilling out into the surrounding parking lots.

There were thousands of exhibitors offering the latest in mixing and spraying and tamping and grinding of a myriad of mixtures of Portland cement. The panoply of machines, some reaching three stories in height, looked like a scene from the age of dinosaurs. These monsters, brought into existence by the recent surge and anticipated increases in the use of concrete, each represented an investment of millions of dollars. Additionally, each was accompanied by accessory systems that added more millions. Hardly anything in the entire show could be bought for under $10,000. It was an expression of exuberance at a time when parallel industries were beginning to undergo contraction.

The goals of the concrete industry were aimed toward the more efficient and quicker deployment of ever more vast amounts of concrete. It was an acceptance and extension of the past. The industry was seemingly unconscious that the materials and the systems for which these monsters were designed had a future that was nothing like a straight-line extension of the past. The problems of profligacy, diminution of available energy and materials, and an overriding need for sustainability were submerged in the soaring demand for concrete.

The concrete industry is designed to serve that present demand. In ordinary circumstances in the past, in which sustainability was not an issue, enthusiastically servicing present demand was rational and profitable. In a world beginning to come to terms with the reality that our time of prodigality is over and that misuse of resources was bringing our planet to its knees, the industry is barely paying lip service to the problem of the enormous tonnage of CO_2 released each year by the production and use of concrete.

In spite of interesting and forward-looking research in universities and even some little in industry-based institutes, these beginning solutions were, for all intents and purposes, ignored in the Las Vegas concrete extravaganza.

Of the thousands of exhibitors huckstering systems and products and machinery, the designs of which for the most part ignore the planet's CO_2 problem, there was a mere and marginal handful that offered so-called green solutions. Only two seminars, sparsely attended, seemed to be aware of the enormous threats looming over the industry. One was a careful and hopeful discussion of the use of the fly ash from our landfills in concrete production, which could immediately, and at minimal cost or confrontation, mitigate the output of CO_2. Not too many paid much attention.

The other was a curious presentation by Wal-Mart of its corporate-wide program, which was touted as Wal-Mart's response to the need for responsible development. As in all other matters, Wal-Mart addressed this global program from its own fierce protection of its bottom line. The presenter was the chief architect of the Wal-Mart organization. After dwelling on how much energy savings accrued from the use of natural light, the architect explained that Wal-Mart would undertake any green activity so long as it was "cost neutral." This looks good PR-wise, but such a program is designed to ignore those overriding and exigent problems that must be addressed but which are not "cost neutral." When the Wal-Mart representative was asked about the use of pervious concrete in their vast parking lots he indicated that this was not within the cost neutral approach. As beneficial as pervious parking lots might be to the protection of aquifers, this was not to be counted as an improvement to the corporation's bottom line. And so Wal-Mart parking lots remain impervious.

This is an example of the concept of noncompulsory self-regulation that regressively permeates not only the concrete industry but all industries and is encouraged by conservative proponents of free market theory. When one considers the cataclysmic changes to our way of life that are about to be forced upon us by our struggling planet, there is simply no "free" mechanism that exists to accommodate these changes. There is no competitive reason why any corporation should accept the additional costs of "greening" so long as their competitors do not do likewise. There is no free market in greening; it will have to be mandated and imposed on all to maintain the free market requirement of a level playing field.

Complicating the matter in the concrete industry is the enormous reluctance of engineers and standard setters to change what they know, from deep experience, is working well. It is especially inertial in an industry in which trouble and failure of construction may not appear for decades. Experts faced with this unmeasurable risk will accept responsibility only in that which has been absolutely proven by generations of use. In a world that no longer has the time for incremental changes over long periods, the revolutionary changes that will be required for our survival cannot come from within the industrial complex. Massive changes will have to be imposed, some with cataclysmic results, on major users of scarce resources.

Since big capital fights tooth and nail for its continued existence it will require big government to institute programs that will seriously ease the burdens on our planet. But big government is inherently dangerous to individual freedoms and comfort and choice. We live in extremely dangerous times as we try to deal with global warming on one hand and the equally scary restriction of individual rights on the other. Wal-Mart is the biggest among very big capital, but the egregious threat of Wal-Mart is that it is much more sophisticated in co-opting the fight against global warming. In the end, Wal-Mart may be the last great corporation betting with its money that its policies, so clearly self-serving, are green and for the good of society. In the end, the much trumpeted campaign to convince America that Wal-Mart is concerned about sustainability turns into a simple cost-cutting program, a process that Wal-Mart has brought to a high art. "What is good for Wal-Mart is what is good for America" seems to echo the claims of that other great corporation that lived and is presently dying by that declaration. Wal-Mart is much richer and infinitely more subtle than General Motors and will not so easily succumb.

· · · · ·

The great engines of economic life that, in a perfect world, are designed to rationalize and restrain exuberance in economic activity are government regulation and enlightened self-interest. Neither work except in the most searing and immediate of crises. In the past decade government regulation has been the tool of industry and the resulting legislation has been weak, short term, and, in the worst cases, voluntary. The problem of global warming, especially as applied to the concrete industry, remains unaddressed by either government or industry even when some easy and cheap, even in some cases cost-reducing, solutions are readily available.

The most glaring case in point is the inclusion of fly ash as a basic constituent of cement. Since fly ash has already been "clinkered" in the searing heat of burning coal, it can replace much of

the limestone used in Portland cement. As a background to the
use of fly ash the following is from Headwater Resources, a major
supplier of fly ash to the industry. These are clear and cogent and
cost-reducing arguments and yet, as we shall see, they are mostly
unheeded by designers, engineers, architects, and, most important, both state and federal regulatory agencies in America.

In making concrete, cement is mixed with water to create
the "glue" that holds strong aggregates together. Fly ash works in
tandem with cement in the production of concrete products.
Concrete containing fly ash is easier to work with because the tiny,
glassy beads create a lubricating effect that causes concrete to flow
and pump better, to fill forms more completely, and to do it all
using up to 10 percent less water. Because the tiny fly ash particles
fill microscopic spaces in the concrete, and because less water is
required, concrete using fly ash is denser and more durable. And
fly ash reacts chemically with lime that is given off by cement
hydration, creating more of the glue that holds concrete together.
That makes concrete containing fly ash stronger over time than
concrete made only with cement.

Because fly ash use displaces cement use, it also reduces the
need for cement production—a major energy user and source of
"greenhouse gas" emissions.

For every ton of cement manufactured, about 6.5 million
BTUs of energy are consumed. For every ton of cement manufactured, about one ton of carbon dioxide is released. Replacing that
ton of cement with fly ash would save enough electricity to power
the average American home for twenty-four days and reduce carbon dioxide emissions equal to two months' use of an automobile.

Experts estimate that cement production contributes to about
7 percent of carbon dioxide emissions from human sources. If all
the fly ash generated each year were used in producing concrete,
the reduction of carbon dioxide released because of decreased
cement production would be equivalent to eliminating 25 percent
of the world's vehicles.

Conserving landfill space is also an important consideration.
Every ton of coal combustion products that is used to improve
our nation's highways and buildings is a ton that is not deposited
in a landfill, saving the same amount of space that the average
American uses over 455 days.

In the face of the serious sustainability problems rushing
down on us, U.S. industry rarely uses more than 5 percent of fly
ash in all of the millions of tons of concrete poured each year.
Canada, for instance, starts at 50 percent of fly ash while we
continue to fill up valuable dump sites disposing of millions of

tons of a material that could instantly mitigate the burden of greenhouse gases on the planet.

On the cutting edge of research into concrete uses and production, there are scores of developments that hold the future promise of making our concrete industry sustainable. In the end, our inertia to make even easy changes does not speak well for our future.

The cement industry, by virtue of its size and because of its enormous output of CO_2, is asking, absent governmental regulation, to become the engine of its own reform. But the evidence is in that, because of the essential timidity of engineers and architects reinforcing the profound corporate resistance against replacement of capital, the industry has little chance of the timely and wrenching revolution in thinking and action that is demanded by the issue of global warming. The many expensive and highly professional research projects that the industry is underwriting have generated much understanding of the threat of CO_2. However, understanding the threat and moving to inconvenient action is the required step not yet taken in the year 2010.

Professor emeritus Bert Bolin of Stockholm University best defined our predicament in terms of both human and planetary inertia.

This inertia of the system also implies that a future change of the climate, induced as a result of human activities, would decline only slowly, even if emissions were suddenly stopped. This inertia is primarily due to the rather slow response of the global circulation of carbon to external disturbances and the great heat capacity of the world oceans. However, society does not either change quickly. A sudden decrease of the greenhouse gas emissions is not possible. The complex infrastructure of modern society and the inertia of social institutions and values also imply that changes cannot not brought about quickly. To replace the present global energy supply system, to almost 80 per cent is based on fossil fuels, by a non–carbon dioxide emitting system, will necessarily take time. In addition, mitigation efforts will hardly be more fully implemented and accordingly have an effect on the course of events, until a decade has gone by.

It is worth noting that it is thirteen years since a first resolution was passed in the United Nations General Assembly in 1987 on environment and development, on which occasion the need to address the issue of human-induced climate change was also recognized for the first time. Mitigation has not yet reduced the rate of increase of carbon dioxide in the atmosphere noticeably. Nor is it likely that the agreements reached in Kyoto by 2010 will have a detectable effect of increase during the first decade of the 21st century, even if the Protocol were fully implemented. Although a future human induced global climate change is recognized by almost all governments of the world, there is still considerable reluctance to take steps that mean a clear change of the present trend of increasing greenhouse gas emissions to the atmosphere.[1]

The cement industry is a perfect microcosm of the reluctant global response to warming. Self-serving and timid have been its responses. The terrifying possibility is that even if the cement industry, along with all human activities, were to put aside self-serving positions and concentrate on long-term solutions, it still might not be enough to prevent ultimate and deleterious changes in the relationship between man and nature.

Even so, this is a gamble with the future that, with odds stacked so fiercely against us, we cannot refuse to take.

HOPEFUL DEVELOPMENTS

There are three pathways to scientific progress. One is the accretion of knowledge through research that is slowly built upon the work of others. Second are the serendipitous accidents that are the unintended consequences of unrelated lines of research, such as the accidental discovery of penicillin. And third is the emergence, absent prior work, of minds so far afield of the norm that in their startling originality they can be thought of only as miraculous gifts.

Yet what gives the best hope that man will survive the repeated threats of a dangerous universe is the ability of science to race beyond itself when Hannibal is at the gate. In our own time, this unique talent of the human spirit emerged in the hothouse production of the atom bomb during World War II, when the world was in peril of regressing into barbarism. In a matter of months an unproved mathematical theory, held by a few researchers with fingers crossed, leaped from blackboard scribble to Hiroshima.

The cloud of global warming that hangs over us today is the most serious of all threats to the continuation of the human experiment. Science has many times pointed the way and provided the solution to serious existential threats over the past couple of centuries. We must now look to science once more for some hints of our future in a potentially too hot world.

The burning of carbon is the eventual end product of all human and natural activity. It is this profoundly central fact that we must address and alter, if we are to survive. The problem with burning carbon to provide us with all the interesting stuff we use is that the process is just too easy. Burn gasoline to get mobility. Burn wood to get charcoal. Burn coal to get energy. Burn carbon to get a panoply of useful, life-enhancing chemicals, and, what interests us here, burn limestone to get cement. We have lit fires all over the globe and fire, the cynical gift of Prometheus, consumes irreplaceable resources as it produces the stuff we have been taught to want. The fires we humans have lit are the fires that, unmitigated, will cook our planet.

Science has already defined the solutions for our need for electricity. France produces 80 percent of its energy needs by atomic burning, generating little deleterious effect on the atmosphere. Denmark's wind generators grind out 40 percent, and growing, of its energy needs. Two other areas of enormous consumption of carbon are individual transport demanded by our peripatetic society and the production and use of concrete.

An audacious solution, signaled by scientific research rising to this ultimate threat, is to replace carbon as the "cementing" element in concrete. On the surface this would seem like suggesting we eliminate water, or even air, from our environment. But in spite of the implausibility of the suggestion it is both theoretically and realistically possible.

The proposal that is the simplest and most immediate to install, at a very low cost, is to replace Portland cement, the ubiquitous glue of concrete, with epoxy. The advantages of epoxy-based concrete are evident. It uses little or no water, an increasingly scarce resource, and it creates minute quantities of CO_2 in its manufacture and no CO_2 in its curing process. It is relatively cheap, has been around a very long time, and its properties are well known. The opposition to eliminating Portland cement comes from the powerful and wealthy organizations whose entire capital structure would be challenged by such change. There would be an elimination of vast amounts of capital stock involved in the manufacture, the distribution, and the pouring of this new, non-greenhouse-gas concrete. There has been little enthusiasm noted so far for anything but incremental improvements in the use of Portland cement. Whatever "greening" there is being pushed by the industry at this time seems to be motivated more by cost savings than by savings in CO_2 production.

There are already dozens of formulations of epoxy-based polymer cements on the market. There are almost one hundred firms in the United States alone that sell polymer cements, but most of their products are designed for repair rather than for original construction. There is at least one formulation, Novalok Polymer Concrete, for which the manufacturer claims that the product is "castable for the chemical-resistant construction of sumps, dikes, containment areas, trenches, walls, floors, and structural support columns or bases. It has been specifically formulated for foundation construction and should be installed with proper reinforcement similar to Portland cement. Mixing and forming methods are also similar to those used for Portland cement installations."

With its potential for planet-saving reductions in CO_2, it is likely that polymer cements will be the construction material for the future thus completing an eonic circle that commenced with the Egyptians' use of polymer materials around 5000 BCE.

In 1981 a patent, #431826, was published describing a sulfur-based concrete. This material was produced at around 140 degrees Centigrade as compared with temperatures of around ten times that for the production of clinker for Portland cement. The saving in CO_2 production compared to the kilning of limestone is enormous. The chemistry has been carefully worked out and has been available for almost thirty years but it has engendered very little interest in the industry.

As has been shown NASA early recognized the logic of using *in situ* building materials for planned structures on the moon. Recognizing that the ultra-high temperatures required for kilning on a very cold lunar surface and the expensive importation of hydrogen, the search for an alternate to Portland cement led researchers to consider sulfur-based concrete. A study done at the Cassanova School of Civil Engineering, Barcelona, Spain, in the late 1990s refers to these problems.

> Although additional technological developments are necessary, the mechanical properties and thermo-chemical stability of cement-based materials make them a very promising candidate (among few) for lunar construction activities. On the other hand, it is clear that any progress on the establishment of a permanent lunar base is necessarily constrained by the availability of *in situ* resources. Major advances have been made in the design of process methods for the production of oxygen, cementitious materials and even water from the lunar regolith. Proper evaluation of natural resources is therefore a major task in the development of strategies for moonbase site selection. As far as raw materials for concrete are concerned, water is undoubtedly the most scarce resource. Even if the existence of ancient cometary ice deposits in the South Pole Aitken basin is confirmed by the Lunar Prospector mission in 1997, the location and abundance of such a resource cast serious doubt on the feasibility of using it as a construction material. *It is, therefore, difficult to envision mass production of conventional concrete in such a dry environment, and new options must be considered.* In this sense, a need arises to

find an alternative material or component to bind the solid ingredients of concrete and subsequently gain strength upon solidification. These criteria constrain the search to relatively abundant volatile substances, capable of undergoing solid-liquid phase transformations at low temperatures. In the lunar geochemical inventory, sulfur is probably the only suitable choice.

Both the epoxy and the sulfur solutions to the proliferation of greenhouse gases deal with familiar materials, of familiar mass and size, acting in predictably familiar ways. But there are investigations under way that are uncovering a vast physical universe that underlies what we understand as normal. These investigations are burrowing into nano engineering, a new science that deals with particles measured in billionths of an inch.

Startling anomalies and curious contradictions to long-held beliefs have been discovered concerning how concrete holds together. Things change fundamentally as we descend from normal ranges of measurement to the awesomely small.

What a group of MIT engineers has discovered about concrete is that its ability to agglomerate lies not in the unique characteristics of the materials used but, in nano size, in their unique organization. This planet-changing concept breaks through many of the problems and limitations of our chemistry-based industries but its potential impact on the global warming problem is enormous. A description of the research cannot be better described than in this report by Denise Brehm on the work of engineer and professor Franz-Josef Ulm of MIT.

One group of engineers at MIT decided to focus its work on the nano-structure of concrete, the world's most widely used material. The production of cement, the primary component of concrete, accounts for 5 to 10 percent of the world's total carbon dioxide emissions; the process is an important contributor to global warming.

In the January issue of the *Journal of the Mechanics and Physics of Solids*, the team reports that the source of concrete's strength and durability lies in the organization of its nanoparticles. The discovery could one day lead to a major reduction in carbon dioxide emissions during manufacturing.

"If everything depends on the organizational structure of the nanoparticles that make up concrete, rather than on the material itself, we can conceivably replace it with a material that has concrete's other characteristics—strength, durability, mass availability and low cost— but does not release so much CO_2 into the atmosphere during manufacture," said Professor Franz-Josef Ulm of civil and environmental engineering.

The work also shows that the study of very common materials at the nano scale has great potential for improving materials in ways we might not have conceived. Ulm refers to this work as the "identification of the geogenomic code of materials, the blueprint of a material's nanomechanical behavior."

Cement is manufactured at the rate of 2.35 billion tons per year, enough to produce 1 cubic meter of concrete for every person in the world. If engineers can reduce carbon dioxide emissions in the world's cement manufacturing by even 10 percent, that would accomplish one-fifth of the Kyoto Protocol's goal of a 5.2 percent reduction in total carbon dioxide emissions.

Ulm considers this a very real possibility. He and Georgios Constantinides, a postdoctoral researcher in materials science and engineering, studied the behavior of the nanostructure of cement. They found that at the nano level, cement particles organize naturally into the most densely packed structure possible for spherical objects, which is similar to a pyramid-shaped pile of oranges.

Cement, the oldest engineered construction material, dating back to the Roman Empire, starts out as limestone and clay that are crushed to a powder and heated to a very high temperature (1500 degrees Celsius) in a kiln. At this high temperature, the mineral undergoes a transformation, storing energy in the powder. When the powder is mixed with water, the energy is released into chemical bonds to form the elementary building block of cement, calcium-silicate-hydrate (C-S-H). At the micro level, C-S-H acts as a glue to bind sand and gravel together to create concrete. Most of the carbon dioxide emissions in this manufacturing process result from heating the kiln to a temperature high enough to transfer energy into the powder.

Ulm and Constantinides gathered a wide range of cement pastes from around the world, and, using a novel nano-indentation technique, poked and prodded the hardened cement paste with a nano-sized needle. An atomic force microscope allowed them to see the nanostructure and judge the strength of each paste by measuring indentations created by the needle, a technique that had been used before on homogenous materials, but not on a heterogeneous material like cement.

To their surprise, they discovered that the C-S-H behavior in all of the different cement pastes consistently displays a unique nanosignature, which they call the material's genomic code. This indicates that the strength of cement paste, and thus of concrete, does not lie in the specific mineral, but in the organization of that mineral as packed nanoparticles.

The C-S-H particles (each about five nanometers, or billionths of a meter, in diameter) have only two packing densities, one for particles placed randomly, say in a box, and another for those stacked symmetrically in a pyramid shape (like a grocer's pile of fruit). These correspond exactly to the mathematically proved highest packing densities allowed by nature for spherical objects: 63 and 74 percent, respectively. In other words, the MIT research shows that materials pack similarly even at the nano scale.

"The construction industry relies heavily on empirical data, but the physics and structure of cement were not well understood," said Constantinides. "Now that the nano-indentation equipment is becoming more widely available—in the late 1990s, there were only four or five machines in the world and now there are five at MIT alone—we can go from studying the mechanics of structures to the mechanics of material at this very small scale."

If the researchers can find—or nanoengineer—a different mineral to use in cement paste, one that has the same packing density but does not require the high temperatures during production, they could conceivably cut world carbon dioxide emissions by up to 10 percent. This aspect of the work is just beginning. Ulm estimates that it will take about five years, and says he's presently looking at magnesium as a possible replacement for the calcium in cement powder. "Magnesium is an earth metal, like calcium, but it is a waste material that people must pay to dispose of," he said.

He recently formed a research team with colleagues in physics, materials science and nuclear engineering to perform atomistic simulations, taking the work a step deeper into the structure of this ubiquitous material.[2]

The gist of the report indicates that the characteristics of materials that appear at a macro, human level of perception are only accidentally related to the combinations of the materials used. The conceptual leap that this represents is mind-boggling when applied to all sorts of chemical and physical industrial processes. When applied precisely to the specific threat of CO_2, it offers hope that we may still be able to rein in the warming of our planet. If we can somehow, as suggested by Professor Ulm, manipulate the "genetic code" of materials rather than their surface characteristics all sorts of solution pathways open up that go considerably beyond the greenhouse gas threat.

Nano engineering is the best hope, and possibly the only hope, for an earth in which our billions of people may continue in the future as they have in the recent past to live in relative comfort.

CHAPTER 13
LUNAR TRANSIT

At the opening of the sixteenth century, as Europe was discovering the new world, the entire population of the old world was a sparse few hundred million souls. The old world was, in modern terms, essentially unpolluted by people. England was a place of glades and glens and woodland and free-running rivers. Roads were much worse than those of Rome, mere tracks in primeval forests. Populations had coalesced around natural trade routes and navigable rivers, creating, among others, the population centers of London and Paris.

Thousand-year-old techniques, a plow often shaped in wood from the notch of a tree, water-driven mills, and horses and oxen, were technology enough to provide food and shelter for a thin and dispersed population. Emerging from the horror of the black death, life had become if not idyllic then a matter of relative ease and survival-rewarding habits.

When mariners hungry for the spices of the East accidentally blew open the new world, they found a vista of glens and glades and woodland and free-running rivers, an almost identical reflection empty of people of the places from which they sailed. Taking up life in this new world was not much more than extending old habits of survival into a land so seemingly familiar that the simple attachment of the word "New" to England and York and Jersey sufficed for identification. The transition into America was a smooth and continuous process that required no new techniques and little innovation. The expansion of Europe was a matter of growth, not discovery. The opening of America represented the last great frontier for Europeans and, since the lands of the new world were like the old, a seamless flow of population from old to new went unhindered by the need for essential changes in how the new immigrants lived.

Now it is five hundred years after the new frontier of America started to fill up. The last quarter of the twentieth century lent shape and meaning to the opening of the twenty-first. Two new frontiers unimagined a century back were postulated, the bottoms of the seas and the illimitable reaches of space. The bottoms of newly fathomed seas are now being opened in a glut of discovery. But for man, discovery without the possibility of further growth of habitation is merely a game. His drive for expansion of borders, go ye forth and conquer, lies deep in his cultural DNA.

Unless it becomes exigent, it is unlikely that we will ever populate the mountains and the valleys of the depths of oceans. We would need to take away the water, and to what end? While in space, the moon and Mars and other empty places yet undefined, we need only to add to what exists, a facility that humankind has raised to high art without always salubrious results.

Thus the moon, less in distance time than the crossing of the Atlantic in a sixteenth-century caravel, hangs out there teasing for population. Unlike the low-hanging fat plum of the new world, the moon does not allow many old habits to be carried over. How we would live on the moon, how we would shelter, how to feed ourselves, indeed where to find the very air each of us needs every five seconds, are serious obstacles for the intended moon men. New, novel, and imaginative solutions would be required. These are all untested fronts that require wrenching departure from established habits.

The earth has granted living things ten million years to reach an accommodation. We, and our biosphere, have interacted for millennia to bring us to the quality of life that defines and succors humankind today. The moon, in contrast, does not give us ten seconds to adjust. We are leaping into a dark abyss of experience and are required, even during the hurtling fall, to substitute instant invention and life-demeaning discomforts for the eons of evolution that slowly accustomed us to our life on earth.

Our moon is the prototypical blank slate upon which, if we obey its rules and uncover its secrets, mankind may write our future and possibly our very survival. We have the technology to re-create moon life merely in imitation of the imperfect life we lead on earth or, if we choose wisely, in a different way altogether that could, ultimately, be much better than the one with which we are now burdened.

In the 1980s, when the word "space" had become a place rather than the absence of place, early interest by the more hawkish among President Reagan's cohorts turned, not surprisingly, to its potential uses in warfare. Space became a place from which war could be waged rather than a place from which peace might be monitored, protected, and encouraged.

The war rooms of Washington invented a pressing need to neutralize a future threat, not yet aborning, of a missile attack from space. Reagan's solution was to posit an antimissile missile shield to protect us from enemy missiles from space. The technology1 required for such a "space war" defense attracted the attention of scientists worldwide, among whom one, Dr. Tung Dzu Lin, was eventually to alter the debate from warlike uses of space on earth to the peaceful uses of space on the moon.

Around 1970 NASA started to receive samples of moonstuff from the return probes named Zond. Prior to that, as early as Surveyor 1, in 1966, descriptions of lunar material were analyzed robotically and transmitted back to earth. This first stream of information concerning the geology of the moon allowed early engineers to take the leap from the makeup of lunar soil to its possible use for the construction of habitats.

The earliest serious discussions commenced with the American engineer of Chinese descent T. D. Lin. Dr. Lin did his work under the aegis of the American Concrete Institute, which demonstrates that bodies such as this institute are good for something other than self-serving lobbying.

The work of Dr. Lin was commenced on a horizon as far removed from practicality as the moon itself is removed from earth. His first conversations with colleagues date from 1984 and in 1987 he published his study entitled "Concrete for Lunar Base Construction." It is the first work in a field that Lin invented and, by some standards, had almost the last word. After Dr. Lin, "all the rest is commentary."

The premise that the use of rockets could raise material for construction of a lunar base was, patently, a nonstarter because of the high cost of exploding large quantities of heavy material aloft. Dr. Lin, extrapolating from the few ounces of moonstuff available, argued that if you wanted to build on the moon you must look to the moon itself for materials with which to build.

This is the way we build on earth. We dig up stuff, do things to it, and recast the results into habitations for earthmen. "The same," Lin explained, "must be done on the Moon. And since all of the elements of concrete are as readily available on the Moon as they are on Earth, then there can be no other path to construction on the Moon than by using existing Moon resources."

Lin started with the thought that what is at the end of a lunar shovel had to be similar to the elements of concrete on earth. His early researches proved that all of the elements save one, hydrogen, could be scraped off the lunar surface. His research also revealed that the complexity of turning lunar regolith, lunar dust, and other materials into a usable form was anything but a simple matter. It was this process that was detailed in a series of scholarly papers.

Lin's recollections of the early events that led him to thoughts of habitating the moon are an insight into the creative side of scientific methodology.

I did not shout "Lunar Concrete" as Archimedes shouted "Eureka." As a matter of fact, when I first spoke with colleagues about the idea of making concrete on the Moon, some said "Interesting," some asked "Are you crazy?" The following tells my story:

One of President Reagan's national policies in the early 1980s was to develop technologies to defend United States from intercontinental missile attacks, known as Star Wars, that attracted serious world attentions. If space war would become real, "wouldn't we need a space station capable of resisting the harmful cosmic and solar radiations including micro-meteoroids?" I asked myself then.

Perhaps, the academic studies for my Ph.D. dissertation that dealt with thermal stress analyses of a missile subjected to tremendous aero-dynamics during the re-entry into Earth atmosphere led me to an imaginative realization for a concrete space station. My laboratory experience also helped me with this respect.

My primary work at Construction Technology Laboratories of the Portland Cement Association involved heavily with fire tests of full scale concrete structural elements. Mixing and casting concrete were part of the routine exercise. The familiarity of sand, aggregate, and cement had led me to read published data on lunar materials with great interest. Surprisingly, I found a similarity between terrestrial and lunar materials, particularly of their chemical compositions.

Subsequently, a paper entitled "Concrete—Potential Construction Material for Orbiting Space Station" was presented at the University of California, in May, 1984. This paper enabled me to go after a dream of lunar concrete research. Eventually, NASA awarded me with 40 grams, the largest amount ever awarded to industrial sectors, of actual lunar soil in 1986. Hopefully, lunar concrete will pave a way for human civilization to reach the Moon and Mars in the foreseeable future.

Lin's Ph.D. dissertation dealt with the aerodynamic stresses encountered by missiles reentering the earth's atmosphere. As a researcher in the cement industry, he came to appreciate that, of all mankind's building materials, concrete had the highest resistance to thermal abuse and an equally high profile of resistance to solar and other radiations.

Putting all of this together it was but a short step to the concept of building a concrete station in space. But then Lin took the longest conceptual step of all. He reasoned that hauling concrete out of the clinging gravity of earth to create a concrete space station would be a Herculean task. Why not, he asked in a series of papers, make the concrete on the moon and, if needed for a space station, haul it into space against only one-sixth of the gravity of the earth.

When Lin conceived of building a space station out of moon-made concrete, peer opinions ranged from "interesting" to "crazy," more to the latter than the former. At this juncture Lin made the final, logical jump from thinking about a concrete space station to the much more exciting possibility of making moon concrete. He turned the debate upside down. That "aha" moment is poetically and portentously described by Dr. Lin himself: "One day in 1983 (I do not remember the date) I happened to watch the beautiful full moon in the night sky. The idea of making concrete using lunar *in situ* materials surfaced in my mind like a butterfly cocoon being pocked through. My argument is that concrete is an excellent material for high energy absorption, good for construction in space." Lin felt that the Japanese hospital building that was subjected to the atomic bomb explosion in 1945 and survived the blast and still stands in the Hiroshima Memorial Peace Park today is convincing evidence that it will be concrete, not some yet to be invented green cheese, that'll survive the empty blasts of cold and heat and radiation on the surface of the moon.

On March 6, 1986, Dr. Lin's dreams were carried forward as he took into his reverent hands a golf ball–sized lump of moon stuff. Lin, rational dreamer and tenacious advocate, was entrusted by the hard-minded engineers of NASA with a few grams of the moon, laboriously and expensively dug out of its surface. If the cost of the American space program was to come down to these precious few ounces, we can conceive of the preposterous idea that a single ounce of moon dust had cost the American people a billion very real dollars.

NASA does not lightly give up a billion dollars but its caution was swept away by the fantastical proposition that great cities on the moon could be built and would avoid the necessity of hauling ruinously expensive material from earth.

Hitherto, the only method of getting anything from the earth to the moon was by balancing it on top of an exploding projectile. These rockets that carried the early astronauts to the moon spent almost all of their mass on propellents and protection, leaving precious little for a payload. For all of the expenditure of dollars and materials, only a little more than eight hundred pounds of lunar soil ever was returned to the earth.

So intrigued were the leaders of NASA that, in Lin's case, they became prodigal of this precious hoard. Since the bucketful of moon soil had to suffice for thousands of researchers for possibly a hundred years, it was prescient that the largest amount granted by NASA to any researcher was the forty grams handed to Dr. Lin.

Lin, a religious man, an anomaly for a hard-headed scientific "prove it" guy, turned poetical. "It's heavenly stuff," he said. "How many people in the entire span of human existence have had the opportunity to touch heavenly stuff?"

From his acceptance remarks in which he paid homage to the support of his Winnetka Bible church and to the evangelical Taiwan church, it can be inferred the Dr. Lin might well have capitalized the word "Heavenly," a concept very real in his lexicon. "I pray," he said on that occasion, "that my work will glorify the name of Jesus Christ."

Dr. Lin also issued a series of far-reaching observations. "A lunar base will come into reality after the turn of the century, if," Lin said, "the federal government approves spending the money." Lin knew he had the technology. All that was required was a fraction of the wealth spent on recent wars.

And he added a remark that has become all too true in the ensuing decades. "The only thing the United States triumphs in is space technology. We cannot as a nation lose this most vital leading factor. God made such a nice orbiting space station for us. It's such a nice stepping stone for mankind to develop technology in space."

Now, as the century has turned, America's moral and political reputation lies in shambles. But, due in some part to the passions of men like Lin, we still "triumph" in space technology.

DR. T. D. LIN

COURTESY DR. T. D. LIN

ENGINEERS, THE INVISIBLE MEN

It would be a good bet that the reader could easily spin off the names of three or more great architects. It is also a good bet that not one in a hundred could recall even one name of a great engineer.

Art and necessity stand at opposite ends of the scale of physical survival. Art is primarily the medium of the architect but necessity is entirely the medium of the engineer.

There will be little energy or motive to expend precious resources that have no direct impact on pure survival. But it is the curious nature of mankind that the calculus of survival seems always to include "the conveyance of spirit."[2] So in spite of the cold logic of the lunar surface art will eventually spring from its own landscape.

As far as imagination can stretch, the preponderance of earth's physical contribution to the moon will be concrete. It follows then that concrete will likely become the matter that will convey spirit. A concrete house of man on the moon looming amid total isolation will surely become a lunar-like evocation of spirit.

The moon, absent a comforting blanket of atmosphere, is bombarded by solar winds, radiation, cosmic rays, and even harder stuff such a micrometeorites. These tiny, micromillimeter-sized pieces of space debris traveling at galactic speeds, and striking the lunar surface uninhibited by atmosphere, are a primary concern in lunar construction. Normal materials such as steel offer some protection from these hurtling projectiles but a suitable thickness of concrete, enhanced by layers of lunar soil, will provide adequate protection. Micrometeorites are fairly common but most would not get through the concrete barriers. For the few that might there could be self-sealing materials layered over the concrete.

Meteoroids, objects around five inches in diameter, bombard the naked moon with undiminished violence but their infrequency would provide less of a threat to potential moon men than do lightning strikes on earth. Meteoroids are a given risk for moon men but absent earthquakes, hurricanes, tornadoes, floods, eruptions, lightning, and other daily earthen confrontations, moon men will, on the average, be less in danger than we are on earth from her repeated violences. In all of the centuries during which we have been peering at the moon we have never witnessed a strike on the moon by an object in the range of the span of a man's hand.

Moon-mined aggregates in lunar concrete, both nonmetallic and nonorganic, are excellent materials for absorbing gamma ray energy. Captured water, which makes up five percent of hardened concrete, is the best substance for absorbing neutron energy. One thought is that the energy released by the impact of radiation on a concrete structure could provide some heat to the structure during the long and cold lunar nights.

LIN'S MOON HOUSE BUILDING ELEVATION AND BUILDING PLAN

IMAGES COURTESY DR. T. D. LIN

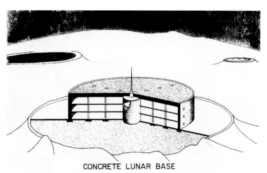

CONCRETE LUNAR BASE

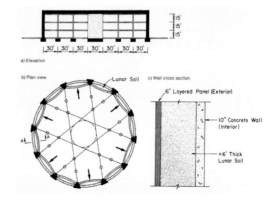

a) Elevation

b) Plan view   Lunar Soil   c) Wall cross section.

6" Layered Panel (Exterior)

10" Concrete Wall (Interior)

>6' Thick Lunar Soil

An important consideration in the use of concrete on the moon is that, of all of the possible building materials made on or hauled to the moon, concrete uses the least energy. This fact combined with the plans to build nuclear power plants on the moon yielding more than enough power for the foreseeable future adds to the inevitable conclusion that moon-made concrete is the only feasible solution to man's propagation into space.

One unique suggestion requires no man-made energy at all. Early man on earth was faced with the problem that the huge rocks that lay all around him were suited to neither his strength nor his needs. It did not take long, for one brighter than the next, to observe that cooking fires, when placed next to rocks, reduced huge to small, a vast improvement over banging two rocks together. It was a short step to rock breaking using fire, which has been the ubiquitous technique even as recently as the nineteenth century.

Because of the incessant and unfiltered raw sunlight that bathes the moon, its use has been suggested for breaking up lunar rocks.

Using direct solar power to break rock required for concrete construction would hugely reduce the cost of making concrete on the moon.

An incidental gift of low gravity is the ease of transport of very heavy stuff. The highest mass of material that would confront moon men would be the making, moving, and use of dense, heavy concrete. Much of the energy consumed on earth in concrete projects is simply moving the stuff around. On earth, engineers are on a constant search for ever lighter construction materials. The one-sixth gravity on the moon argues for ever

ROCK BREAKING (MATSUMOTO, YOSHIDA, AND TAKIGI)

COURTESY DR. T. D. LIN

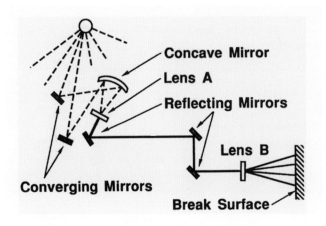

Concave Mirror

Lens A

Reflecting Mirrors

Lens B

Converging Mirrors

Break Surface

heavier construction. Concrete, in all of its myriad weights and forms, becomes the obvious material for all lunar construction.

Limestone, the quintessential material in the making of concrete, is the unintended gift of untold trillions of small marine fauna whose bodies built up layers of sediment on the bottoms of earth's many seas. Broken up, burned, and milled, it is the cement that converts aggregate to concrete. While cementitious material can be derived from other materials, limestone remains one of the most valuable gifts of Gaia.

Selene, however, makes no such prodigal gift. There were few or no oceans on the moon and it is yet to be shown that there were any small animals to populate them. Limestone, therefore, does not occur on the moon so we must seek less obvious sources for its cements.

T. D. Lin, writing in 1987,[3] observed that information brought back by early lunar explorations indicated that while limestone is absent there are many moon rocks that can produce cement. The essentials of cement are silicate, alumina, and calcium oxide, all of which, lunar research has shown, appear in most lunar rock. The stuff is there; the technologies exist and the production of moon concrete is a simply a matter of applying long-used processes to an endless supply of moon material.

Except for one enormous obstacle. There is little usable hydrogen on the moon and without hydrogen there is no water and without water there is no conventional concrete.

However, in the late 1980s, there had developed an intense interest in the chemical engineering community of the makeup of the lunar landscape. In a study (Agosto, 1984) that points the way toward the production of lunar concrete, a method was proposed that involved the hydrogen reduction of ilmenite. In lay terms this was a process by which water could be manufactured from lunar material with the addition of only one lightweight element from earth. With this magic little formula[4] the production of lunar concrete becomes a near reality, with only the importation of liquid hydrogen from earth.

Until technologies evolve, such as various proposals for waterless cement and nanotechnologies that will open a whole new waterless horizon, and finally cut the hydrogen umbilical with earth, this convenient chemistry will allow mankind to at least gain a foothold, tenuous and still dependent upon Gaia, on our closest neighbor.

EPILOGUE

Concrete rose in the chronological highlands of Egypt and flowed down through millennia and spread out onto the floodplains of the twentieth century. Natural concretions existed in caves and caverns from the beginning of time and will exist in myriad forms as long as anything exists on earth.

It is the essential primeval material, nature's own construction material, of which we are only now beginning to appreciate its milliard uses. Concrete, in forms not yet conceived, will carry us to the profoundest depths of the oceans and to the moon and beyond. Under new guises it will play an ever increasing part in the restoration of a survivable ecological balance to our damaged earth.

We will have concrete that you can see through and concrete that sucks acid rain from the air we breathe. Concrete is already in use in which thin plastic strands, almost weightless, replace heavy iron rebars that suck up so much energy to produce.

We will have computer-driven machines that will, untouched by the hands of men, pour concrete to form and build structures of any shapes and any sizes that we can twist out of our fecund imaginings. These machines, 3D printers using concrete as ink, will be able to completely construct a one-story, two-thousand-square-foot home on site, in one day and without using human hands, a process that will, at the same time, eliminate almost one quarter of the solid waste stream in the United States created by the construction industry. These concrete homes will contain our heat and keep us cool and whose roofs and sides will be coated with a concrete that directly converts sunlight to power.

These same three-dimensional copying machines, guided by X-ray and CT scan data, are already replicating human bones that have been destroyed or eaten by disease. Strong, lightweight, and porous, the "printed" bones have characteristics similar to natural bone and, because they are tailored to fit exactly where they need to go, they are quick to integrate with the surrounding bone. The printed bone is also designed to be resorbed by the body as the surrounding bone slowly grows into and replaces it.

In a like manner, computer-driven contour copying machines will be able to build complete plastic body shells for the light-weight cars of the future and for almost any consumable or industrial object that is in use today.

We will have concrete roads and parking lots that refill our aquifers and filter polluted rainwater directly back to the earth. We already have concrete materials that can stabilize toxic wastes into nontoxic solids and prevent the leaching of poisons into our water supply.

We will have concrete made of paper and concrete made of Styrofoam and concrete made of shredded tires. We will have soft concrete furniture to sit upon and concrete canvas that, with the addition of water, self-inflates into instant shelters. We will adorn ourselves with concretions around our necks and hands, wearing concrete as proudly as we now wear diamonds.

We will have concrete that heals itself by self-sealing cracks and concrete that senses problems and radios us when things are about to go badly. We are beginning to enlist microbes to agglomerate loose sand into a paradigm concrete that promises to halt earth and mud avalanches and, perhaps some time in the future, can be trained to do the same for snow.

We already have the beginnings of concrete that transmits light, thus altering our relationship of windows to walls and a soft and friable concrete that mires and halts huge jet aircrafts that overrun the end of runways.

Our engineers will build the great dikes that will keep the oceans at bay until we can suck the carbon out of the air. Concrete will be our ecological lifeboat while we labor to re-form the glistening coats of the polar antipodes and recap the icy carapace of Greenland.

At the other end of the scale our nanoengineers, dealing in billionths of a meter, are discovering that the concrete we see and feel is not a product of the chemical characteristics of the materials that go into it. Scientists have found that the source of concrete's strength and durability lies in the organization of its nanoparticles and that it would be possible to significantly cut world carbon dioxide emissions within five years by replacing present materials that depend on oxidation to achieve the crystallization that causes contemporary concrete to adhere.

All that is catalogued here is already on the shelves of our warehouses or in the warehouses of the minds of our engineers and chemists. These are not miracles. These are hard stones already abuilding.

APPENDICES

Mercer

In the world of concrete in the twentieth century, there were two men who recognized the implications of the new concrete technology. The two men could not have been more different as personalities and in their approach to their work. Both made breathtaking contributions to the developing history of concrete, which contributions, ironically, were stillborn. Both men in their very earliest constructions were so far ahead of their time that the builders of concrete could not digest their work. It would take two generations of engineers before the seminal work of Henry Chapman Mercer and Thomas Alva Edison was recognized and carried forward.

Henry Chapman Mercer's work was a marriage of art and craft born out of the passion that drives some folk to undertake the impossible. He was born of solid Quaker stock in Bucks County, Pennsylvania, in 1856. The family was well-to-do and the young man was educated to the best of his time. He was sent to private schools and eventually took an AB degree at Harvard, reading in law but concentrating most of his studies in history.

He had that best of relatives, an adoring aunt of considerable means. His Aunt El, Elizabeth Mercer Chapman, was something of a bon vivant whose husband had been appointed the American ambassador to Italy by Abraham Lincoln.

She took upon herself the job of carrying forward the education of Henry by taking him along on her many tours of Europe. At that time, around 1875, touring in Europe for a young American was at the very farthest end of anticipation and Mercer returned with two souvenirs that were to indelibly limn his life, a deep passion for the baronial architecture of Germany and a case of gonorrhea from which he suffered for the rest of his life.

The disease forced him into a bachelor's existence as this fastidious and aristocratic man would not allow a wife to be exposed to the disease. He remained celibate and sublimated the passions of sex into other fields. It is interesting to toy with the notion that the gonorrhea, which turned him from the normalcy and constraints of marriage, unleashed the wild fancies for which he is remembered—his home, Fonthill, and the great Mercer Museum,

The disease "desocialized" Mercer and, without the strictures of the Victorian society into which he had been born and with the aid of a 1907 bequest from Aunt El, he was "free to do foolish things."

Why would a man, untrained in architecture and in engineering, decide to build three startling structures using an untried and novel method of construction. The answer lies in the four threads of his life that inevitably came together in what have been called "American architectural treasures": his love of castles, his interest in archaeology, his early involvement in the maga-

zine *Cement Age*, and his dismay at the passing of the ingenious mechanical solutions of the preindustrial age.

Mercer was, first and foremost, a conservator. When he built Fonthill, a concrete home of some forty rooms, he encased within its walls a cottage built in 1740 on the site. The cottage remains at the core of Fonthill. Unwilling to destroy this palpable tie with the past he actually poured concrete around and over it to form three large arches that support the roof of the later construction. Shuttered windows, an original door, and one stone wall of the cottage remain visible. Mercer could not let old and, to his eye, beautiful things die.

In the same spirit he began to collect examples of how Americans of preceding centuries, using the most primitive of tools and machinery, solved the problems of daily living. Indeed, what is now the Mercer Museum grew out of Mercer's need to create a repository for the mostly common wooden objects that he collected. Since an uncle had lost an irreplaceable collection of art objects to fire, Mercer began to investigate the fireproof qualities of concrete and it was for him a short step from thought to actuality.

Even before the concept was invented in our own time, Mercer had originated the science of neo archaeology, the preservation of objects of the immediate past. The great concrete museum that rose out of the rolling hills of Bucks County was dedicated to that process and stands today as one of the very few repositories of the tools with which frontier America was built. Mercer was obsessed with how so much technology becomes so quickly obsolete. He was the first to recognize that there was a wealth of history in the so-called junk that was rapidly accumulating as a result of the swift industrialization of America. He began "rummaging bake ovens, wagon houses, cellars, hay lofts, smoke houses, garrets and chimney corners" for cast-off artifacts of the eighteenth and nineteenth centuries.

Mercer's prescient concern for rapid obsolescence is only today coming into focus as we, in the opening years of the twenty-first century, risk losing much of our history to the fact that technologies made obsolete describe the very essence of the years in which they flourished. Early computers, much software, and an enormous amount of stored data are not now easily available to us as changes in our technologies overlap themselves. Floppy discs, widespread only a few years ago, today lack the ubiquitous machines that made the data they hold available. What Mercer instinctively recognized is that the essential continuity, so important to understanding our past, was being increasingly lost with each succeeding wave of technological "improvements."

The Mercer Museum was among the first examples of poured concrete structures in America. But while others may have been a bit earlier or a bit more architecturally refined, none rivaled the sheer audacity of its conception. Soaring six stories it now accommodates and protects more than forty thousand objects in its fifty-five galleries.

The enormous structure was built by Mercer himself as designer and supervisor and eight laborers assisted only by a patient horse named Lucy. The concrete was hand mixed in pails and carried aloft by a

MERCER AND FONTHILL MUSEUMS, DOYLESTOWN, PENNSYLVANIA
PHOTOGRAPH REESE PALLEY

simple pulley powered by Lucy. The great pillars and arches that surround the six-story central atrium were formed by wooden slats bound together with wire into which concrete was poured. The hand mixing was not always perfect and much variation can be seen in the surfaces. But the structure was obviously well conceived and constructed. It has lasted, with little attention, for a hundred years.

The museum had one feature that had rarely appeared in a public structure up to that time. It contains a sloping six-story-high ramp that wound gently around the scores of exhibition alcoves. The intention was to make the viewing of the objects an easy downward stroll. Half a century later Frank Lloyd Wright incorporated a similar ramp that wound around the interior of the Guggenheim Museum,[1] a doff of his architectural hat to Mercer's ingenuity.

There is a brutal logic to the building that is expressed in every unfinished surface and in the naked clarity of its seeming accidental engineering. Mercer was flying by

the seat of his pants and, had he been a better-trained engineer or more knowledgeable about the novel material with which he was experimenting, the job would likely never have been started.

As important to the history of concrete as this building is, Mercer's contribution to the salvation of the handworks of history is, perhaps, more important. In predicting, against all logic, that the contents of his museum would be "worth its weight in gold a hundred years hence," he argued his view of history thus.

You may go down into Independence Hall in Philadelphia, and stand in the room in which the Declaration of Independence was signed and there look up at the portraits of the signers. But do you think that you are nearer to the essence of the matter than you are here [in the Museum] when you realize that ten hundred thousand arms, seizing upon axes of this type, with an immense amount of labor and effort made it worthwhile to have a Declaration of Independence by cutting down one of the greatest forests in the North Temperate Zone. You may go hear a lecture on the War of 1812...but do you think that you are more vividly confronted with the truth of the whole story than when you are here when you realize, looking at those spinning-wheels, that once upon a time here was a vast noise of humming from the work of ten hundred thousand women at least, spinning upon those wheels... to make it possible for men to be adequately protected from the cold so that they could go out and fight any battles at all by sea or by land... Perhaps these things can be adequately described by history but a sight of the actual object conveys an impression, otherwise indescribable[2]

In the years between 1900 and 1916 Mercer completed three construction projects involving poured concrete, besides the museum, he built Fonthill, a forty-two-room castellated home that, in architecture, lies somewhere between the Monrovian castles of which he was so fond and a French château. Lacking the stonemasons of the century past, and the money that it would have cost to closely replicate his dreams, he found that poured concrete was both within his means and sufficiently approximated the European originals to satisfy him. The seven-thousand-ton six-story museum was built for under $40,000 and completed in less than three years. To hew, haul, and fit mined natural stone would likely have cost ten times that sum and many more years even if Mercer had been able to find the skilled workmen needed.

What sketches survive of Mercer's conception of his house are mere hen scratches on note paper drawn as he sat with his workmen in the midst of construction. He had built a solid clay model that gave some sense of its outward appearance but not a hint of scale or loads or bearing surfaces or any of the prefiguring that keep buildings from falling down. Fonthill and the Mercer Museum,[3] built to instinct

rather than to science, never did and perhaps never will fall down. The concrete will, decade after decade, continue to harden.

[1] Shortly before the Guggenheim was built Wright redesigned an old building in San Francisco that recalled the Mercer Museum. The reconstruction was designed for the Morris Jewelry firm and fell into disrepair until it was brought back to its original condition in the sixties by the Reese Palley Galleries. Its central feature, as in the Mercer Museum, was a winding ramp surrounding a central atrium that ran from the bottom floor to just under the ceiling. Curiously, for neither the Morris building nor the Mercer Museum were there ever any formal architectural drawings made.

[2] *The Mercer Mile*, Bucks County Historical Society, Doylestown, Penn., 1998.

[3] The third of Mercer's concrete buildings was the Monrovian Pottery and Tile Works. One story high and built to actual use rather than fancy, the works add a commercial cant to the legacy of Henry Mercer.

APPENDIX II
Roman Underwater

University of Colorado at Boulder history professor Robert Hohlfelder, an internationally known underwater archaeologist, has said scholars have long been in awe of the engineering feats of the early Romans. A former codirector of the international Caesarea Ancient Harbor Excavation Project, he said the research effort was spurred by the stunning hydraulic concrete efforts undertaken at Caesarea Harbor in present-day Israel and elsewhere in the Mediterranean before the time of Christ.

Hohlfelder, who teamed up on the project with London architect and archaeologist Christopher Brandon

and Greek and Roman studies professor John Peter Oleson of Canada's University of Victoria, also said the writings of the ancient Roman Vitruvius provided a key starting point. Vitruvius published ten books on architecture circa 25 BC describing the building and engineering methods practiced during the Roman empire, including ancient harbor construction. "The writings of Vitruvius are a window on the engineering efforts of ancient Romans," said Hohlfelder. "But we still had a number of questions about the use of ancient hydraulic concrete, and felt the only way to answer them was to attempt our own project based on what the ancients did and the materials they used."

The three researchers formed the Roman Maritime Concrete Structure Study, or ROMACONS, in 2002, and began collecting and testing hydraulic concrete cores from early Roman structures around the Mediterranean region. In addition to analyzing the composition and strength of different cores, they also were able to trace raw materials to specific Mediterranean sources with the help of CU–Boulder geology professor Charles Stern, illuminating ancient trading patterns.

Vitruvius explained how to build the wooden forms for underwater concrete structures, but he did not specify how they were anchored to the seafloor, how the mortar was poured, how aggregate materials such as stone chunks were added, or how long it took the concrete to cure.

In 2004 the team obtained a study site through the Italcementi Group, an Italian concrete company with a marine testing station in the harbor of Brindisi, Italy, to build a freestanding concrete pier, or "pila" —a common feature in ancient Roman harbors. They designed the pila to be small, about two meters on a side and two meters high, reaching just above the water's surface at high tide.

In September 2004 the team drove wooden planks into the submerged seafloor to make the forms, which were reinforced with horizontal beams to form a box. "We had seen impressions of these vertical wooden planks in Roman concrete, and wondered if the cracks between planks had to be caulked to prevent concrete leakage," Hohlfelder said. "But the thick mix they used may have made this unnecessary."

They used the Roman recipe for concrete passed down by Vitruvius. It included seawater, lime and sand (pozzolana), and chunks of volcanic rock from the Bay of Naples— the same source for material used in ancient construction efforts at Caesarea and elsewhere in the region. The lime powder combined with sand and water made up the mortar, which would bind the aggregate into a solid mass of concrete.

Individual loads of the mortar were plopped into the form by the team using a wicker basket rigged with a "trip line" modeled after ancient Roman illustrations of construction scenes with similar baskets and from actual artifacts recovered by archaeologists from an ancient shipwreck site near Pisa. The team used hand tools to tamp the aggregate into the mortar as the structure slowly rose from the seafloor.

The three men finished the pila in September 2004 after using thirteen tons of raw material and expending 273 work hours, capping the top with paving stones in the manner of the early Romans. "We believe this is the first structure built with these materials and techniques in at least sixteen hundred years," said Hohlfelder. The team will extract cores from the pila and analyze them to assess the underwater curing rate of the concrete.

"We think we have a better idea now about what went on day-to-day when Caesarea Harbor and other ports in the Mediterranean were being constructed," Hohlfelder said.

Hohlfelder has studied ancient shipwreck remains off Cyprus, Greece, and Israel and ten ancient harbors—including the submerged town of Aperlæ in present-day Turkey —during his academic career at the University of Colorado at Boulder.

The hundred-acre Caesarea Harbor, the world's first port constructed in the open sea, is considered one of the most innovative and successful engineering feats of the ancient world. Framed by two artificial breakwaters and containing a lighthouse, towers, and warehouses that served ships throughout the Mediterranean for more than twelve hundred years, the harbor was completed about 15 BCE.[4]

[4] Originated from a press release and posted on the Internet, May 4, 2008, by David Meadows

APPENDIX III

David Moore

The author's first step in starting to think about *A Seven-Thousand-Year History of Concrete* was to ask our Internet search engines to respond to the inquiry "concrete." The search reported that 16,500,000 references were found. (Two years later the number had grown to 171,000,000.) This both encouraged and discouraged the writer in pursuing the project. I was intmidated by the sheer volume of available information and, at the same time, uplifted by the breadth, and thus the implied importance, of concrete in the history of cultures.

On the assumption, imperfectly arrived at, that the Romans would surely have something to say about concrete, I typed in "Roman concrete." The Internet reported "only"

13,200 entries, a number that was at least conceivable if not manageable. The first two references were works by David Moore and most other of the initial references contained material about or by David Moore.

When Maimonides was asked to discourse on the Old Testament his answer was, "Treat thy neighbor as thyself and all the rest is commentary." This is the way it is with regard to Roman concrete—"Read Moore and all the rest is commentary."

I immediately searched for his book *The Pantheon: The Triumph of Concrete* in the usual book searches on the Web and discovered to my surprise that this important book on the history of concrete was nowhere to be found.

It was not until much later, when I ran across an obscure interview with David Moore by Stephan Miller of *Constructor* magazine (September 2002), that I learned Moore had decommercialized the work by self-publishing it. The result was that, seeing no profit, there was no commercial distribution of the book. And thereby hangs a tale.

David Moore retired after a forty-year career as an engineer and was on his way to Saudi Arabia for a post-career appointment when he made his life-changing error of stopping in Rome. A quick visit to the Pantheon whetted his appetite for some explanation as to why this curious construct has lasted eighteen hundred years. He searched for answers and found almost no convincing literature on why Roman concrete was able to accomplish that which we moderns were seemingly incapable.

Ten years later, after correcting the translations of contemporary writings of Vitruvius and Pliny, Moore completed his volume on the Pantheon, which has definitively answered the questions of how the Pantheon was built as well as why the concrete used has lasted all these centuries.

He asked a nephew who runs an office supply firm in Pindale, Wyoming, to publish it at the nephew's cost. Moore would take no royalties. The problem with self-published books is the lack of a distribution mechanism. At this point, John Moore, engineer and photographer and the son of David, created a Web site and the book has become available to all. I responded to a link that advised "buy this book" and discovered that it was still available at the most welcome low price of $25.

That is where research for this volume commenced and, in return, I would like to dedicate the chapter on Roman concrete to the modest and unassuming family Moore. *"Altissima quaeque flumina minimo sono labi."**

*Still water runs deep.

The Builders of Eddystone

Eddystone Rocks

"The fury of the sea is the least thing our sailors fear: Keep them but from a Lee Shore, or touching upon a Sand, they'll venture all the rest."

—Daniel Defoe, *The Storm* (1704)

Sailors know that they are more safe a thousand miles at sea than they are a thousand feet from a harbor.

In the deep oceans in which dangerous seas flatten out into enormous but gentle hills, a well-found vessel will ride up one side and down the other hardly noticing the seismic events over which it is sailing. There is little danger from waves in deep water where there is both no bottom to drag the seas into breaking crests or toothy rocks to tear out botttoms.

The danger is ever and always the proximity of land, especially in those shallowing approaches where the mariner is attempting a landfall into a safe haven. Until our present microsecond of historical time, when geopositioning by satellites has provided clear pathways into the world's ports, a landfall, after a stately passage across blue water, was a time of deep concern bordering too many times on outright terror.

By the sixteenth century the locations of deadly rocks and reefs were well known to mariners, but the location of their vessels in relation to these dangers was a matter mostly of hard learned art and shipmasterly guesswork.

Darkness was the ultimate enemy of an inward-bound vessel. In daylight, if the winds were kindly for sailing vessels, shallows and reefs known from the deep experience of knowledgeable skippers could be avoided. At night the mariner was a blind man groping and guessing at the edge of a cliff.

From early times, when occasional bonfires would hint at a harbor, a light on shore if it could be identified was the only true indictor of a ship's position. When these lights were moved outward and set upon the dangers to shipping that surrounded safe harbors, lighthouses, warning of specific dangers, sprang up along treacherous coasts.

In the third century BC, Ptolemy II built on the little island of Pharos one of the earliest permanent lighthouses. The Pharos lighthouse became the progenitor of all the tall structures subsequently built to hold a welcoming flame. Some of these were relatively easy to build on good hard rock mounted either at sea level or on the high promontories of capes. But to protect against the occasional reef and rock that rose far out at sea, construction was profoundly more difficult.

Perhaps the most killing and toilsome danger to mariners in all of Europe is the Eddystone reef.

The Eddystone Rocks lie fourteen miles south-southwest of Plymouth harbor and 10 miles due south of Rame Head. It is dead center in the great bay of England's most dangerpous coast. Fifteen hundred wrecks lie east and west of Rame Head, many, if not most, caught on the jagged teeth of Eddystone or wrecked in desperate and blind efforts to avoid them.

At high tide and in a calm sea only two rocks are visable but disappear with even a modest swell from a distant storm. A dangerous crown of small sabertoothed rocks that surround them lies normally beneath the sea and emerges only at low tide.

"Eddystone," Adam Hart-Davis said, "was a perfectly placed peril" with which sailors played an endless game of approach and avoidance. With an equally dangerous French coast to the south and inhospitable Devon to the east and west, sailing vessels were hard put to find a safe passage.

Our own Pilgrim fathers setting out from Plymouth in 1620 were well aware of its threat. In the *Mayflower*'s log, the captain noted: "a wicked reef of twenty three rust-red rocks lying nine and one half miles south of Rame head on the Devon mainland, great ragged stones around which the sea constantly eddies, a great danger to all ships hereabouts, for they sit astride of this harbour and are exposed to the full force of the westerly winds and must always be dreaded by mariners. Leaving Plymouth, we managed to avoid this reef but ships making harbour must stand well to the south and this is difficult in stormy weather, for if any vessel makes too far to the southas likely as not she will be caught in the prevailing strong current and swept to her doom on those evil rocks."

Note that the captain speaks of the dangerous "eddies" ever present around the reef; hence the name Eddystone.

Early lighthouses, even those in the most industrialized countries, were lighted by burning candles. The first three of the Eddystone lights, by Winstanley, Rudyard and Smeaton, on the Eddystone Rocks, were also all lit by fire.

Prior to 1815, when Parliament began to look into the payment of fees or tolls by shipping, the private builders of lighthouses were empowered to extract a fee from passing ships. After 1815 most ligh-houses in England were supported by a fee, based on tonnage, which was collected by docking vessels. This fee was directed either to the commisoners of the port or to an arrangment with a private entre-peneur who had been granted, or who had purchased, the right to construct a lighthouse.

As early as 1665 the Admiralty was petitioned to erect lighthouses on the southern and southwestern coasts of England. At that time the coasts were entirely unlit, and while the Admiralty agreed that lights were needed and offered permis-sions to construct them lighthouses failed to attract builders due to the niggardliness of the fees that could be collected. In 1692 an applicant named Whitfield sought permission to build on Eddystone Rocks but withdrew when he realized it might take decades, if ever, to recoup his investment.

The task fell ultimately to a shipowner who, in 1695, as the telling goes, was having a drink at a pub on the waterfront when two shipwrecked sailors approached him with bad news.

> Then stepped two mariners down
>   the street
> With looks of grief and fear:
> "Now if Winstanley be your name,
> We bring you evil cheer."

The "evil cheer" was the news that the second of Henry Winstanley's ships, the *Constant*, had been wrecked on Eddystone. Earlier that same year his other vessel, *Snowdrop*, had been lost wth her entire crew of sixty.

> "I will take horse," Winstanley said,
> "And see this deadly rock."

See it he did and, in search of fame and fortune and mired in ignorance and inexperience, he set out to build the first lighthouse ever to be situated on Eddysone Rocks. Commenting on Winstanley's hubris, Adam Hart-Davis said, "Had Winstanley known anything at all, in practical terms, about lighthouses, about rocks or about storms at sea, he would surely never have tried to satisfy his craving for fame by dab-bling in such dangerous difficulties."

Perhaps that is too harsh a judg-ment for the brave, adventuresome, and sometimes wildly impractical entrepeneurs of the eighteenth century. For without those men rushing blindly into activities for which there simply was no previous experience, the "wonderful century" could never have aspired to, and reached, its stars.

The first of the four Eddystone navigational lights, all built by private contracters, was undertaken for profit by the least likely of candi-dates, this businessman who, it is reported, loved fantasy, showman-ship, and practical jokes. Henry Winstanley whose antics and person-ality defined him as the prototypical English eccentric came at the proj-ect from anger at his lost ships and from the desire to attract the atten-tion of Charles II, who had declared the need for a light on Eddystone. In the events that transpired, Winstanley was to pay dearly for his cockiness and his conceit.

Henry Winstanley was neither architect nor engineer. He was an engraver, gadgeteer, inventor, and illusionist. In the days when all architectural plans were engraved by hand, perhaps his interest in matters architectural led him to envision himself as an enginneer. In the early eighteenth century a man's trade was generally that which he called himself.

Winstanley made his first for-tunes from operating an odd theater in Piccadilly called Winstanley's Waterworkes, where, for a small sum, patrons were treated to a wild combination of fireworks, fountains, and illusions. He did well enough at this venture to buy and equip two ships to take part in the expanding sea trade that was changing Europe.

As luck, and history, would have it, when Winstanley lost his first two ships on Eddystone Rocks, he decided that something had to be done and he was the man to do it. He convinced the Admiralty that his homemade plans were the answer to the shipwrecks. The Admiralty agreed and Winstanley went to work.

The task was daunting as the following passage makes clear.

> Given the extraordinary technological sophistication of modern times, it takes a leap of imagination to appreci-ate the scale of the problems faced by Henry Winstanley when he began work on the first Eddystone Light— a building of his own design—in the summer of 1696. To begin with, he was no architect. He was in the light-house business for one reason only: Two of his ships had been wrecked on the Eddystone and he was determined to lose no more.
>
> His first problem was the reef itself. Of all the rocks in its three jagged

ridges, the only one high enough to remain exposed at high tide, and which might serve as a base for a tower, was the dauntingly small and of the wrong shape. It stuck out of the water like a right-angled triangle. Barely ten paces wide at its broadest, it sloped into the sea at an angle of 30. It was hardly the ideal foundation for a tower. Then there was the difficulty of getting small sailing vessels loaded with heavy stone blocks, supplies and workmen to and from the Eddystone on a regular basis. In 1696 this was a major operation in itself, without then having to find a way to land them on that sloping, sea-swept rock to build a tower.

Add to this the limited working time available (about three hours each tide), the absolute requirement for perfect weather, notoriously absent in the Channel, the lack of any power other than human backs force, the fact that nothing could be left on the rock between working sessions unless permanently secured, and the lack of anything resembling quick-drying waterproof cement, and one begins to appreciate just a few of the difficulties involved.

Despite this, it took Winstanley only three working seasons to construct a 1om tower, which first showed a light on 14 November 1698. Strengthened and almost doubled in height the following year, this lighthouse turned the Eddystone into a wreck-free zone for the first time in its history. It was the 17th century equivalent of putting a man on the moon or building the Channel tunnel.*

To add to his woes, and as he was supervising the initial founda- tion, French privateers who roamed the waters of the English coast dis- covered him at work. They kidnapped him and his workmen, held them hostage, and destroyed all that had been so far built. The Admiralty negotiated his release and he went promptly back to work.

Winstanley was a playful man. He was addicted to practical jokes and he once built a chair in which

the unknowing victim was suddenly imprisoned and shot backward out a window. The light, Winstanley's Tower, as it came to be known, has the appearance of a practical joke itself. It was strange and unexpected, a piece of rococo planted in the middle of an empty sea. Hung about with hoists, flying his personal emblem and the flags of England, it looks more like fantasy than fact. Inside, Winstanley had constructed for himself a luxurious parlor in which he entertained friends who were brave enough to make the treacherous transfer from the sea to his tower.

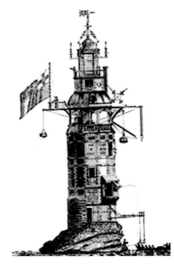

**THE WINSTANLEY LIGHT
1698-1703**

Winstanley, arrogant, self- assured, and flamboyant, boasted that it was his one wish to be in his famous lighthouse during "the greatest storm that ever was."

In a merciless twist of fate his wish was granted. On the night of November 26, 1703, just five years after the light was completed, Winstanley against the advice of local fishermen, who did not like the look of the weather, was in his light- house supervising repair work when

the south of England was devastated by a dreadful tempest.

When dawn broke the next day the Winstanley light and Winstanley himself had been swept out to sea in a storm that also took eight thou- sand English lives.

For five years before the Great Storm of November 1703, there hadn't been a shipwreck at the Rocks, well protected as they were by the Winstanley Tower. But only two days passed after the destruction of the light before the Eddystone Rocks claimed their first victim in half a decade. Sailing home from the sea the merchantman, *Winchelsea* piled up on the unlighted rocks and sank. There were only two survivors.

*Museum of Diving and Underwater Exploration.

The Second Eddystone Light

John Rudyard's lighthouse on Eddystone Rocks was built in 1709, shortly after Winstanley and his lighthouse were blown out to sea. Rudyard, one of those accomplished Englishmen who managed to be more renaissance than specialist, was born to a dismaying family of thieves and wantons in Cornwall on the south coast of England. His siblings and relatives were described by their own pastor as "a worthless set of ragged beggers whom almost nobody would employ, on account of the bad ness of their character."

Young John, the lone white sheep of the family, suffered endless abuse by a brutish father and bully- ing brothers because, for whatever reasons and from where ever he got the strength, he refused to take part in their illegal activities. Penniless, he ran away to Plymouth, preferring to face penury and loneliness to the ill treatment of his family.

In a Horatio Alger scenario the ragged and penniles street urchin was hired as a domestic servant by a man who sensed that Rudyard was more than he seemed at the surface. He was schooled by his employer, a condition reserved at the time by the children of the rich. His mentor, uncharacteristically for the time, set him up in his own business.

His moral character, ability, and personality led him to succeed as a silk merchant on Ludgate Hill in London. It was an astounding bootstrap effort (with a little help from his friend). It was because of this same concatenation of good qualities that, when Winstanley's lighthouse was swept to sea, Rudyard was able to attract the attention of one Captain John Lovett, who had obtained a patent charter for Eddystone Rocks. Captain Lovett, through an act of Parliament, was given a ninety-nine-year lease, which included a clause that permitted him to charge a penny per ton of all shipping that proceeded both inward and outward from the Cornwall. With the penny as an incentive Lovett, a man with no engineering training, hired Rudyard, who had even fewer professional qualifications, to design a new lighthouse.

Rudyard hired two experienced shiprights from the Admiralty and, betwen the three of them, designed and built on the premise that a lighthouse should be most like a boat in its relationship to the sea. As a result, Rudyard designed a tower much like a vertical hull. The resulting tower, built of "good Devon oak," stood guard over shipping for forty-seven years and, if it had not burned down in 1755, might be standing still.

The lanterns of all lighthouses at this time were lit by candle fire. The Rudyard tower was wood made waterproof with pitch, the same method of waterproofing used by

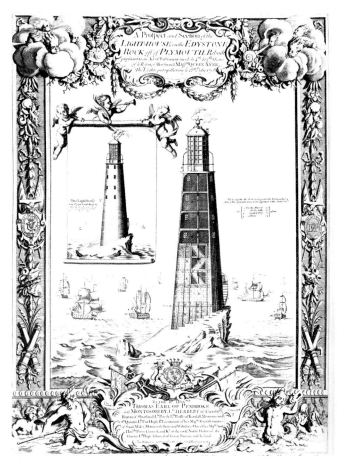

JOHN RUDYARD'S TOWER PLAN

shipbuilders. The combination of wood, pitch, and candles was destined to bring down the tower. The wonder is that it took so long.

A candle-lit lantern required hourly care. One evening a keeper got a bit sloppy and when he returned an hour later the lantern was in flames. Fed by the highly inflammable pitch and fanned by a draft created by the hollow chimney-like tube of the lighthouse itself, Rudyard's Tower burned to the ground.

A contemporary report notes that one keeper, standing mouth agape below the fire when the leaden roof melted, received molten lead about his boby and claimed, though no one at the time believed him, that he had swallowed a lump of hot lead. However, he eventually died of his burns and the surgeon doing the autopsy did, in fact, discover a seven-ounce lump of lead in his stomach.

A very bad end for the keeper and a bad end for Rudyard's Tower but it also signaled the end of experimenting with wood and the beginning of the use of stone and cementitious materials, ultimately the only material than can resist the conditions amid which, perforce, lighthouses are sighted.

John Smeaton

"He had not...to force his way up through the obstructions of poverty, toil and parental neglect; but was led gently by the hand from his earliest years, and carefully trained and cultured after the best methods then known."

— *Lives of the Engineers*, 1861

The eventual winner in the race to historical recognition was John Smeaton, who had been an early competitor since the 1770s. Smeaton was beaten to patent by Higgins and bested in quality by both Parker and Aspdin. But Smeaton had a not-so-secret weapon that had already impressed itself on the consciousness of the English people. It was an inescapable image that stood out like a glorious sore thumb in the English Channel off the entrance to the Port of Plymouth. He had used his knowledge of waterproof cement to construct a light to benefit navigation that stood guard over English shipping for a century and a half.

Smeaton, by far the most interesting of the English rockmakers, was the first man in history to build an indestructible lighthouse on the inhospitable site of Eddystone Rocks. It was cleverly built with interlocking blocks of Portland stone cemented together with a hydraulic cement. Smeaton had obviously read Vitruvius, probably in the Giocondo translation, since he went so far in imitation of classical Roman cement as to import pozzolanic material from Civitavecchia near Rome. The success of this project established Smeaton as "a Man of his Season." His career covered seven decades and dozens of major works in ports and canals and bridges. During these years he dominated, if not invented, the infant field of civil engineering but in the end it was the lighthouse at Eddystone for which he is now remembered best.

"It remains a curious question, which I must leave to the learned naturalist and chemist, why an intermediate mixture of clay...in limestone... should render it capable of setting in water in a manner no pure lime I have yet seen...has been capable of doing. It is easy to add clay... to a pure lime, but it produces no such effect."

— John Smeaton

John Smeaton was born in Leeds to Scottish parents in 1724. His father was a Yorkshire lawyer who presented young John with the proverbial silver spoon at birth. After a sound primary education he was sent to London for training in the courts of law. He was expected, as the firstborn son, to take up his family trade but early in life John's interest in the law, a most respected profession, was superseded by his passion for things mechanical. "Mechanicks" were considered mere tradesmen, or worse, and it took some convincing to receive his father's blessing to abandon the law. John wanted to design and construct scientific instruments, especially those related to navigation.

Smeaton's mind could not be long contained in the small world of instrument making and he soon turned his interest to the larger field of works of public engineering. Here he found room to swing his intellectual cat and, by 1756, in spite of no previous experience, he bravely bid on the rebuilding of the Eddystone lighthouse. No less a luminary than the president of the Royal Society accepted his bid and charged him with the reconstruction of the light that had continually fallen into the sea.

That he was chosen over two much more experienced firms was probably the result of his growing reputation in the expanding world of natural philosophy. At an early age he had read papers before the Royal Society and, at age twenty-nine, in 1753, he became a fellow, the youngest member of that august body. In 1759 he presented a paper entitled "An experimental enquiry concerning the Natural Powers of Water and Wind to turn Wheels."

This was no distant, academic study. Smeaton was an early aficionado of what was to come to be known as the scientific method, to wit: research, observation, and repeatable experimentation. His paper resulted in a significant revolution in the construction of waterwheels in Europe, a primary source of power at the time. Prior to Smeaton, undershot wheels were constructed in which the power was derived from the rush of the water passing beneath the wheel. Smeaton was able to scientifically demonstrate that by directing water to the top of a waterwheel, thus using the weight of the water as well as its movement, this doubled the efficiency of the device. For this contribution Smeaton received the Royal Society's Copely Medal at the young age of thirty-five.

Smeaton was uncomfortable with the appellation "engineer," which was commonly used by the graduates of military colleges. All public infrastructure stretching from the Roman times up to the industrial revolution had traditionally been the purview of the military. Suddenly, there were firms and individuals outside of the military undertaking large public projects for whom there was no clear professional title. Smeaton in 1768 invented the term "civil engineer" for himself and that title has come down to us today, separating military projects such as forts and defenses from the broader civil field. The profession was further bifurcated at the time with mechanical engineering when railroads and hydropower plants appeared and into electrical engineering, pioneered by Thomas Edison.

A few years ago, under the title *A Guide to Life, the Universe and Everything*, the British Broadcasting System described John Smeaton's legacy thus:

Smeaton's Legacy

Today, having coined the term, Smeaton remains one of civil engineering's heavyweights—the breadth and depth of his influence are phenomenal. As the prototype for a flurry of like-minded 19th Century engineers (e.g. Henry Palmer, Thomas Telford, the Brunels) Smeaton, in his career, designed the first successful Eddystone Lighthouse, he greatly improved on Newcomen's steam engine, he designed windmills, watermills, canals and bridges as well as pumps, ports, mines and jetties.

John Smeaton died on October 28, 1792, after he suffered a stroke while walking in the garden of his family home at Austhorpe. His enduring legacy is more than the engineering works, some of which remain standing as monuments to the great man himself. Not only is he widely regarded as the founder of the civil engineering profession, but his methods of construction site management and supervision are still in use today. John Smeaton clearly understood that managing people correctly was as important as design and construction.

> "Stone, wood and iron are wrought and put together by mechanical methods, but the greatest work is to keep right the animal part of the machinery."
>
> —John Smeaton

It was Smeaton's desire for the practice of professional engineers dining together—so that they might get to know one another better and thereby avoid potential hostility that might arise in their public dealings —that spawned the formation of the Society of Civil Engineers in March 1771. The society met fortnightly at the King's Head in Holborn and encouraged "conversation, argument and social communication of ideas and knowledge."

While the Eddystone light was a prominent marker in the commerce of the oceans, the Great North Road was, in a sense, the solid link that knit together the north and the south of England.

If Smeaton were alive today he might well argue that the lighthouse, while interesting and useful, could not compare with his solution for ending the seasonal flooding of the Great North Road. This main artery of English inland traffic crosses the Trent River floodplain. From the beginning of memory of inland transport the river flooded the plain, impeding transit and sometimes wiping out the road itself. It was a problem that needed solving and, in 1768, as the leading engineer of his day, Smeaton was consulted and produced an elegant engineering solution.

After a series of flood events in the last half of the eighteenth century caused major disruptions to passage along the Great North Road to the city of Newark, causing major loss of business to the town, John Smeaton was commissioned to find a means of allowing traffic to continue unimpeded and yet allow the floodwaters to drain. He came up with the hitherto unheard notion of building a causeway punctuated by arches across the floodplain.

In the largest piece of road engineering since the Romans, he designed and oversaw the construction of the Smeaton Viaduct, a series of bridges and overpasses that allowed land traffic to proceed unimpeded yet allow floodwaters to continue to drain the area unimpeded by roadways. The origin of this enormous and productive project is all but forgotten today and yet it can be argued that it was, while relatively short-lived, the major contribution of this remarkable man. The work was completed by 1800, it involved a causeway one kilometer or so long, crossing three parishes, and a grand total of 125 arches.*

There is little left of the original construction. There are some walls and some arches that remained when the rebuilding took place in the nineteenth century but the viaduct and the road it supported, made possible by Smeaton's waterproof cement, did its job and made a major contribution to the industrialization of England.

*Ursilla Spence and Mike Bishop, *East Midlands Archaeological Research Framework: An Archaeological Resource Assessment of Modern Nottinghamshire*

Timeline:

A Chronological Sequence of the History of Cement and Concrete*

5000 TO 3000 BCE

Egyptians mixed mud with straw to bind dried bricks. They also used gypsum mortars and mortars of lime in the pyramids. Chinese used cementitious materials to hold bamboo together in their boats and in the Great Wall.

800 BCE

Greeks used lime mortars, which were much harder than later Roman mortars.

300 BCE

Babylonians and Assyrians used bitumen to bind stones and bricks.

300 BCE – 476 AD

Romans used pozzolan cement from Pozzuoli, Italy, near Mount Vesuvius to build the Appian Way, Roman baths, the Colosseum and Pantheon in Rome, and the Pont du Gard aqueduct in southern France. They used lime as a cementitious material. Pliny reported a mortar mixture of one part lime to four parts sand. Vitruvius reported two parts pozzolan to one part lime. Animal fat, milk, and blood were used as admixtures. These structures still exist today!

1200 – 1500

The quality of cementing materials deteriorated. The use of burning lime and pozzolan (admixture) was lost but reintroduced in the 1300s.

1678

Joseph Moxon wrote about a hidden fire in heated lime that appears upon the addition of water.

1779

Bry Higgins was issued a patent for hydraulic cement (stucco) for exterior plastering use.

1780

Bry Higgins published "Experiments and Observations Made with the View of Improving the Art of Composing and Applying Calcereous Cements and Preparing Quicklime."

1793

John Smeaton found that the calcination of limestone containing clay gave a lime that hardened underwater (hydraulic lime). He used hydraulic lime to rebuild the Eddystone lighthouse in Cornwall, England, which he had been commissioned to build in 1756, but had first to invent a material that would not be affected by water. He wrote a book about his work.

1796

James Parker from England patented a natural hydraulic cement by calcining nodules of impure limestone containing clay, called Parker's cement or Roman cement.

1802

In France, a similar Roman cement process was used.

1810

Edgar Dobbs received a patent for hydraulic mortars, stucco, and plaster, although they were of poor quality due to lack of kiln precautions.

1812 – 1813

Louis Vicat of France prepared artificial hydraulic lime by calcining synthetic mixtures of limestone and clay.

1818

Maurice St. Leger was issued patents for hydraulic cement. Natural cement was produced in the United States.

Natural cement is limestone that naturally has the appropriate amounts of clay to make the same type of concrete as John Smeaton discovered.

1820 – 1821

John Tickell and Abraham Chambers were issued more hydraulic cement patents.

1822

James Frost of England prepared artificial hydraulic lime like Vicat's and called it British cement.

1824

Joseph Aspdin of England invented Portland cement by burning finely ground chalk with finely divided clay in a limekiln until carbon dioxide was driven off. The sintered product was then ground and he named it after the high-quality building stones quarried at Portland, England.

1828

I. K. Brunel is credited with the first engineering application of Portland cement, which was used to fill a breach in the Thames Tunnel.

1830

The first production of lime and hydraulic cement took place in Canada.

1836

The first systematic tests of tensile and compressive strength took place in Germany.

1843

J. M. Mauder, Son & Co. was licensed to produce patented Portland cement.

1845

Isaac Johnson claims to have burned the raw materials of Portland cement to clinkering temperatures.

1849

Pettenkofer & Fuches performed the first accurate chemical analysis of Portland cement.

1860

The beginning of the era of Portland cements of modern composition.

1862

Blake Stonebreaker of England introduced the jawbreakers to crush clinkers.

1867

Joseph Monier of France reinforced William Wand's (USA) flowerpots with wire, ushering in the idea of iron reinforcing bars (rebar).

1871

David Saylor was issued the first American patent for Portland cement. He showed the importance of true clinkering.

1880

J. Grant of England showed the importance of using the hardest and densest portions of the clinker. Key ingredients were being chemically analyzed.

1886

The first rotary kiln was introduced in England to replace the vertical shaft kilns.

1887

Henry Le Chatelier of France established oxide ratios to prepare the proper amount of lime to produce Portland cement. He named the components: alite (tricalcium silicate), belite (dicalcium silicate), and celite (tetracalcium aluminoferrite). He proposed that hardening is caused by the formation of crystalline products of the reaction between cement and water.

1889

The first concrete reinforced bridge is built.

1890

The addition of gypsum when grinding clinker to act as a retardant to the setting of concrete was introduced in the United States. Vertical shaft kilns were replaced with rotary kilns and ball mills were used for grinding cement.

1891

George Bartholomew placed the first concrete street in the United States in Bellefontaine, Ohio. It still exists today!

1893

William Michaelis claimed that hydrated metasilicates form a gelatinous mass (gel) that dehydrates over time to harden.

1900

Basic cement tests were standardized.

1903

The first concrete high-rise was built in Cincinnati, Ohio.

1908

Thomas Edison built cheap, cozy concrete houses in Union, New Jersey.

1909

Thomas Edison was issued a patent for rotary kilns.

1929

Dr. Linus Pauling of the United States formulated a set of principles for the structures of complex silicates.

1930

Air entraining agents were introduced to improve concrete's resistance to freeze/thaw damage.

1936

The first major concrete dams, Hoover Dam and Grand Coulee Dam, were built. They still exist today!

1956

U.S. Congress enacted the Federal Interstate Highway Act.

1967

First concrete domed sport structure, the Assembly Hall, was constructed at the University of Illinois, Urbana-Champaign.

1970S

Fiber reinforcement in concrete was introduced.

1975

CN Tower in Toronto, Canada, the tallest slip-form building, was constructed. Water Tower Place in Chicago, Illinois, the tallest building, was constructed.

1980S

Superplasticizers were introduced as admixtures.

1985

Silica fume was introduced as a pozzolanic additive. The "highest strength" concrete was used in building Union Plaza in Seattle, Washington.

1992

The tallest reinforced concrete building in the world was constructed at 311 S. Wacker Drive, Chicago, Illinois.

✱Courtesy of Dr. N.K. Shrivastava and Kiran Bhujun

CHAPTER NOTES

CHAPTER ONE

1. In 1798 Napoleon Bonaparte conquered Egypt with an army of 55,000 men. With them was a party of three hundred men of science and letters whose objective it was to record the present culture and the archeological past of Egypt. The result was an extensive series of writings and engravings entitled *Description de L'Egypte.*

2. The two incursions did not penetrate into the inner burial chmber of Tutankhamun. The air that Carnvon and Carter breathed as they unsealed the inner tomb was the same air that the burial priests breathed as they laid Tut to rest.

3. Erich von Daniken, *Chariots of the Gods?*, 1970.

4. Moustafa Gadalla, *Pyramid Illusions: A Journey to the Truth*, 1997.

5. Joseph Davidovits and Margie Morris, *The Pyramids: An Enigma Solved*, 1988.

CHAPTER TWO

1. Rose Macaulay, *Pleasure of Ruins*, 1966.

2. Themba Wakashe, "Incense Route – Desert Cities in the Negev," UNESCO 2005.

CHAPTER THREE

1. Rodolfo Lanciani, *The Ruins and Excavations of Ancient Rome*, 1897.

2. C. B. Wilby, *Concrete for Structural Engineers*. London: Newnes Butterworths, 1977.

3. Kenneth G. Holum et al., *King Herod's Dream: Caesarea by the Sea*, 1988. Page 101.

4. *Herod's Dream*, p. 105.

CHAPTER SIX

1. Bryan Higgins, *Experiments and Observations Made with the View of Improving the Art of Composing and Applying Calcerouis Cements and Preparing Quicklime*, London, 1780.

2. *The Writings of George Washington*, Putnam Sons, 1889.

3. Dublin: printed by J. Chambers for James Williams, 1776.

4. Captain's log of the *Mayflower*, 1620.

5. *The Romance of Cement*, Edison Portland Cement Company, Livermore & Knight, New York, 1926.

CHAPTER SEVEN

1. Amy E. Slaton, *Reinforced Concrete and the Modernization of American Building, 1900–1930.*

2. Slaton, *Reinforced Concrete.*

3. Slaton, *Reinforced Concrete.*

4. The justification for inclusion of this report in a history of concrete is that, although Pykrete contains no cement, the essential ingredient of cementitious material, it is clearly a concretion as defined by the Oxford English Dictionary: "a solid mass formed by aggregation and cohesion of particles."

5. This quote and much of the background color described here are derived from an article entitled "The Floating Island" by Paul Collins, published in the *Cabinet Online Magazine* (Summer 2002).

6. Collins points out that the spelling of "Habbakuk"—rather than the biblical "Habakkuk"—was due to an Admiralty clerk's error.

7. Habakkuk was a minor Old Testament prophet who is best remembered for his conversa-

tions with God. At one point he complains that justice is being subverted and that he is puzzled that God is doing nothing about it. Yahweh replies that a "new and startling display of His justice is about to take place." The "new and startling display" was, of course, Pyke's ice island, which would smite the Hitlerian Myrmidons.

8. Bartolomeo de Neocastro, *Historia Sicula*, c. 1293.

CHAPTER EIGHT

1. Francis Arthur Jones, *Thomas Alva Edison: Sixty Years of an Inventor's Life*, Thomas Y. Crowell, New York, 1908.

2. It is most interesting to note that this is true only in the industrialized world. The third world, lacking both skill and the capital infrastructure needed for sophisticated housing construction, has discovered the ease and economy of the basic concrete box as a minimal but serviceable habitat.

3. Michael Petersen's description of experimentation.

4. Michael Petersen, *Invention and Technology* magazine, vol. 11, 1996.

CHAPTER NINE

1. Dinsmoor had prepared well for his death. Emulating, perhaps unconsciously, the pharaohs, he built a forty-foot-high limestone mausoleum in the midst of his *Garden of Eden*. When he died, he was embalmed and put on display in an open concrete coffin. The mausoleum contained a glass window through which, even after almost a century, his decomposed remains may be viewed by those blessed with a strong stomach.

2. © Malvina Reynolds.

3. In an attempt to ameliorate the featureless insipidity of style in his Silver Towers complex in New

York, Pei placed the *Portrait of Sylvette*, a curvy, involuted sculpture conceived by Picasso and realized by Carl Nesjar.

4. The church was paid for primarily by its own congregation. It was not an easy task but with a little help from the government and many contributions from Scandinavian artists and artisans, the church rose under its 200-foot-high steeple. Individual contributions were welcomed for the organ. Contributors had dedicated to them one of the 5,000 pipes, the size of the pipe being directly related to the size of the donation. Contributors have had the opportunity to listen, in all of its solitary glory, to their very own pipe.

5. Population about 300,000.

CHAPTER TEN

1. "Concrete Ships," Sixty-fifth U.S. Congress, 1917.

2. From *History of the World War* by Francis A. Marck, Ph.D. (The United States Publishers of the United States and Canada, 1918): "In addition to the steel and wood vessels the Emergency Fleet Corporation also constructed a number of concrete ships. The first step in this direction was taken on April 3, when the construction of four 7,500-ton concrete ships at a Pacific coast shipyard was authorized. This action was taken as a result of a report on the trials made with the concrete ship *Faith*, which was built in San Francisco by private capital. The test of this ship had been satisfactory and Mr. R. J. Wig, an agent of the Emergency Fleet Corporation, who had made a careful inspection of the *Faith* and watched the tests, reported his confidence in the new cargo carrier. The successful trial trip of the *Faith* led, on the 17th of May, to the government order that fifty-eight more such ships be constructed. Sites for yards were leased and contracts awarded.

The concrete ship turned out to be a great success."

3. The great ocean liners do the passage in five days. Any respectable modern freighter will do it in eight days and this writer, in a thirty-two-foot cutter, made the same crossing under sail in twenty-one days. The excruciatingly slow progress was not set by the recently built two concrete ships, which could easily make six to eight knots.

CHAPTER ELEVEN

1. San Francisco proceedings of CANMET/ACI, September 2001.

2. Italcementi Group, with a production capacity of approximately 70 million tons of cement annually, is the fifth largest cement producer in the world.

3. Titanium dioxide is one of the top fifty chemicals produced worldwide. It is a white mineral found as rutile and anatase. Both forms contain pure titanium dioxide that is bound to impurities. Titanium dioxide is chemically processed to remove these impurities, leaving the pure, white pigment available for use. Titanium dioxide has a variety of uses, as it is odorless and absorbent. This mineral can be found in many products, ranging from paint to food to cosmetics. In cosmetics, it serves several purposes; it is a white pigment, an opacifier, and a sunscreen.

4. Joann Gonchar, AIA.

5. American Waterworks Association, May 2001.

6. Massachusetts Institute of Technology, "America's Infrastructure Engineering Dilemma," Ernest G. Frankel. September/October 2007.

7. *National Geographic* online.

8. Jonathan Overpeck, director of the Institute for the Study of Planet Earth at the University of Arizona in Tucson.

CHAPTER TWELVE

1. Bert Bolin has also been director of the International Meteorological Institute in Stockholm, a member of the Swedish Research Committee, and chairman of the UN Evaluation Commission for global climate changes. He is a member of the Royal Swedish Academy of Sciences.

2. Denise Brehm, *Civil and Environmental Engineering Department*, MIT, Cambridge, Mass.

CHAPTER THIRTEEN

1. The technology, after almost three decades, has not yet provided the protection for which it was heralded.

2. Salvador de Madariaga: "Art is the conveyance of spirit by means of matter."

3. Of Dr. Lin, R. A. Kaden writes, "Lunar concrete is an international topic. Mooncrete will challenge the entire scientific community interested in advanced concrete technology. It has received more interest within the last three years since T. D. Lin (1987) wrote his article entitled 'Making Concrete on the Moon.' This was truly the initial feasibility study that has advanced this idea from a laboratory study, to a dream for scientific and engineering communities alike. The severe lunar temperature extremes, limited natural materials, and the absence of an atmosphere are important design parameters to be considered."

4. $FeTiO_3 + H_2$ Yields TiO_2 + Iron + *Water*!

BIBLIOGRAPHY

Alexander, Christopher, et al. *A Pattern Language* (New York: Oxford University Press, 1977)

Anderson, Robert, and Ibrahim Fawzy. *Egypt Revealed: Scenes from Napoleon's Description de l'Egypte* (Cairo: American University in Cairo Press, 1987)

Beaver, Patrick. *A History of Lighthouses* (Secaucus, N.J.: Citadel Press, 1973)

Berry, John. *Playing Cards of the World* (London: Guildhall, 1995)

Besset, Maurice. *Le Corbusier: To Live With Light* (New York: Rizzoli International Publications, 1987)

Campbell, John A. Hulks. *The Breakwater Ships of Powell River* (Powell River, B.C.: Works Publishing, 2003)

Cheng, Fu-Tung. *Concrete at Home* (Newtown, Conn.: The Taunton Press, 2005)

Croft, Catherine. *Concrete Architecture* (Salt Lake City: Gibbs Smith, 2004)

Dyke, Linda F. *Henry Chapman Mercer* (Doylestown, Penn.: Tower Hill Press, 1989)

Eddison Portland Cement Company. *The Romance of Cement* (New York: Livermore & Knight Company, 1926)

Fairweather, Sally. *Picasso's Concrete Sculptures* (New York: Hudson Hills Press, 1982)

Front, Carol M., Joan Minton Christopher, and Martha Capwell Fox. *The Lehigh Valley Cement Industry* (Chicago: Arcadia Publishing, 2006)

Gallagher, Dan. *Florida's Great Ocean Railway* (Sarasota, Fla.: Pineapple Press, 2003)

Gemmill, Helen K. *The Mercer Mile* (Doylestown, Penn.: Bucks County Historical Society, 1998)

Gold, Lorne W. *The Canadian Habbakuk Project* (Cambridge, U.K.: International Geological Society, 1993)

Goss, Andrew. *Concrete Handbook for Artists* (Owen Sound, Ontario: Goss Design Studio, 2002)

Goss, Andrew, and Stuart Reed. *Heavy Duty* (Ontario: Tom Thomsen Memorial Art Gallery, 2003)

Hanks, David A. *The Decorative Designs of Frank Lloyd Wright* (New York: E. P. Dutton, 1979)

Hart-Davis, Adam. *Henry Winstanley and the Eddystone Lighthouse* (Gloucestershire, U.K.: Sutton Publishing, 2002)

Holum, Kenneth G., et al. *King Herod's Dream: Caesarea by the Sea* (New York: W. W. Norton and Company, 1988)

Kaden, Richard A. *Lunar Concrete* (Detroit: American Concrete Institute, 1991)

Kaufmann, Edgar, and Ben Raeburn. *Frank Lloyd Wright: Writings and Buildings* (New York: Meridian Books, 1960)

Kelly, Connie Considine. *The History of Concrete Ships* (Cape May, N.J.: Kelly, 1999)

Kristjansson, Rev. Gunnar. *Churches of Iceland* (Reykjavík: Iceland Review, 1988)

Larn, Richard. *Devon Shipwrecks* (Newton Abbot, U.K., North Pomfret, Vt.: David & Charles, 1974)

Macaulay, Rose. *Pleasure of Ruins* (New York: Barnes & Noble, 1996)

Mays, Larry W. *Urban Water Supply Handbook* (New York: McGraw Hill, 2002)

Meehan, Patrick J. *The Master Architect: Conversations with Frank Lloyd Wright* (New York: John Wiley and Sons, 1984)

Mendell, W. W., ed. *Lunar Bases and Space Activities of the 21st Century* (Houston: Lunar and Planetary Institute, 1985)

Moore, David. *The Roman Pantheon* (Big Piney, Wy.: David Moore, 1995)

Murray, Peter. *The Architecture of the Italian Renaissance* (New York: Schocken Press, 1963)

Pfeiffer, Bruce Brooks, and Gerald Nordland, eds. *Frank Lloyd Wright: In the Realm of Ideas* (Carbondale: Southern Illinois University Press, 1987)

Poos, Thomas G. *Fonthill the Home of Henry Chapman Mercer* (Feasterville, Penn.: Manor House Publishing, 2000)

Pyke, Geoffrey. *To Ruhleben and Back* (Brooklyn: McSweeney Books, reprint ed. 2003)

Scott, Phil. *Hemmingway's Hurricane* (New York: McGraw-Hill, 2006)

Slaton, Amy E. *Reinforced Concrete and the Modernization of American Building, 1900–1930* (Baltimore: Johns Hopkins University Press, 2001)

Smithson, Alison, and Peter Smithson. *The Heroic Period of Modern Architecture* (New York: Rizzoli Books, 1981)

Standiford, Les. *Last Train to Paradise* (New York: Three Rivers Press, 2002)

Stone, Lisa. *Sacred Spaces and Other Places* (Chicago: School of the Art Institute of Chicago, 1993)

Tafel, Edgar. *Years with Frank Lloyd Wright* (New York: Dover, 1979)

Vincent, Carole. *Concrete Works* (Cornwall, U.K.: Alison Hodge, 2003)

Vitruvius. *The Ten Books of Architecture* (Boston: Harvard University Press, 1914)

Wittkower, Rudolf, *Architectural Principles in the Age of Humanism* (New York: W.W. Norton and Company, 1971)

Wright, Frank Lloyd. *The Future of Architecture* (New York: Horizon Press, 1953)

INDEX

Page numbers in *italics* refer to illustrations.

Aalto, Alvar, 120
adobe, 49, 114, 127, 128, 130
Agrippa, Marcus Vipsanius, 30
Ahkenaten, Pharaoh of Egypt, 14
air pollution, 168, 181–82
Alexander, Christopher, 130
Alexander the Great, 24–25
Alfred Kahn, S.S., 153–54
Ally, Mustapha, 88–89
American Concrete Institute, 205
American Waterworks Association, 184–85
Amun, 20
antipollutant photocatalysts, 181–82
aqueducts, 35, *35*, 49
aquifers, 163, 167–69, 193, 213
arsenic salts, 23, 27
art, 64, 68, 98–139
    image and technique in, 100
    see also architecture; sculpture
Aspdin, Joseph, 44, 50, 54–55, 153, 222
Assyrians, 28
Atlantis, S.S., 148–49
Australia, 119–22, 136
Auth, Tony, *84*
Bache, Anja, *103*, 119
Bache, Hans H., 174–80
bamboo, 159
Barr, Alfred H., Jr., 113
Bartolommeo de Neocastro, 85–86
basalt, 21
Bauhaus movement, 13, 135
Beaux Arts style, 116
Belgium, 71, 72, 143
bendable concrete, *174*, 176
berms, 37
Betograve process, 111–13
Bjarnarnes Church, 137–39, *138*
Blaauw, Menno, 22
boats, 158–59
Bolin, Bert, 196–97, 227n
bones, 183, 212
Boroton, *100, 101*
Brandon, Christopher, 216–17
Brehm, Denise, 200–202
bricks, 20, 22, 24, 33, 43, 45–46, 48–49,
    64, 116, 118, 175
    adobe, 49, 114, 127, 128, 130
bridge construction, 38–39, 41, 59, 64, 153,
    184, 185–86, 190–91, *191*
Brunelleschi, Filippo, 30
bubbles, diving, 158
building codes, local, 63, 64
bunkers, 68–69, *71*, 72, 73–78
Burj Al Arab Hotel, 122, *122*
Bust of Sylvette (Picasso), 111, 112–13, *112, 113*

Caesarea, 34–37, *35*, 216–17
    filling underwater caissons at, 36–37,
    36, 41
    Sebastos Teringo port of, 34, *34*, 35–37, 41
Calatrava, Santiago, 191
Canada, 100, *153*, 154–56, *155*, 195, 216
canal construction, 55, 56, 57, 92
canoes, 146, 158, 159–60, *160*
Cape Fear, S.S., 149, 157
Carnarvon, Lord, 12–13
Carroll, Lewis, 75
Carter, Howard, 12–13
Cassanova School of Civil Engineering,
    199–200
Castellano, Paul, 87
cement, 47–57, 78, 84, 128, 137, 142, 143–
    44, 176, 178, 180, 182–83, 211
    current consumption of, 164–65, 182
    fly ash in, 128, 179, 180, 183, 189, 193,
    194–96
    hydraulic, 48–50, 51–53, 54, 222
    nanoparticles of, 183, 200–202, 213
    natural, 17, 54–57, 91–92
    Portland, *see* Portland Cement
    setting speed of, 55, 56, 57
    silicon-based, 153
Cement Age, 214
cementitious materials, 24, 25, 28, 42, 47–
    48, 49, 80, 159, 168, 211, 221, 226n
Chaldean architecture, 24
chalk, 18, 54
Chapman, Elizabeth Mercer, 214
Chariots of the Gods? (von Däniken), 14–15
Charles II, King of England, 219
Charles of Anjou, 85–86
China, 122, 158–59, 177, 182
Christianity, 29, 33
    churches of, 131–39
Churchill, Winston, 69, 79–80
Cincinnati, Ohio, 114–16, *115*
Circle Fish (Peterman), *99*
cisterns, 27–28, 33
clinker, 179–80, 187, 189
Coignet, François, 115
Columbo crime family, 87
computers, 59–60, 212–13, 215
Comyn, Leslie, 147
concrete:
    aging of, 184–85
    air bubbles in, 19, 31, 32
    components of, 142–44
    delivery of, 64, 86–89, 243–44
    ductility of, 175, 176–77
    in eighteenth century, 45–53
    fireproof quality of, 95, 96, 134, 214

first evidence of, 11
future of, 212–13
green, 179
historical appearance and disappearance
    of, 22–23, 25, 26, 33, 41, 44, 45–46, 48,
    93
hydration of, 11, 176, 184
hydraulic, 23, 36–37, *36*, 41, 48–50
hydrostatic pressure resistance of, 171–72
impact load resistance of, 176–77
lightweight, 124, 127, 128, 130, 158
mixture content of, 78, 128, 142, 143–44,
    175, 176
new chemistry of, 163–65, 166, 174–83
in nineteenth century, 48, 52, 53–57
precasting of, 63–64, 132
present world consumption of, 179, 182
proliferation of, 60–67, 163–65, 181, 182,
    189–91, 192
setting of, 32, 50
social changes caused by, 62–63, 114
standardized formulations of, 57, 61–62,
    128, 147, 166
strength of, 31, 93, 114–15, 128, 158, 169–
    70, 175, 180
tamping of, 31, 32, 37, 64
timeline of, 224–25
unreinforced, 30–33, 93
concrete boot, 83–85, *84*
"Concrete for Lunar Base Construction"
    (Lin), 205
concrete industry, 179–80, 184–85, 192–202
    annual trade show of, 192–93
    green solutions for, 193, 194–96, 198
    hopeful developments in, 163, 197–202
    noncompulsory self-regulation of, 193–
    94, 196
    Wal-Mart and, 193–94
Concrete Technologies Laboratory, 156
Considere, S.S., 155–56
Constantinides, Georgios, 201–2
construction industry, 91, 98 143, 166, 177,
    201–2, 212, 223
Cooper, Henry N., 115–16
Coplay Cement Company, 154
craft unions, 61, 62, 63–64
CRC (compact reinforced concrete), 174–
    80, *174, 176, 177, 178*
Cuba, 147–48, 150
Cuyamaca, S.S., 149
Daley, Richard, 169
Danish Centre for Green Concrete, 179
Darius, King of Persia, 24–25
David, Sylvette, 112
David O. Saylor, S.S., 154
Davidovitz, Joseph, 17–22, *21*
Davidsson, Hannes Kr., 138
De architectura (Vitruvius), 38, 39–41, 43–44
deep shelters, 73–74, *73*
Defense Department, U.S., 65
Defoe, Daniel, 218
de Gaulle, Charles, 70

democracy, 25, 69, 186
Denmark, 119–22, 136, 174–80, *174, 175, 177,* 198
Denser, S.S., 149
Depression era, 13, 64, 140, 145–46
Dickens, Charles, 47
dikes, 164–65, 186, 213
Dinosaur (Stark), *106, 107*
Dinsmoor, Samuel Perry, *104,* 105, *105,* 226n
Diodorus Siculus, 27
Dobbs, Edgar, 54
dome houses, 97, *124,* 125
domes, 114
  Pantheon, 30–33, *30, 31, 32*
Doylestown, Pa., 58–59, *58*
Dubai, 122, *122*
Dunn, Christopher, 15
earth, 61, 187
  agglomeration of, 10–11, 64
  latitude and longitude lines of, 31
  see also global warming; sustainability
East Coast Railway, 140–41
Eckel, Edwin Clarence, 153
Eddystone Lights, 51–53, *51, 53,* 154
  builders of, 218–23
Eddystone Rocks, 218–20, 222
Edison, Thomas Alva, 90–97, 214, 223
  concrete piano proposed by, 95, 96
  electric light bulb invented by, 90, 92
  low-income concrete houses of, 64, 91, 93–94, 96–97, *96,* 98
  scientific method of, 90–91, 92
  Victrola of, 9, 95, *95*
Edison Portland Cement Company, 91, 92–95, 96
  rotary kilns of, 53, 57, 92–93, 95
Edwin Clarence Eckel, S.S., 153
Egypt, ancient, 8, 12–23, 25, 26, 114, 131, 199, 212, 218
  bronze tools of, 19, 20
  copper tools of, 16, 17, 19, 20
  gods of, 14, 20
  Nabateans and, 28–29
  New Kingdom, 18, 19
  priesthood of, 12, 16–17, 20, 22, 23, 24, 38
  sun-dried bricks of, 20, 24, 33
  see also pyramids, Egyptian
Egyptology, 12–13, 14, 15, 16, 17, 18–22
Einstein, Albert, 21, 59, 75
Eisenhower, Dwight D., 65, 74
Ellmer, Wilfried, 170–73, *174*
Emile N. Vidale, S.S., 155–56
Empire State Building, 116
England, 8, 42–44, 46–53, 54–55, 59–60, 69, 115, 132, 203
epoxy-based polymer concrete, 198–99, 200
Erie Canal, 55
factory buildings, 61–62
Faith, 147–48, *148,* 227n
Fallingwater, 119, 122–24, *123,* 136, 190
faraday cages, 76

ferro-cement, 158–60
Fidler, Eugene, 110–11
Finland, 120
Finnbogason, Rognvaldur, 138
Flagler, Henry M., 140–46
  private railroad car of, 140, *141,* 145
floating islands, 81, 83
Florence, Cathedral of, 30
Florida, 140–46, 150, 151, 164
fly ash, 128, 179, 180, 183, 189, 193, 194–96
Fonthill, *58,* 214, *215,* 216
Ford, Henry, 94, 128, 154
Fougner, N. K., 146–47
France, 17, 38, 41, 44, 47–48, 50, 54, 85–86, 93, 110, 115, 117, 135, *135,* 153, 158, 198, 220
Francois Hennebique, S.S., 153
Franklin, Benjamin, 42
Frost, James, 54
Fuller, Buckminster, 146
furniture, 98, 213
Gadalla, Moustafafa, 16
Galloway, Nathan Ed, 106, *106*
"Garden of Eden" (Dinsmoor), *104,* 105, *105*
Gaudi i Cornet, Antoni, 122, 125–27, *125*
Gehry, Frank, 122
Genesis (Nozick), *102*
geochemical analyses, 19
Geopolymer Institute of Saint-Quentin, 18
geopolymer theory, 18, 21
Giocondo, Fra Giovanni, 38–41, 42, 44, 222
Giza Power Plant, The (Dunn), 15
global warming, 177–83, 194–202
  atmospheric carbon dioxide in, 163–65, 167, 169–70, 172, 174, 178–80, 181, 182–83, 187, 192–93, 195, 196–97, 199, 202, 213
  rising sea level in, 164–65, 186–89
gneiss, anorthositic, 21
Goddess of Liberty (Dinsmoor), *105*
Good Old Days (Stark), *105, 107*
Goss, Andrew, 100–101, *103*
Gothic style, 131–32
Grassroots art movement, 100–101, 104–7, 108
Great Ocean Railway, 141–46, *142, 143*
  hurricanes and, 144–46, *144*
Greco-Roman style, 117
Greeks, ancient, 18, 24, 25, 27, 29, 30, 33, 37, 50
Greenbrier Hotel and Spa, 76–78
green buildings, 179
Greenland ice sheet, 187–88, 213
Guevara, Che, 150
Guggenheim Museum (Bilbao), 114
Guggenheim Museum (New York City), 58, *215,* 216
guilds, craft, 46, 61, 63
Guyana, 88–89
Habbakuk, H.M.S., 81–82, 226n

Hadrian, Emperor of Rome, 30
Hallgrímur, Church of, 136–37, *137*
Handy Work (Moxon), 42, 43–44
Hart-Davis, Adam, 52, 218, 219
Headwater Resources, 195–96
Hearst, William Randolph, 116–18, *117*
Henry Le Chatelier, S.S., 153, *153,* 155–56
Henry VI, King of England, 46
Henry VIII, King of England, 132
Herod, King of Judaea, 33–37, *35,* 41
Herodotus, 16–17
Hesselberg, Erik, 110–11
Heyerdahl, Thor, 109–10, 146
Higgins, Bry, 48–50, 222
Hisma desert, 26–27
Hitler, Adolf, 65, 70, 72, 73, 79
  bunker of, 68
Hohlfelder, Robert, 216–17
Hoover Dam, 64, 190, *190*
Household Words, 47
houses, 93–95, *104,* 105, *105,* 212
  Fallingwater, 119, 122–24, *123,* 136, 190
  Fonthill, 58, 214, *215,* 216
  low-income, 64, 91, 93–94, 96–97, *96,* 98, 124–25, *124*
  San Simeon, 116–18, *116, 117*
  self-built, 125–30
House 2 (Whiteread), 108–9, *108*
hydrogen, 199, 211
Iceland, 136–39, *137, 138*
igneous rock, 10
Imhotep, 20, 38
India, 97, *124,* 125, 139, 158, 182
industrial revolution, 44, 45, 47, 52, 53–58
Ingalls, Melville, 114–16, *115*
International suite, 119
Italcementi Group, 181, 216, 227n
Italy, 52, 181, 216–17
James I, King of England, 47
Jerusalem Temple, 37
Jews, 29, 33–37, 153–54
John Aspdin, S.S., 153
John Smeaton, S.S., 154, 155–56
Johonnot, Rodney, 133–34
Josephus, 36
Kahn, Alfred, 153–54
Kahnweiler, Daniel-Henry, 112
"Karley's Marker" (Nozick), *102*
Keeper of the Eddystone Light, The, 52–53
keeps, medieval, 69, 70, 165
Kelvedon Hatch, 75–76
Kessler, Clyde, 160
Khufu, Great Pyramid of, 17, 22
King, Ernest, 81–82
Kingo houses, 120
Koch, Ed, 87–88
Kon-Tiki, 109–10, 146
Kornher, Steve, 127, 129–30
Kornher House, *126,* 127, 129–30
Kyoto Agreement, 179–80, 196
Lambot, Jean-Louis, 115, 158
landfills, 179, 183, 193, 195–96

Le Chatelier, Henry, 153, *153*, 155–56
Le Corbusier, 131–32, 134–36
Leonardo da Vinci, 40, *40*, 99
Levittown, 129
Liberty ships, 81
Light Seats (Bache), *103*, 119
limekilns, 8, 22–23, 27, 48
    clinker produced by, 179–80, 187, 189
    rotary, 53, 57, 92–93, 95
    vertical "bottle," 55, 56–57, 91–92, *91*
limestone, 26, 55–56, 194–95, 211
    burning of, 22–23, 27, 42, 55, 92, 182, 187
    finding substitute for, 182–83, 187
    stratification of, 19
limestone mortar, 18, 24–25, 43–44
Lin, Tung Dzu, 205–8, *208, 209*, 211, 227n
Lipschutz, Heinz, 157
listening posts, 67–68, *67*
Lithium, S.S., 149–50
L.J. Vicat, S.S., 154, 155–56
London, 32, 43, 69, 75, 79, 222
Loriot, Antoine-Joseph, 50
Louis XII, King of France, 38, 41
Lovett, John, 221
McCloskey and Company, 151–53
Mafia, 85–89
Maginot, André, 70
Maginot Line, 69–72, *71*
Maimonides, 217
Malthus, Thomas, 60
Mannheim Line, 69–70
Maritime Commission, U.S., 151, 155
Marlborough Blenheim Hotel, 92, *93*
Mars, 9, 60, 204, 206
Masada, 37, 66, 69
Massachusetts Institute of Technology
    (MIT), 183, 185–86, 200–201
Mayflower, 218–19
mechane, 16–17
Mercer, Henry Chapman, 58, 214–16
Mercer Museum, 58–59, 214–16, *215*
Mesha, King of Moab, 27
Mexico, *126*, 127, 129–30, 139, *139*
Mies van der Rohe, Ludwig, 136
Miff, S.S., 150
Miller, Stephan, 217
mirrored constructions, 35
molds, 16–17, 19, 32–33, 93, 94, 97
    of hard stone vessels, 20–21, *21*
    underwater caissons, 36–37, *36*, 41
monopolies, 46–47, 162
moon, 60, 199, 203–11, 212
    habitats on, 205–11, *209*
    rock breaking on, 210, *210*
Moore, David, 217–18
Moore, Henry, *73*
Moore, John, 218
Moorish style, 92, *93*, 117
Morello, Antonio and Giuseppe, 86
Morgan, Julia, 117–18
Mountbatten, Lord, 79–80, 81
Moxon, Joseph, 42–44, 48

murder, by concrete boot, 83–85, *84*
Nabateans, 26–29, 33–34
Namsenfjord, 146–47, *147*
nanotechnologies, 183, 200–202, 211, 213
Napoleon I, Emperor of the French, 12
    Russian defeat of, 68–69
NASA, 60, 199, 205, 206, 207–8
natron salts, 11, 18
Navy, U.S., 147
Nazi Germany, 65–74, 79
    blitzkrieg of, 67–68, 69, 70, 71–72, 73–74
    Siegfried Line of, 69–70, 72–73
    U-boats of, 79, 81, 150–51, 152
Nesjar, Carl, 110–13, 226n
Netherlands, 71, 72, 186–87
New Orleans, La., 164, 185, 188
New York, N.Y., 92, 96, 136, 226n
    Empire State Building, 116
    Mafia in, 86–89
New York Times, 89, 113
Nicoya parish church, 139, *139*
Norway, 110–11, 136, 146–47
Notre Dame du Haut, 131–32, *134*, 136
Novalok Polymer Concrete, 198–99
Nozick, Lori, *102*
nuclear holocaust, 66, 73, 75–78, 165
nuclear power plants, 177, 210
    floating, 82–83
ocean transportation, 166, 172–74, 180–81
oil drilling platforms, 149–50, 171
    Pykrete islands as, 83
oil industry, 172, 181
Oleson, John Peter, 216–17
Operation Habbakuk, 82
Oppenheimer, Robert, 165
Overocker, Betty, 84–85
Overpeck, Jonathon, 188
Palestine, 26–29, 33–37
Palley, Marilyn Arnold, *103*
Palo Alto, S.S., 150
Panama Canal, 55
Pantheon, 30–33, *30, 31, 32*, 161, 184, 217–18
Pantheon, The: The Triumph of Concrete
    (Moore), 217–18
Papercrete, 128
Papercrete, 128
Parker, James, 50, 222
Parrish family, 75, 76
patents, 46–50, 54, 56, 115, 153, 154, 157,
    199, 222
Pattern Language, A (Alexander), 130
Patton, George S., 69
Peeled Orchid (Boroton), *100*
Pei, I.M., 112–13, 136, 226n
Perutz, Martin, 79, 81
pervious concrete, 163, 167, 168–70, 182, 193
Peterman, Stuart, *99*
Petersen, Michael, 96
Pétursson, Hallgrímur, 136–37
Pharos lighthouse, 218
Philippines, 159
Picasso, Pablo, 100, 108, 109–13, *112, 113*,
    129, 226n

pillboxes, 66–67, *66*
Polias, S.S., 150
pollution, environmental, 161, 163–65, 167,
    168, 177, 181–82, 213
Pompeii, 24–25
Pont Notre-Dame, 41
"Poor Man's Tale of a Patent, A"
    (Dickens), 47
Portland Cement, 50, *50*, 54–55, 56, 57, 80,
    143, 153, 154, 166, 168, 183, 192, 195,
    198, 199
Powell River breakwater, *153*, 154–56, *155*
Powers, Richard R., 157
Pritzker Prize, 122
Prince of Peace Church, 132
Prince of Peace Church, 132
Pritzker Prize, 122
Ptolemy II, Pharaoh of Egypt, 218
Pyke, Geoffrey, 79–82, 226n
Pykrete, 78–83, 226n
    as floating islands, 81, 83, 226n
    in H.M.S. *Habbakuk*, 81–82
"pyramidiots," 12, 14–15
pyramids, architectural, 137–39, *138*
pyramids, Egyptian, 8, 11, 12–23, 190–91
    hard stone vessels found in, 20–21, *21*
    as royal tombs, 13, 20
    unknown function of, 12, 13–14, 15
    Zoser step, 20–21
pyramids, Egyptian, construction of, 12, 13,
    14–22, 29, 38
    by ancient astronauts, 14–15, 20
    Herodotus's account of, 16–17
    hewn-stone theory of, 15–16, 20
    hydrolysis theory of, 15
    poured concrete theory of, 16–22, 24
radar, 67, 68, 79, 151
railroads, 57, 59, 65, 162, 167
Ransome, Ernest R., 115
Ready Mix trucks, 77, 86–87, 89, 143–44
Reagan, Ronald, 204–5, 206
reinforced concrete, 61–62, 93, 95, 114–16,
    130, 153–54, 158, 159
    CRC, 174–80, *176, 177*
    plastic strands in, 212
    rebars of, 93, 116, 152, 212
Renaissance, 18, 38–41, 42
rock breaking, 210, *210*
rock cycle, 10–11
Rockefeller, John D., 140
Rogers, Will, 106–7
Rolls-Royce cars, 176
ROMACONS (Roman Maritime Concrete
    Structure Study), 216–17
Roman concrete, 30–37, 42, 49, 216–18
    aqueducts of, 35, *35*
    high tensile strength of, 31, 37
    hydraulic, 36–37, *36*, 41, 216–17
    tamping of, 31, 32, 37
    Vitruvius's recorded formula for, 38–41,
        43–44, 216, 217, 222
    volcanic ash in, 26–27, 28, 31, 33, 128

waterproof pozzolan, 26–27, 35, 37, 38, 40, 43–44, 50, 52, 85, 222
  see also Caesarea; Pantheon
Romans, ancient, 8, 18, 22–23, 24, 25, 30, 37, 70, 114, 190
  cisterns of, 27, 33
  Nabateans and, 28–29, 33–34
  roads of, 39, 203, 223
Rommel, Erwin, 69
Roosevelt, Franklin Delano, 65
Root, Ed, 104, 107
Rosenblatt, Joel, 83
Rudyerd, John, 219, 220–21m, 221
Rudyerd Light, 51, 52, 220–21, 221
Saarinen, Eero, 120
sailboats, ferro-cement, 158–59
Samuelsson, Gudjon, 137
San Pasquale, S.S., 150
San Simeon (Hearst's Castle), 116–18, 116, 117
Sapona, S.S., 150
Saylor, David O., 154
Schulson, Erland, 80
sculpture, 98–113, 99, 100, 101, 102, 103
sea level, rise in, 164–65, 186–89
seawall, repair of, 130–31, 131
sedimentary rock, 10
self-built homes, 125–30
Selma, S.S., 150
sewage sludge, 180
sewer systems, 162, 163, 167, 169
ships, 146–60, 166, 227n
  alternative uses of, 147–50, 153–56
  construction of, 148, 151–53, 152
  consumables in, 155–56
  egg-shaped hulls as design of, 149, 157–58
  of ferro-cement, 158–60
  maintenance of, 157
  in Powell River breakwater, 153, 154–56, 155
  submarines, see submarines
  water displaced by, 157–58
  weather conditions encountered by, 173–74
  in World War I, 147–50, 151, 157
  in World War II, 150–57
Sicilian Vespers, 85–86
siege warfare, 69
Siegfried Line, 69–70, 72–73
silica, 26–27
silica fume, 183
Sinai, mines of, 23, 26, 37
slag cement, 183
slate, 21
Slaton, Amy E., 61–63
Sliced Wall (Boroton), 101
Smeaton, John, 44, 49–50, 52, 154, 155–56, 219, 222–23
Smeaton's Tower, 51, 52, 53
Smeaton Viaduct, 223
Smith, Adam, 45, 54
Smith, Fred, 106

smog control, 181–82
sound mirrors, 67–68, 67
Soviet Union, 9, 75, 76–77, 136
  in World War II, 65, 68, 73
space program, 9, 60
  warfare and, 204–5, 206
  see also moon
space station, 206, 207
Spain, 114, 117, 125, 199–200
spice routes, ancient, 26, 27, 28, 36
stained glass, 46
Stalin, Joseph, 9
Stark, Glenn, 106–7, 106
Stern, Charles, 216
stones, hewn, 15–17, 18–22, 32, 44, 64, 118, 131, 175
stone vessels, hard, 20–21, 21
STRAHNET (Strategic Highway Network), 65–66
Strato's Tower, 36
St. Sophia, 32
stucco, 48–49
submarines, 149, 157–58, 170–74, 170, 171
  in ocean transportation, 172–74, 181
sulfur-based concrete, 199–200
supplementary cementitious materials (SCMs), 183
Surveyor I, 205
Switzerland, 39, 40, 59, 66–67, 85
Sydney Opera House, 119–22, 122, 136
Syria, 24
Tafel, Edgar, 123
Terranova, Vincenzo and Ciro, 86
Thaddeus Merriman, S.S., 155–56
Third International Congress of Egyptologists (1982), 18
Three Gorges Dam, 61, 189–90, 189
Tiki, 110–11
titanium dioxide, 181–82, 227n
Totem Pole (Galloway), 106
trade unions, 62, 63–64
trench warfare, 67, 69, 70
Troy, 67, 69
trucking industry, 161–62
Tuchman, Barbara, 150
Tutankhamen, Pharaoh of Egypt, 12–13
TXActive, 181
Ulm, Franz-Josef, 183, 200–202
UHPC (ultra-high-performance concretes), 177
United Nations, 136, 196
  Intergovernmental Panel on Climate Change of, 187
United States, 59
United States Shipping Board (USSB), 147, 148
Unity Temple, 132–34, 133
Utzon, Jørn, 119–22, 136
Utzon-Frank, Einar, 119–20
Vesuvius, Mount, 26–27, 28, 33, 37
Vicat, Louis J., 50, 54, 154
Vicat needle, 50, 50, 154

Victoria, Queen of England, 52, 53
Victrola, 9, 95, 95
Viksjo, Erling, 111–12
Villa Savoye, 135, 135
Visigoths, 25
Vitruvian man, 40, 40
Vitruvius, 38–41, 43–44, 216, 217, 222
Vitruvius, S.S., 154
volcanic ash, 26–27, 28, 31, 33, 128
von Däniken, Erich, 14–15
Wal-Mart, 193–94
Washington, George, 49
waste materials, 179, 183, 212, 213
waterproof concrete, 48–57, 141, 143, 167, 222
  in bridge construction, 38, 41
  Nabatean, 26–29, 33–34
  Roman pozzolan, 26–27, 35, 37, 38, 40, 43–44, 50, 52, 85, 222
  stucco, 48–49
water supply, 166–70, 178, 191
  aging infrastructure of, 184–85
  aquifers of, 163, 167–69, 193, 213
  transport in distribution of, 83, 180–81
waterwheels, 222–23
Welch, Sir William, 81–82
whales, 174
White, Canvas, 55–56
white concrete, 181–82
white gold, 50
Whiteread, Rachel, 100, 108–9, 108
Wickline, Randy, 77
Wilkinson, William B., 115
Wilson, Woodrow, 148
Winstanley, Henry, 219–20
Winstanley Light, 51, 52, 219–20, 220, 221
Winstanley's Waterworks, 219
wood, 8, 22–23, 45–46, 64, 66, 80, 114, 130, 152, 221
  in construction, 48, 91, 149
  as limekiln fuel, 48, 91–92
  in underwater caissons, 36–37, 36, 41
World of Concrete trade show, 192–93
World Trade Center Towers, 35
World War I, 79, 98, 145–46
  concrete ships in, 147–50, 151, 157
  trench warfare of, 67, 69, 70
World War II, 64–74, 76, 77, 79–82, 129, 166, 185, 197
  Allied shipping lost in, 79, 150–51, 152
  concrete ships in, 150–57
  Pykrete and, 78–83
  see also defensive fortifications, fixed; Nazi Germany
Wright, Frank Lloyd, 119, 120, 122–24, 132–34, 133, 136, 190, 215, 216
Zond moon probes, 205
Zoser step pyramid, 20–21